CHASING RAINBOWS

CHASING RAINBOWS

FROM INNOCENCE TO PURGATORY AND REDEMPTION AS A COMPULSIVE SPORTS FAN

BEN DOBSON

Copyright © 2022 Ben Dobson

The moral right of the author has been asserted.

Apart from any fair dealing for the purposes of research or private study, or criticism or review, as permitted under the Copyright, Designs and Patents Act 1988, this publication may only be reproduced, stored or transmitted, in any form or by any means, with the prior permission in writing of the publishers, or in the case of reprographic reproduction in accordance with the terms of licences issued by the Copyright Licensing Agency. Enquiries concerning reproduction outside those terms should be sent to the publishers.

Matador
Unit E2 Airfield Business Park,
Harrison Road, Market Harborough,
Leicestershire. LE16 7UL
Tel: 0116 2792299
Email: books@troubador.co.uk
Web: www.troubador.co.uk/matador
Twitter: @matadorbooks

ISBN 978 1803131 412

British Library Cataloguing in Publication Data.
A catalogue record for this book is available from the British Library.

Printed and bound in the UK by TJ Book Limited, Padstow, Cornwall
Typeset in 12pt Adobe Jenson Pro by Troubador Publishing Ltd, Leicester, UK

Matador is an imprint of Troubador Publishing Ltd

For Dad, who introduced me to all this.
I loved sharing it with you and I almost forgive you…

FOREWORD
STUART BROAD, MBE

Sports fans reading this book should not feel odd about having idiosyncratic feelings around matches. Why? Because I can tell you that players experience them too and it's completely normal! Let's face it, when it comes to game day, we all act irrationally and behave in manners we feel will have a positive influence on the result. Even though deep down, we must know they won't.

Superstitions and habits run deep. Take my former England and Nottinghamshire teammate Graeme Swann as an example. He used to wear the same cycling shorts every time he bowled – unless he bowled badly of course, then he'd change them. Not only that, though; if he'd had a bad day, the next he would try a different route to the ground. Somehow, you see, it was the fault of his underwear and the traffic if things had gone awry.

In contrast, I've always tried to be relaxed as a player and not let too much affect me. I'm someone whose mentality is very strong in competitive mode. My mind is full of positive thoughts towards winning– bowling good deliveries, the momentum I can bring to the game, how I can change the course of a contest – I never think about losing moments until they actually happen. But the minute I go and watch Nottingham Forest, I'm a different kettle of fish. When I go to games, I wear red socks. Really? Is that going to have any bearing on the result? Of course not. But I cannot stop myself thinking it will. If Forest are playing on telly, and winning, I won't go and make a cup of tea because I fear the opposition will score if I move from the living room. Is that not nonsense? The game is happening in Reading, and I'm sat on a sofa more than a hundred miles away.

My stepdad Nick Joyce – wearer of the letter D in his heyday and the second most selected second row at Leicester Tigers behind Martin Johnson – goes a stage further. He remains so passionate about the fortunes of the club and yet refuses to go and watch their home fixtures because he's got it into his head that when he goes, they lose.

My friend Ben Dobson is cut from similar cloth. Someone who selects two mutually exclusive events and attributes some illogical significance between them. Ben was at The Oval – the first game he'd seen me play live, I believe – when I took five Australian wickets to alter the course of the final 2009 Ashes Test and also witnessed my first Test hundred against Pakistan first-hand. It led to him developing a theory that I play better when he is there. Naturally, I have suspected this has simply been a ploy to persuade me to provide hospitality tickets yet, as stupid as it sounds, I can't help thinking that along the way, he's brought me some luck.

I first met Ben when he was a support member of the British & Irish Lions tour of 2009. Around that time, the England cricket team were also kitted out by adidas. We hit it off and our friendship developed through our shared love for a variety of sports, or should I say a love of our teams winning, because as we all know – and as is illustrated in the following pages – it's hard to love sport when they lose. Although he has never played top level sport and is just a fan, Ben has always recognised the support that's needed at the top level. He is empathetic about the pressures of playing for England and has always been supportive. That has undoubtedly been developed through his own business roles. Some of my favourite memories are watching the England rugby team alongside Ben.

He's probably the most nervous watcher I've come across too, to be honest. I have seen some in my time, don't get me wrong: Alastair Cook bouncing a tennis ball when we were nine wickets down in Cardiff, with Jimmy Anderson and Monty Panesar trying to save the 2009 Ashes match, or Jos Buttler – who I was sat next to at Headingley in 2019 when his best mate Jack Leach was batting, trying to get Ben Stokes back on strike to beat Australia and keep us in with a chance of regaining the urn – fidgeting.

I've watched live sport in some pretty tense environments, but Ben would have to top anyone I could name for foreseeing potential disaster. He tends to go quiet for long periods, and that is when his brain's working overtime, figuring out things like who might be scoring first or next, why his team should definitely win today but mainly what could make them lose. Pre-match, he discusses every possible outcome as if he is Mystic Meg. He will just come out with stuff like: 'what if Ben Youngs can only last an hour and someone else has to play for the last twenty minutes? Then what?'. Well, I don't know, do I?

We are all guilty of predicting the ifs and buts of certain paths a match can take: what if they delay the new ball? What if they take two wickets in the final half hour? What if…

The biggest 'what if' when we have been in each other's company actually came during England's 2015 Rugby World Cup game against Wales at Twickenham. Behind late on, England kicked for touch when awarded a penalty. Of course, in hindsight, if they had taken the kick for goal, to tie the game, the future may well have told a different story. Then again, it might not. We always want to have our cake and eat it as fans, do we not?

When it comes to our sports teams, nobody knows better the trials and tribulations they bring us or conveys their passion for their teams like Ben. He lives and breathes their fortunes. Poor guy.

Nottingham, June 2021

PREFACE

There are a lot of books about sport. I know this because I think I've read most of them. Many are written by, or about, those who *did*: the people who had the talent, those who made it and told the rest of us what it was like. But there are far more of us who *couldn't* and *didn't*. We watched, we followed and, let's be honest, we pretended on the beaches, fields and playgrounds of our youth, and sometimes just in our own heads, that we were them. Some of us still do. And the truth for *us* is that our lives became every bit as defined by sport as did those of the people good enough to play it. They have no monopoly on the reality that sport can dominate a life. In retirement, they then sell us back their stories. So, for the rest of us, here's mine. And perhaps yours too.

I have tried to convince myself on many occasions that I'm past all this now, that in reflective middle age I can develop a healthier relationship with sport. But I have no illusions anymore. I'm an obsessive follower of sport, and specifically English sport, and for fifty-odd years, I've attempted to use this as a shield against the realities of life. That English sport has only occasionally offered its devotees anything other than pain, frustration and heartbreak means I now accept this was never going to be a very effective tactic. This book is for all those who recognise this condition and have ever had their mood ruined for a day, a week, a month or a year, to a totally inappropriate extent, by their addiction to their teams or their heroes and by some perceived sporting 'disaster'.

AUTHOR'S NOTE

Thankful…

I've just finished reading a book by my friend, former professional cricketer and successful businessman, David Nash. I'm glad I did as it helped me find the perspective I was searching for in writing my own story. There were parallels between us that struck me immediately. In his book, Nashy reveals that the effervescent personality and the general bonhomie and 'life and soul' he offers to those around him mask deeper insecurities. He also suggests, rather too modestly, that his only real skills are in interacting with others in a successful way. People tell me I too am capable of holding a room on occasions and delivering the odd one-liner to keep the party going, and if that's true, I'm both surprised and delighted, but I also hide a few anxieties and can relate to my mate's experience completely. We've both had an 'anxiety' connected to sport. This, however, is where similarity becomes divergence. Sport became his reality and his day job, and the pressures it exerted upon him were real and serious, true mental health issues which he rightly cares about deeply and which drive his empathetic character and passion for supporting others. Although I've also made my living from sport, in truth, what follows is not really about that, or the sort of on-pitch performance in which David was involved, but about *following* sport and the very much less serious 'pain' this has sometimes inflicted. Suddenly, it concerned me that nobody reading what follows should take this too seriously, as any sense that I was suggesting my own 'unburdenings' might be comparable would belittle the more real issue.

So, let's be clear at the outset: his story is an inspirational one and reads like the world's longest thank-you note; mine, I realised, is not and does not and might be seen more as a letter of complaint, which it is not meant to be. His tale is important and matters; mine, I am aware, is more self-indulgent, although I hope still with a little merit. Therefore, this book should be seen as a true and heartfelt take on a life dominated by sport, perhaps touched rather too much by the negativity of the pessimistic sports fan, but I hope it also reflects my own understanding of the absurdity of taking such a position. Because for all the 'angst' referred to in these pages – perfectly genuine but ultimately of a pretty frivolous nature – putting this down on paper has had the desired effect of that better sense of perspective and a true appreciation of the life force sport can be. As I read Nashy's book, I realised he and his friendship were living examples of what sport has given me of greatest value. What matters is not the outcome of the Ashes series (although unfortunately it actually still does to an extent) but the people it has allowed me to meet, the experiences I've had and the cherished relationships I've been fortunate enough to build. The fact I can count as a mate the legend who was willing to write the foreword for this book is down to sport – nothing else. No sport would have meant no Nashy and no Broady, and life would have been very much the poorer, and for every one of those friendships there are many others too.

Nashy and Stuart are solid people who measure the value of what they do in the positive impact it can have on others. Reading his book, one Nash pearl of wisdom which could have been aimed at me was, 'don't take yourself too seriously. No one else does.' Thank you for the timely reminder.

With that in mind, whilst I hope you might find some recognition, empathy and, who knows, even enjoyment in what follows, please take the curmudgeonly, whining author telling the story with a large pinch of salt and believe that deep down there is a happy, well-adjusted and very grateful soul in there somewhere. Sport – specifically the people it brings together – is special, and I'm truly thankful.

INTRODUCTION
CHASING RAINBOWS

'You're the worst cricket fan in the world' so says my good mate from South London, fellow cricket follower, Surrey member and England supporter home and abroad. To those who know me as a cricket-mad aficionado and walking encyclopaedia, this might seem an odd assertion. However, he holds this opinion because he lives for the moments of greatest excitement and seems able to meet the triumphs and disasters with equanimity, the game being the thing, accepting that the beauty lies in its unpredictability and its highs and lows. I used to be the same in my early days of innocence. But today, when it comes to those moments of greatest tension, I simply can't watch, or it will surely all go wrong. Where he positively seeks and revels in these moments, I do anything I can to avoid them; in the sports I claim to follow, when it comes down to the wire, I know I will find no actual enjoyment in these tightrope walks. So, I look away. As a carefree spirit with the ultimate c'est la vie attitude to life, Den has no time for my cowardice and pessimism, and I see his point. It poses the questions: 'why bother?' and 'how did it ever come to this?'. These are questions I am only now coming close to answering, with this book being a final attempt at closure and a fresh attitude. The other theme which, until recently at least, has seemed to run through my sporting experience is a strange pattern of Svengali-like happenings, a rather surreal ability to transform the fortunes of various participants either through my support or simply just my presence in their midst.

Looking back, the number of examples of this phenomenon are almost unnerving and make me wonder if I was put on this earth as some sort of guardian angel for the likes of Messrs McMenemy and Ferguson. If so, sadly those powers have waned as I've grown older and as the journey from innocence to reality has progressed.

The signs of a developing addiction were undoubtedly there when, at the age of nine, I managed to make the output of my entire school year's efforts one long football commentary. Each half-term's work would be on a different theme and ideally result in a body of associated work strung into a cardboard folder by those staples of the 1970s called treasury tags. The folder had to have a cover. In Hollybrook Middle School, year two, my six topics across the year included such diverse matters as City of Southampton, Fibres and Fabrics and Holidays in Europe. My form teacher's initial mild amusement morphed into increasing irritation as I delivered six covers (and much content inside) which I managed to present in a football context regardless of the subject matter. 'Southampton' was something of a tap-in with our football team somehow having won the FA Cup five months prior, thereby putting the city on the map and into the national consciousness in a way last seen with the launching of the Titanic. (Unfortunately, this connection was reinforced by the way Saints were also to sink dramatically straight after their moment in the spotlight.) I therefore felt wholly justified in making them the centrepiece of my first term's study folder. Using an annotated diagram of the fabric make-up of their home kit for 'Fibres and Fabrics' was admittedly more tenuous, and by the time I illustrated 'Holidays in Europe' with pictures of each city left in the last sixteen of the European Cup Winners' Cup that contained a team that might be drawn against Southampton, the idea was wearing a bit thin. Few nine-year-olds are endowed with the ability to judge where the line should be drawn on such occasions; certainly, this one wasn't. It was, however, an early example of my desire and ability to see, and encourage others to see, all of life's various experiences through the lens of sport.

Sports following can be a fickle mistress to its obsessives, and the acceptability of a devotion to it seems to become more questionable as you move through life's journey. In youth, it is like having a girlfriend,

INTRODUCTION

something to look forward to at the end of a long school day and to plan weekends around, which then leaves you with an empty feeling in the stomach when ultimately, and inevitably, it all goes wrong. But once in married middle age, it is more like an extra-marital affair – there is guilt at the time it forces you to spend apart and the emotion wasted on it which should be saved for others, and however it ends, you wonder what on earth you were doing. But, for some, its temptations are still hard to resist. (I am reasonably confident my wife, Mary, will not be reading this but, just in case, I would like to stress that this last bit is purely a metaphor and that sport has been my one and only dalliance, at the time of writing.)

One of my favourite philosophers and life coaches, Homer J Simpson, once raised a glass and hailed alcohol as 'the cause of, and solution to, all of life's problems'. This is perhaps a little less acceptable as a statement in today's world but is still funny in my book. In my world, I sometimes think I could say the same about sport. I love sport, and at certain times I hate sport, but I can't be ungrateful to it, and I certainly can't disown it, so here I am trying to work out whether I've been clever, as well as incredibly lucky, in living my dream or have alternatively been a total waster with no grasp on life's priorities, letting something which doesn't really matter and I can't control dictate the best part of my existence. I now believe the answer to be *both* to varying degrees. At the age of fifty-three, I can't help but question whether sport is a serious enough business for the all-consuming role it has played to have been worthwhile or even healthy – certainly as regards watching it – and whether the occasional moments of elation are worth the almost constant angst. Then I remind myself how much poorer life would have been without it. Nonetheless, being an English sports follower is not a simple matter. Some may think it's just a case of going to the game or turning the telly on and enjoying the entertainment. Why would it be any more complex than that? Why indeed? But some of us know different. Does it really matter? Is watching sport indeed not meant to be entertainment? If so, does that not imply it should be enjoyable? After all, it involves an apparently voluntary decision to be involved which some would say is completely within the control of the individual. For me it certainly began that way – perhaps not a conscious decision, more an imperceptible drift into its clutches – but as something exciting and fun. So how did it become a journey to a place where I could sometimes barely watch in any way which could be deemed pleasurable but rather with the charmlessness of a five-year-old who has been denied their heart's desire? It's something which runs contrary to the idea of gaining maturity as you grow older. Instead, I've realised I've become less able to treat its slings and arrows with the slightest hint of grace, which is something I need to address. My relationship with sport seemed far healthier and more well-adjusted at seven years old than it does at fifty-three. Should this evolution, or regression, worry me? Is it reflective of more than just my sports following – does it shine a light on a life-approach which needs to lighten up a bit? The revisiting of how this came about is an attempt to get a handle on it and, if necessary, reverse it with the hope of maximising the enjoyment before time runs out. One of Britain's greatest middle-distance runners, Steve Ovett, whose phlegmatic outlook and apparent lack of self-importance made him my clear favourite in the rivalry with Sebastian Coe in the seventies and eighties, explained his relatively early departure from athletics and his general outlook when he said, 'there is no way sport is so important that it can be allowed to dominate the rest of your life'. I understand that, Steve, and commend you on your own sense of perspective, but for the addicted amongst us followers, it is easier said than done.

My life has been utterly dominated by sport. For forty-seven years, it has been the constant in my life's journey. In fact, it wouldn't be an exaggeration to suggest that since my first encounters with it in 1974, sport has, in some way, shape or form, played a part in most of the days of my life. Not because I was good at it – this is not an athlete's autobiography – but through a childhood so sport-obsessed that *Star Wars*, *Knight Rider* and train sets didn't even register. I wish I'd been blessed with the gifts of a Best, a Woods, or even a Pringle, but I wasn't. No matter – ever since my entrapment, I've somehow managed to make sport the most omnipresent and central pillar of my existence and I've been playing, watching, recording, collecting, arguing, fantasising, punching the walls, living, and even *working* under its umbrella ever since. I played at school; I managed to blag my way into Loughborough University to spend three years on a Sports Science course – which often consisted of playing sport all day, trained by some of the finest coaches in the country – in the company of people far better qualified to be there and with real sporting potential; and then I secured entry into a 'real world', which was perhaps no such thing, by landing my first permanent job at a small sports marketing company. Admittedly, that involved a decision to leave the cosseted world of home and Southampton for a back-to-back terrace in Oldham, but if it was to ensure life thereafter meant sport, I would've moved to a hole in the ground. Some might say that this was a pretty good description of Oldham at the time; I couldn't possibly comment. Looking back, it wasn't my worst call, given that for the next thirty-plus years I was actually paid to enjoy some of the greatest sporting events and experience some of them in a personal capacity that I could never once have imagined, and meet and work with people who would otherwise undoubtedly have been distant heroes. As a result, I've not had a 'working' day since 1986 in which sport hasn't been a part. Had I been offered that when going through the careers department talks and the vague anxiety of having to imagine what I was going to make of my life when an unworldly teenager, I would scarcely have believed it. I remember once, as a young boy, listening to a family friend's friend on a holiday who worked in sports sponsorship for Mars. I couldn't have been more impressed if he had revealed himself as Neil Armstrong (or even David Armstrong). It stuck with me... imagine spending your life in nothing but the world of sport when you had not the slightest chance of actually playing it for a living. It hasn't, however, always been a life conducive to keeping an appropriate sense of proportion when it comes to sport. Am I a sports *fan*? I'm certainly a fan of its existence, otherwise I would have been left with the problem of how to fill the larger part of my life and how to express any human emotion in its absence. I liked *playing* sport, and even had my moments, but that's different. We are talking here about sports *following*, not *doing*. And there comes a point for some of us when *following* – which suggests a level of mild interest and entertainment – becomes something more than that, when, without you realising how it's happened, the whole thing has run a little out of control. So perhaps addict, obsessive or poor, deluded soul are better epithets than fan. I once read that 'sport is something that does not matter but is performed [and I would add, followed] as if it does. In that contradiction lies its beauty'. That's about right. And Danny Blanchflower clearly had a better adjusted take on it than mine when he referred to sport as 'that glorious irrelevance'. When I first saw this description, I couldn't work out if it was a perfect summation or a simplistic misrepresentation and a belittling of my life choices. It *does* matter. To me, it matters immensely. It matters out of all proportion to its real significance. For the obsessive, it dominates your waking hours for much of your life, and for those whose subconscious constantly attempts to rewrite the more upsetting outcomes, it dominates many of your sleeping ones as well. Even today, the last thing I'm thinking of as I drift off to sleep? Maybe the best England forward line of my lifetime, the top five best England rugby back divisions or, when all other obvious selections have been made, perhaps the best ever left-handed, bearded cricketing XIs (I kid you not. It's the only XI in which I've ever found a place for Ray Bright). That first self-check of the day as you open your eyes – *how am I feeling today?* – mine is usually determined by the previous night's results as they come floating back into my consciousness.

Friends have been chosen and occasionally rejected as a result of sport's influence. Numerous personal plans and events, including the very biggest according to my wife, have been organised around it. Having spent years spouting incredulity that unconcerned friends and relatives had arranged their weddings on days of significant sporting events, it was only when it came round to my own that I learnt that to get the venue you wanted, you had to book these things so far in advance that you ran the risk of that year's sporting calendar not having been finalised at the required time of booking. So it was that I got my comeuppance on Saturday the 18th of November, 2000 when I had to explain to my guests why this was happening on a day which started that morning with an England Test match in Pakistan, followed at midday by the Manchester derby and completed at around the time the vows were being made by England v Australia at Twickenham. Given this was the first Manchester derby in several years, City having just been promoted, and that all of my in-laws were season ticket holders at Maine Road who had been waiting for this occasion – the game, not the wedding – for a long time, dragging them all to the edge of the Lake District was not best appreciated. The fact they made it is to their credit. I was in two minds myself.

INTRODUCTION

Playing sport has virtues which are easy to extol, and it is a source of regret that my love of sport has never been matched by sufficient brilliance at being able to perform it. OK, I could play up to a point and did so reasonably through school, university and beyond. Loughborough Old Boys' games are now a last occasional rage against the dying of this particular light, after having been retired from my beloved five-a-sides a decade ago by a combination of my knees and my wife, both of whom I remain attached to for better and for worse. The physical well-being, competition and challenges of playing, the camaraderie and even the release of those pleasurable little fellows called endorphins make us feel truly alive. It's the same simple joy that a dog finds in playing ball. But Fido doesn't decide, when he realises he's not much good at this, to spend the rest of his life watching other dogs doing precisely the same for hours on end and going into a week-long sulk whenever they lose out to their owners. *Watching* sport is peculiar to humans and is a very different matter. If you are serene enough to enjoy the spectacle simply to marvel at the sight of a triumph of human skill and endeavour, you may find it an uplifting experience. But let's face it, not many of us fall into that dubious category. In the main, it turns us into couch-bound know-alls full of tension, disappointment, bitterness and even hatred. Nice. It can even encourage those who find it impossible to resist the call of the radio phone-in. (A few of this breed show the sports supporter in absolutely our worst light and point enough of a mirror back at me that it almost cures me of my own pettiness. The football phone-in can often be the living proof of Lord Halifax's assertion that 'anger is never without an argument, but seldom a good one'.) However, we should not upbraid ourselves too much. The writer Nick Hornby may well be the definitive voice on this, and in his autobiographical novel *Fever Pitch*, he suggests that, in sport, watching *is* doing – his point being that the dedicated followers amongst us put every bit as much time, effort and emotional energy into our teams as do those who play for them. We are involved.

In my experience, there are several categories of character when it comes to sports watching: those whose experience of life is wholly dictated by it and will be moved to tears by a last minute equaliser; those who have these moments but like to think they see the bigger picture;

those who know their sport and will watch with neutrality and claim to be able to take it or leave it; and those who have no clue, no interest and would prefer to be out cycling the Pennine Way. I myself am trying to see the colour of the trees in autumn as more important these days, and for a while, it seems to work… I'm so close… and then, to my shame and despite this new-found middle-aged approach, a failure to score at home to West Brom still takes a large percentage of the enjoyment out of my Saturday night. Pathetic. Those of us who can't shake this are addicted. Like any drug, we know we can get a fleeting moment of happiness, even ecstasy, but also that it will more often deliver extreme tension, sweating, irritability, disappointment, anger and mood swings whilst severely trying the patience of our loved ones. And, like many junkies, in my case the acceptance that I may have a problem is still something that until now I have found it easier to avoid than to acknowledge.

Being an *English* sports fan seems to me to be a particularly acute strain of this disease. Unless you are a German with Australian parents, brought up in Liverpool in the seventies and eighties before moving to Manchester in the nineties (reincarnating as a United fan after being heavily concussed unloading the removal van), and with distant family connections to Roger Federer, Michael Schumacher and Stephen Hendry, following sport is not going to be one long, happy party. But that in a sense explains it – without spending a good amount of time lying in the sporting gutter, those stars you gaze at lose their sparkle. OK, if I was from Munich, the 1999 Champions League final might well have scarred me for life, but overall, being a German fan cannot surely remotely compare to our experience. They have neither our fatalism nor our justifiable reasons for it. In my forty years of obsession, I've had perhaps six or seven moments of extreme elation: Wembley 1976, Headingley 1981, Barcelona 1999, Sydney 2003, The Oval 2005, Lord's and Headingley 2019. I still now, in the aftermath of another disappointment, tell myself it's just a game, just entertainment to be consumed and enjoyed as part of life's experience and no more than that. And yet, my reality tells me something different. If the new De Niro film is a disappointment, the Counting Crows gig I've been waiting for is a let-down, if Al Murray's routine isn't as side-splitting as usual, it doesn't eat away at me for months. And this all comes under the banner of entertainment. So, does sport perhaps sit in another category? I wish I could consume sport as an enjoyable social diversion and put it in what many consider its proper place, but I'm rather concerned that to dismiss it as pointless would be also to dismiss the life in which it has been the common denominator, the constant thread. I say I love it, but my relationship with it is not as simple as that. It can empty my stomach, ruin my weekend, make me bitter and twisted. I get so chewed up at times I can't actually watch, which defies its point. I've never walked out of a concert because I'm too nervous about the outcome. I don't mutter, 'come on, Springsteen, concentrate, don't give it away….'.

Although I'd say I'm a pretty easy-going sort, in the past, my competitiveness meant I could sometimes barely involve myself in sport – whether playing or watching – or completely enjoy it without severely irritating someone around me. This led to the rather defensive mindset I am ready to leave behind. In my more active sporting days, it often felt better to play someone too good for you against whom you could play and improve without the risk of any shame in defeat, or occasionally enjoy being so comfortably superior you could feel safe (examples include letting my sister admire my cover drive on the beach and then having to go and fetch the ball from the sea), than to be involved in anything which could go either way. Because then, the only person who can fail you is you. Cricket on the beach was heaven; cricket for the first XI, waiting to bat, was purgatory, and if it was all over and I never actually made it to the crease lower down the order, my pretence at disappointment hid an almighty relief. In which case, why ever did I decide to be there in the first place? I've discovered this sometimes applies to supporting too. A Saturday when you wake up to the realisation you are playing Liverpool away is a far more relaxed and enjoyable one than a day when you're at home to Brighton. Far better to expect to lose a game everyone else expects you to than to live through the risk of not winning one you have to. This is the perverse reality of the addicted sports supporter. The prospect of losing is almost more comfortable than the prospect of winning. The excitement only ever comes with concomitant risk, panic and usually, ultimately, disappointment. It holds up a mirror to your immaturities and insecurities.

I know it takes all sorts, and admittedly there are some people who are either sane or insane enough not to care. I actually know people – remarkably some are even friends – for whom sport certainly *is* an irrelevance, and not even a glorious one. They fascinate me. For twenty-five years, I've been with a girl I love unconditionally and on whom my sports-centric existence has made so much impact that she will undoubtedly be found watching *Celebrity Antiques Road Trip* should England ever be winning another World Cup. (Whatever I might like to think, the idea that the whole nation is gripped at such times is a fallacy. I know this because she told me so.) There's no earthly reason why your uncomprehending loved ones should have the quality of their lives hanging on the result of the Third Test Match at Old Trafford. I have a very good friend who is completely untouched by sport, and he still seems to consider his life rich and fulfilling. I'm not sure quite how I feel about that – bemused, sympathetic or envious. He's a top bloke is Steve, but what does he know of life who knows not the joy of a victory over Australia? How does he measure the success of his weekend if Jeff Stelling breaking the news of losing to a ninety-seventh-minute offside goal means nothing to him? Does the fact I ask these questions make me less mature than him? I fear so. Increasingly, I feel I would prefer to be in his position, and I'm now trying to convince myself I am heading in that direction at last.

That great social commentator of the seventies, Reginald Iolanthe Perrin, once mused on why people are the only species neurotic enough to require a purpose in life. Wildebeest don't suffer mid-life crises. My dog has never bothered himself with the pain of a last-minute defeat – he knows nothing of an England batting collapse and cares even less. I doubt that anyone whose life is enhanced by a horse, cat, rabbit or tortoise has ever seen them concerned about how the Ryder Cup four-balls are going. A giraffe, unless it is called Jack Charlton, does not ruminate on sloppy defending or a disastrous penalty shoot-out. Koalas, despite their upbringing, do not spend months fretting over the possible outcome of an Ashes series. So why do so many human beings – we are led to believe the most developed and intelligent species on the planet – have major issues with such matters? But what do the Steves of this world *do*? Where are

INTRODUCTION

the uncontrollable highs and lows in their lives? How do they get through the post-Christmas blues without two months of the Six Nations or without the hope and trepidation of turning on the BBC Sport app to check the Ashes score from Australia? Is there something wrong with these people? Because this is where it leads the rest of us, who somehow, in the mists of time, got life's values and priorities wrong, to a place where a sunrise over the Himalayas would happily be traded for Jimmy White beating Stephen Hendry. The non-afflicted think we are over-egging this and that it's some sort of cry for attention. They don't understand. I have striven for an alternative, but the fact is, if I hear the words 'black spot', I instinctively think not about a potential car accident but rather where to leave the cue ball.

If it feels like I'm starting to depress you and to do sport down, please bear with me as last year, without warning, something called a global pandemic came along and gave sport and its role in my life, and in society in general, a fresh perspective – a chance to reassess the *for* and *against* and offer it some gratitude for being there after all. Don't speak too soon, but I think I might, just might, be ready to complete the journey's circle back to innocence, get over myself and use this as a springboard to see the world's glass as half full, even fully full, again in the future. No less a prophet than Muhammad Ali said that the man who views the world at fifty the same as he did at twenty has wasted thirty years of his life. Fair point from the big man but a little uncomfortable for me. This made me realise I'd actually been *immaturing* through the passage of time rather than the other way around, as is more traditional, and that in middle age, there is something unnerving about having let a 'glorious irrelevance' dominate my life. So, it's time to grow up.

Art (which in my world usually means sport) imitating life is a concept which has gained credence with me whilst writing the book. Maybe Aristotle had something after all. It struck me how the sport I've followed has reflected my life's journey in an almost unreal manner. It's a strange corollary; a journey from the happy innocence of youth, and those 'sweet childish days' that Wordsworth remembered as being 'as long as twenty days are now', through the harsher reality of a real, grown-up world, an unimagined period of living the dream and finally, a search for some sort of balance and, I hope, my arrival back at that happy place from which I started out. All the way, the highs and lows of following English sport seem to have tracked my life experience like a path that follows a river. This is why the book is written the way it is, through four distinct phases, and I hope its narrative articulates what I am trying to say. It is ultimately a catharsis of sorts, so thank you for indulging me. In his fascinating and engaging appearance on *Desert Island Discs*, Arsene Wenger talked of three distinct types of pupil he coached at various stages in his career: the child, who wants simply to play and is completely in the present; the teenager, who sees things in black and white and for whom you are either stupid or a genius; and the adult, who lives with an internal suffering but has to find a compromise with the external world and, if he's capable of that, can find a balanced life. That struck me as a perceptive summing up of my journey. Why and where it started, how it became so important to me and why now I want to give it its due is the main substance to the story that follows.

The proverb says what can't be cured must be endured. Before I started writing, I felt that endurance was my only option. Now, my ambition is to use this process as the cure. In the meantime, I'll accept and enjoy the fact that we're always hanging on for that glorious moment – just around the corner, we're sure – which makes it all worthwhile. The Scottish writer Norman McCaig suggested 'experience teaches us that it doesn't', whilst Pope (Alexander rather than Nick or Ollie in this instance) told us that hope springs eternal. Both valid assertions. Following English sport is the definitive triumph of hope over experience. I, however, remain addicted to the hope. Forever chasing rainbows.

PART ONE
SEASONS IN THE SUN
1974–1985

> 'Youth would be an ideal state
> if it came a little later in life'
> H.H. ASQUITH

HAPPY NEW YEAR...

Welcome 1974. We start here because it's about as far back as I can remember – the earliest, if rather vague, memories of my parents' famous, occasionally infamous, annual New Year's Eve house party, full of reassuring seventies icons such as the Cinzano Bianco, on which, out of sight four years later, I got horrendously drunk for the first time at the age of eleven and proceeded to treat the assembled guests to a centre-of-lounge-floor performance of *Greased Lightning*, complete with black plastic jacket and slicked back hair. Recalling the 31st of December, 1973 is not a bad effort given I was just six and a half at the time. I mean, could *you* imagine a Christmas when 'Merry Xmas Everybody' and 'I Wish It Could Be Christmas Every Day' were actually *new releases?*

I remember the post-party, parental hangover hush of the house on New Year's Day morning, along with two other emotions which were to be New Year traditions for years to come. Firstly, the realisation that Christmas was over, brutally and abruptly, it seemed to me. All the fairy-tale magic of the past week had gone, and the sense of anticlimax which was to recur for the next forty-seven years crept in. The childlike excitement of putting up and decorating the tree was about to be matched by the melancholy of doing the reverse. Even the taste of the glue you had to lick to link up the 1970's paper chains was finally beginning to fade. Secondly, it was the first time ever I was conscious of the one thing that was going to pull me out of this pessimistic torpor and remind me that life goes on – the upcoming weekend heralded the third round of the FA Cup. Whichever genius first decided on this bit of scheduling has my undying gratitude, as for years, it stood as a metaphor for renewal, hope and future possibilities. So it was for me for the first time as we stepped into 1974. The future was uncertain but full of possibilities. Who knew where life might take me? 1974 was when it all began and was the year that shaped things to come forever after.

TRAPPED

Looking back, I'm not sure I stood a chance. I was born on the 3rd of May, 1967. That's just shy of nine months after the 30th of July, 1966, which for the uninitiated is the date of what is usually considered the greatest moment in English sporting history. Given I was a slightly early arrival, it's a pretty good bet that I was conceived in the immediate afterglow of this (literally) seminal moment. So perhaps I was always destined to be wedded to sport and have it shadowing the passage of my life, starting as it did with those two most significant moments joined together. So, as I say, it's not my fault. Theses have been written on weaker premises than this.

My predilection for using sport as a barrier against the realities of life was encouraged by my early experiences during which, for several years, sport's true colours – notably its capacity to cause me significant distress – were kept hidden from me, which I now consider was entrapment pure and simple. I was ensnared, not least by an almost unreal correlation between my formative years following sport and the hard-to-fathom success of my local football club. Those first few years contained myriad special first experiences for a wide-eyed young disciple following in his father's sport-loving footsteps and taking him as an example. I absorbed them all and was myself absorbed. They are all now defining moments seared into my memory. In '74, sport and everything that came with it had the innocence of a first love affair. (My never-to-be-forgotten encounter with Louise Bowden at the edge of the Hollybrook playground that same year another example of sport and real life running in parallel.) It was a time when watching sport was a simple, pleasurable pastime, particularly as the right people always seemed to win. The idea that there might be any flip side, any inherent risk, never occurred to me, hence the scale of the shock when it started happening a couple of years later. Nor was there yet any need for hatred. It was a blank canvas. That spring also heralded the first number-one single I can remember hearing. In retrospect, none could have been more apposite than Terry Jacks's 'Seasons in the Sun'.

If I didn't quite come out of the womb as a member of various England supporters' clubs, I can't recall a formative memory from a time before I was conscious of sport. I must have been semi-aware of it before 1974, as I vaguely remember opening the batting on the beach as Brian Luckhurst, whose last Test Match for England was in 1973, and it was on a camping trip that summer that I first gave notice of how I intended to rank the importance of sport versus life itself, in this case quite literally. Camping in the majesty of the Swiss Alps with my family and my dad's best mate, my first reaction to any new location chosen for the night was not to take in the view but to assess where best to pitch the wicket as opposed to the tent. My string bag of bat, four stumps and tennis ball was not being hauled around the continent for nothing. On this occasion, we were setting up on a small patch of greenery halfway up an alpine hillside at about five thousand feet above sea level, with the ground falling away significantly on all sides. The wicket clearly had to go in the middle of what space there was. At this height, the opportunities for replacing lost tennis balls were limited so the one I had was precious. In the manner of all six-year-olds, I'd decided I should bat, with my dad's mate keeping wicket. One of Dad's 'Harold Larwoods' was too much both for my batting prowess and his mate's wicketkeeping abilities and it went for byes at some velocity. 'Uncle' Brian dutifully gave chase before plunging out of view rather more quickly than seemed propitious. With a look of horror, Dad sprinted to the precipice and saw his friend clinging to the cliff with the help of various bits of vegetation. He was in the process – ultimately successful, I might add – of dragging him back up when I'm advised my face appeared over the edge and made the enquiry, 'can you see it yet?'. I've had to live with that story for a long time without ever being told if I gave any indication as to whether the retention of my uncle was any recompense for the loss of my last tennis ball.

So yes, 1973 may have seen the start of my active sporting career, but my conscious memories of sports watching begin in '74, and I remember the day as if it were yesterday. The day the entrapment truly began.

FIRST TIME

The 4th of May, 1974, Wembley, and I'm aware of the FA Cup final for the first time. Liverpool and Newcastle live on the telly, early second half, 0-0. I'm seven years and one day old; I'm a Liverpool fan (that day); and I'm a little excited. 'Our' full back Alec Lindsay – as close to a journeyman performer as Liverpool got at that time, or for many years afterwards – was through on goal. An unstoppable shot, a fantastic goal – my first ever.

I'm up in a flash; I feel something unusual which, in future years, my Loughborough seminars will identify as a rush of adrenaline, and I make for the lounge table and my lovingly prepared piece of paper. I scribble *Liverpool 1-0, Lindsay, forty-six minutes*, and the world is a good place to be. Then, confusion – why is it still 0-0? Why is Dad smirking at me? What the hell is 'offside'? Suddenly, my excitement seemed wasted, even silly, and my match report was ruined given the absence of Tippex from my pencil case in 1974. For the very first time, I experienced that cocktail of feelings: elation, worry, a tension in the pit of the stomach and finally, miserable disappointment as I realised it was all for nothing. It had taken just over three quarters of an hour of my sports-watching life. Had Kevin Keegan not put everything right seven minutes later, the first sport-induced tears may well have followed, who knows? As it was, that moment had to wait for another three years, but I would get there soon enough, the inevitability of which I probably ought to have understood subconsciously in that moment. The Roman poet Persius advised that disease should be confronted at its onset. Advice that I clearly failed to heed.

That's precisely where it started. I am not a person of great faith, but had I had the faculty or inclination to consider the portents in this episode, I might have seen it as a warning from above and caught it just in time. Not all kids fall in love with sport, and here was my moment to plump for cars or science fiction instead, my chance to forego the whole business forever. There it was in microcosm, clearly laid out for me what the next forty-seven plus years were going to offer if I chose this path. Groundless hope followed by frequent sorrow – the way forward from here.

Those reading this book backwards would be surprised at my love of all things Liverpool that May afternoon. I'm not a Liverpool fan, as will become apparent; quite the contrary. But back then, they had Kevin Keegan. KK was the star; he was England; he had his own column in my *Shoot* magazine which informed me each week that he was 'writing for me'; through this, I knew he had sheepdogs and a nice farm in North Wales. Never mind my hero, he was virtually my best mate. I was mad on Kevin, so I supported his team. Now I see how easy the journey has been from the kid with the love of watching sport for its own sake – and the innocent support I offered to anyone English or any player that excited me regardless of his team – to the bitter old fifty-something who today can barely watch for fear that someone who antagonises him might have a successful day.

From that afternoon onwards, nothing could stop the train that was to transport me through sport for the rest of my days. That Cup final was followed a month later by a World Cup. This was another level – was I really to be allowed to watch game after game of live football for days on end at all times of the day and night? Instead of my sister putting me through *Crossroads*, I got four men on the telly sat around in chairs just *talking* about football for hours. Having only woken up to football that spring, it never occurred to me to ask why England were not taking part, but, England or no England, this was *international* sport. Noise, flags, odd-looking television pictures and crackly commentators. And countries, some of whom clearly appeared not to like each other very much. Strange new words such as 'Zaire' and 'Haiti' and more ethnicity and bizarre hairstyles than the middle-class suburban seven-year-old mind could take in.

And my first ever Panini sticker book, World Cup '74, which had the same value for me as their first edition Chaucers and Shakespeares do to the Getty Library. The glossy touch and the vibrant colours were compelling, and it didn't leave my side for a month, in which time I realised I actually had to play an active role in completing the treasure by buying groups of stickers in little paper wrappers at 3p a time. It may not seem a lot, but it stretched my seven-year-old pocket money to the limit. Suddenly, Texan and Amazin' Raisin bars had to take a sabbatical as all funds were diverted to the ambition of filling up the book, leading to significant tension in the lottery of opening the pack for which you had emptied your piggy bank. If anyone had wanted to introduce a kid to the kick of gambling, this was a pretty good way to go about it, because you had no idea what you were getting for your money, which was a cute and cruel piece of addictive marketing. The holy grail were the Scots and the Brazilians. If you opened your packet to find instead a collection of hirsute faces from Yugoslavia and Chile, as seemed to be my lot every time, you wanted to go again – waiting until the next week's money was available was unimaginable, especially if Graham Brennan had just landed a Peter Lorimer. And there was the increasing likelihood, or statistical fact, that as your book filled up, most of any future packet's contents would just contain duplicates of the players you already had. What the odds grew to of actually completing your book, without the use of subterfuge before bankrupting the family, I've never tried to calculate. Yes, there were 'swaps' in the playground, but that was simply a catalyst for fights and an invitation to bullies so had to be executed with great care and didn't always deliver an acceptable outcome. And anyway, there were exchange rate issues which would have challenged Norman Lamont – how many Haitians do you have to offer up to get a Rivelino or a Billy Bremner? This led to my first brush with crime (and punishment) as, having thrown my latest packet away in disgust and therefore having nothing to show for my investment, I decided to tell Dad that I didn't have any stickers because they had been taken off me by the boy who lived across the road, and might I therefore have some replacement funds? The schemes of seven-year-olds are rarely thought through with an eye for detail, hence why I didn't anticipate Dad marching over to confront the lad's parents. A headmaster who doesn't enjoy being lied to, and who has just been embarrassed by throwing false accusations at the neighbours, made for a scary judge and jury. And for the first time, but not the last, sport had driven me to behaviour of which I couldn't be proud. Needless to say, there were no more stickers, and I had to save up enough to take the cop-out route of sending away for all the stickers I still needed. By which time, the 1978 version wasn't so very far away.

As for the tournament itself, the clues to what sport might do to me in the future were again all there. Clearly the most deserving team with easily the best player (for the next six months in the playground I was Johan Cruyff, as was everyone else which rather diluted the effect) did not win the cup. I didn't see why this should happen. My assumption was that results should be fair. Flair and excitement had met their nemesis in a solid, serious, ruthless, and to me it seemed, cold-hearted, team called… West Germany, versions of which were going to prove something of a thorn in the side in years to come. But my addiction was still growing.

That World Cup meant I'd had my introduction to global football before my introduction to England, which was to be the next chapter in my education. This happened on a never-to-be-forgotten evening which now looks slightly surreal. At 4.30am that morning, the most iconic boxing bout in history had taken place in Zaire (what was it with this place?). Muhammad Ali and George Foreman fought out the Rumble in the Jungle in front of one of the first ever pay TV audiences in America and around the world. What the UK got was delayed transmission on BBC One that evening. So, what we ended up with was a Wednesday night with no *Holby City* or *Masterchef* but one of the greatest sporting events in history at 8pm, and England v Czechoslovakia on *Sportsnight* at 10pm. I'm still puzzled as to how it happened, but somehow, I was allowed to stay up to watch all of this. As I was used to being packed off to bed not too long after Bob Wellings and Frank Bough had wrapped up *Nationwide*, this was another world and it dawned on me that sport might afford me more such opportunities to taste the adult life before my time, which was another tick in the positives column. I had no idea at the time what an incongruous night this was: *Ask The Family*, world heavyweight boxing and *Sportsnight*. Robert Robinson, Muhammad Ali and Barry Davies may not have been everyone's idea of the Holy Trinity but for me, these were riches indeed. The boxing mesmerised me. The colour, noise and violence of it made me feel almost guilty to be watching. And there was this strangely beautiful bloke in white satin shorts everyone was calling The Greatest. I never missed one of his fights after that and was only ever in his corner. Then, at 10 pm on 30th October 1974 came England and the first of sport's great confidence tricks. With my sports watching still at the embryonic stage, England v Poland a year before meant little to me. I had been protected from the national shockwave and the first talk, but not the last, of the nadir of English football. To me, England just meant all my favourite players getting together to play for an all-star team. I did, however, catch the pervading sense of optimism and renewal, even if I didn't understand it. For this was, I understood later, my initiation to the concept of the sporting new dawn – a delusional construct, designed to erase past ignominies from the memory and restart the cycle of hope, regardless of any basis in fact, which was to recur on an almost annual basis for the next four decades. Having failed to qualify for the summer's World Cup, England came back not only with a new manager and revamped team but a new kit… often a fundamental element of any new dawn. This one actually marked the start of the true replica kit, and it was responsible for one of my very few sporting disappointments in those early days. Kits were important, but until then, it had been necessary to be creative if I was going to look like a first-division player. If I fancied being Arsenal when I went to the park with my ball, I had to put my red T-shirt over my best white school shirt to get the required look, or rather something not quite approximating to it. However, this kit launch was big news, and most of my schoolmates were going to be getting it without fuss. Within months, it was *the* look on games day and down at the rec. Unfortunately, I had a mother whose post-war upbringing had imbued her with a somewhat frugal character, and she didn't quite get that the real thing was the only thing… she was adamant that paying for the actual kit was crazy when she could make it just as well. Head of Design at Admiral she wasn't, and my own England shirt emerged as a basic white nylon top with a couple of satin ribbons from the C&A haberdashery sewn onto each arm to 'replicate' the dashing new design feature. I'm not sure she had her pantone book with her as the colours were at best an approximation, with the red stripe a less than masculine rose pink. Her attempt at a Three Lions badge shrivelled to the size of my left nipple in the wash. It was an open invitation to ridicule, and I'm still not sure why I ever put it on, but it may help explain how I came to be a rather sensitive and self-conscious young individual.

But for now, in the comforting company of Harry Carpenter and Barry Davies, it seemed to me that England were to be just another unbridled success story. My first night game broadcast from Wembley looked like an exotic fairyland and Wembley itself forbidding in its size and majesty. Mick Channon had recently scribbled his name in biro on my first Southampton shirt in The Dell car park, thereby cementing his place ahead of Kevin Keegan at the top of my revised hero list. Now both of them were playing together for England and Mick followed my script by scoring and helping England beat Czechoslovakia (a team whose players' names it seemed to me were just the alphabet spelt backwards) 3-0. I never considered anything could burst this bubble of positivity, and although putting my faith wholly in the person of Gerry Francis was ultimately proven to be misguided, over the next year, a strolling victory against the world champions West Germany and a 5-1 thrashing of Scotland just seemed to confirm this was the way things were meant to be. I may even have heard Davies mention something about a 'new dawn'. Then of course, exactly a year to the day after my debut, they lost in Bratislava and disappeared from another tournament before it had started. Another amber signal which at the time passed me by.

SOUND & VISION

For the time being, television was to continue to be the vehicle for these firsts, and the next one arrived on the 4th of January, 1975: my second FA Cup third round but the first time I had dedicated my whole day to its unfolding. It was an intoxicating kaleidoscope of thirty-two matches all happening at the same time (remember that?). Such a thing required a bit of extra work and recognition on my part, so with my *Shoot!* magazine in my right hand, open on the page listing all the games, I positioned myself in front of Mum's typewriter. The machine was a little daunting, but I'd seen Mum tapping away on it so it couldn't be that tricky. Having recently had my first glimpse of the *Grandstand* vidiprinter unveiling the full-time scores in a delightfully random manner which wrung out every last drop of tension (the words coming in one letter at a time, frequently pausing for thought halfway through a result, thus building anticipation steadily as you tried to second guess if the Saints score was finally coming through or you were about to learn how York City had fared at Southend), I had decided to reproduce my own fantasy version that Saturday morning well in advance of the games. To be honest, even though I began this endeavour at 9am, if Frank Bough had had to rely on me for any legible information, it would have come in roughly around the time of the quarter-finals. I never was offered that job on *Grandstand*, which at the time could've sufficed as my life's ambition. Fingers were cut to ribbons and ribbons were stuck to paper, the big black smudges of ink giving me nothing like the portentous piece of paper I wanted to hand over to my father like a busy sub-editor. In fact, given my penchant at that point for dressing up in character in the most literal way, I'd be surprised if I didn't have my holiday sun visor standing by. So, Mum had to step in and, instead of predicting the results, the adjusted timescale had us copying out the real results, but I did end up with my piece of paper, goalscorers and minutes included. This may be why Derek Posse's otherwise unremarkable double for Orient against Derby has somehow stayed with me ever since. That Saturday was a red-letter day for another reason; my first ever *Match of the Day*. Why I had been allowed to stay up all evening for that first England game I can't recall, but it wasn't going to happen again anytime soon. So, I had come to an arrangement with the powers that be at home. Shortly after Tom Baker had finished with the Daleks, I was packed off to bed. Then Dad would arrive at 10pm to shake me awake and plant a cup of cocoa in my hand. This seemed a good compromise, but in reality, if you've ever been woken from a deep sleep after three hours, you'll appreciate I was often a little dazed and confused. It did, though, introduce me to the cosy comfort of a long-term routine. Bed, wake up, hot chocolate, *Match of the Day*, bed again. My total faith in this routine was responsible for the only other mental scar left from that period. To be fair, Mum and Dad were faultless in their timekeeping, consistency and the quality of their cocoa. But if I was dazed and confused when I *was* woken up, that was nothing compared to the confusion when I *wasn't*. The reason escapes me, but one weekend, we were packed off to stay with my maternal grandparents; I wasn't overexcited about this as it would be fair to say the Scottish Presbyterians from deepest, sleepy Sussex were less laugh a minute than Dad's Geordie parents who were more my idea of what grandparents were meant to be. More importantly, I was well aware that 'Grandpa Mac' knew as much about sport as I knew about Presbyterianism and cared even less. Here was a man who I wasn't sure belonged in our family or with whom I could possibly have a blood tie. If a football had floated through his window, he wouldn't have had the faintest idea what it was. Being able to grow yellow tomatoes was all very well but wasn't enough to gain him credibility or affection in my eyes. In fact, I sensed he felt my interest in such frivolities as football was bad for my character, and he was barely able to conceal an air of disapproval and completely unable to conceal one of indifference. So, alarm bells were ringing. I checked with Mum and Dad every fifteen minutes on the journey that they had given full instructions for the *Match of the Day* routine, and again as they departed the scene, I was assured that this was all in hand. Having gone to bed at the appointed time – the time linked directly to the 'wake me up again' part of the bargain – I woke to what appeared to be light coming through my curtains. The sense of bewilderment was overwhelming. Even though it was plain that this had all the telltale signs of a Sunday morning, if I didn't admit that to myself, perhaps it wouldn't be true. I couldn't have been more stunned if Jimmy Hill himself had appeared to invite me down to watch the programme… a disorientation followed by horror as it struck me what had happened. This was akin to the moment not too long previously when I realised Father Christmas didn't exist – I could see how it might make sense but simply didn't want to admit the truth of it. This was a *Match of the Day* I was never going to get back. In those days of no video recorders, no repeats, no magazine goals shows, that weekend's football had gone forever and may as well never have happened. I don't know whether they did it on purpose, but I wasn't about to give them the benefit of the doubt and never really forgave them. If it still rankles in my fifties, it must have been apocalyptic at the time, and if you can sense an element of never quite having let go of this, you are right. Another sign that maybe this sports-following thing was going to lose its lifelong battle for any sense of proportion.

That episode confirmed how sport and the telly were by now the epicentre of my world. *Match of the Day* was duly supplemented with *Football Focus* and *On The Ball* as Saturdays got going, and the Sunday routine was now also firmly embedded: 'three and in' at the rec (white shirt with red tee over the top or home-made England), back in time for Sunday roast and then pudding on knees in front of Brian Moore and *The Big Match*. That theme tune had a melodiousness wasted on a football highlights show but also the melancholy which announced the beginning of the end of the weekend. The absolute bonus ball was a *Sportsnight* or *Midweek Sports Special* for an England match or a Cup replay, even if I had more chance of Mum and Dad suggesting we all went down to the ODEON to take in *A Clockwork Orange* than of getting a ticket to stay up for those on a school night.

Which is where the radio made its entrance. If anything, radio has an even greater nostalgic resonance. Firstly, since live football on the telly meant either the FA Cup final or England v Scotland, radio was the only vehicle on which to follow things as they happened ninety-nine per cent of the time. And even then, you had no guarantees. The radio listings in the paper always seemed some way behind the whims of the Radio 2 scheduler, so you could place little trust in them and therefore on any given night when I knew significant football was due to be played, I would tune in full of anticipation at 8.02pm. The feeling of deflation when *Listen To The Band* came across the airwaves instead was total. But England games and European nights featuring English teams were a pretty safe bet. For a few years, it felt as though I had gained a couple of extra uncles as the mellifluous tones of Peter Jones and less mellifluous ones of Alan Parry joined me for some memorable evenings. Tucked up in bed, radio positioned at just the angle needed to be able to pick up any mellifluousness at all, the pictures were my own to create, but the sound will never leave me. Nor will the theme tune, which always seemed to presage another glory night for Liverpool in the European Cup. It was to be about ten years before I actually watched the goals from the night David Fairclough pulled it out of the fire against St Etienne, but that didn't make it any less real or exciting as The Kop seemed to have joined me in my bedroom. It's the way

I will always remember that match, no matter how many times I see the pictures. The tension was only increased by the fact that the commentary couldn't help but be a fraction behind the crowd and the action, and with no images, I had to get used to split seconds when imagination replaced reality and any number of outcomes were possible. These were second-guessing moments when time seemed to expand, and you were dropped slap bang in the middle of the hope-despair continuum. At the time it was a buzz, but like so many elements of my sports watching, as time went on, it moved from excited anticipation to wretched angst. In other words, as I 'matured', I became less able to deal with such a trivial matter, to the point where listening to anything truly important via this medium could not be suffered any longer. Today, a podcast goes on until it is absolutely certain that the live stuff has finished, at which point the decision is simple – if things turn out as hoped, you listen to two hours of reaction and debate in a warm and protected glow; if not, it's back to Stephen Fry and pretend it never happened. It's my 'overnight Ashes' technique.

The second role of the radio was to be the solution when you couldn't be in front of the telly even if something *was* live. Before the Sky Sports app or BBC online on a phone, inconveniences such as days out or holidays were a serious problem. For one, the football season always seemed to start whilst we were in a tent somewhere. My frustration at that was only increased by the fact that every game seemed to have been played in glorious sunshine in the same country in which I was huddled under canvas in every layer of clothing I'd brought with me, listening to the only sound that could rival Peter Jones for the title of most vivid memory of my adolescence: rain on a tent.

Then there was the cricket. There was a time when even a small, portable radio was either unavailable or frowned upon on the summer camping holidays, and to be fair, most of the places we ended up probably can't get a reception to this day, so the only way of listening to *Test Match Special*, the definitive sound of my early summers, was on the car radio. In the campsite, this usually meant you could glean a maximum of four words out of ten. Even then, my family friend James and I tried hard to ignore the great outdoors in favour of sitting in the front seats for as much of the day as possible. If this was never going to fly for long, it met its end when

Dad's attempted trip to pick up the night's gin from the supermarket was confounded by the flattest of flat batteries. So, given these were usually touring holidays, the best solution was to be travelling and the goal was to encourage our respective parents to move on a Test match day, ideally taking long enough to dismantle the tents and pack the car to ensure a set-off time of around 10.55am. The longer the trip, the better. Some would see it as a shame, I suppose, that instead of the occasionally sun-kissed beaches of the Gower peninsula or the mountains of the Lake District, the highlight of my holidays would be a day in the back of a Datsun with Johnners, Fred Trueman and Trevor Bailey. The only real tension with a *TMS* day came when it was raining, and I began to wonder how long they would be willing to chat before they were replaced by classical music on Radio 3. These were genuinely the things I used to worry about when considering what could possibly spoil my summer holidays.

Our ability to manage this process probably reached its apogee during the summer of 1977 and that summer's Ashes series when we roamed around Wales barely, it seemed, stopping to get out of the car. It's probably why I can recall such Australian greats as Craig Serjeant and Mick Malone as readily as Shane Warne or Ricky Ponting, which is a faculty not bestowed on many, even if I haven't found a use for it yet.

Greater difficulty arose during those summers which included a trip to see friends in the South of France. Living in Southampton, that was a pretty simple trip, although it involved the best part of eight hours in the car on the other side of the Channel. At first glance, it appeared this could be the perfect summer day if you could pick the day of a Test and make those eight hours between 10am and 6pm. The problem was that the range of the UK's long wave radio signal would not reach as far as Provence, and there was a helpless foreboding as the car reached the outskirts of Rennes, which I knew from bitter experience was roughly the spot, and Christopher Martin-Jenkins would gradually fade out to be replaced by a local Alain Partridge. Worse still, you could be pretty certain this would happen just as Ian Botham was coming in to bat. From that point on, for two weeks, the only tactic left was to encourage visits into the biggest town possible from the beautiful Languedoc countryside in search of the holy grail: a French tabac in which you could find an English newspaper.

Ninety per cent of the time, this would end in disappointment, so when eventually, one of the revolving metal stands spun round to reveal *The Times* hiding behind *Le Monde*, the heart leapt, and what did it matter if it was four days old and four times more expensive than back home? You had to temper the good news with the fact that it might reveal something you really should have seen for yourself. When in 1981 I found just such a paper with the headline 'Was Botham's Innings the Greatest Ever?', it produced decidedly mixed emotions.

The radio's most indelible impression of all, though, was as part of the match-going ritual. Again, there was a quaintness about how you were or weren't able to keep up with goings-on elsewhere if you were actually at a game. I would be all for football grounds banning any electronic devices and returning to the system of some bloke in a white coat bending over at half-time to hang two numbers below each letter of the alphabet, each corresponding to a match listed in your programme. The collective reaction of the whole crowd as each integer was slowly positioned – cheers for Portsmouth 2-0 down, gasps for Liverpool trailing at home and so on – was an important part of the day, taking my mind off the decision as to whether the need for the loo was worth the queue, the aroma and the strange language. But at the end of the game, it was all about the radio. We would get out of the ground and begin the walk back up Hill Lane to the car as the results were coming in – the ideal being to reach the car in time for *Sports Report*. In the meantime, in the land of the returning football supporter, he who owned the small transistor radio was king. I've no idea why I didn't have one; I can't even remember ever making the request – perhaps I thought Mum would try to make a home-made one. So, the tactic was to fall in step with the owner of the best and loudest radio and follow them all the way. A difference in stride length often meant falling in step involved running to ensure you could pick up the headmasterly voice of Bryon Butler spreading the news. There was no other sound quite like it. There were two types of radio-possessors, and you needed to pick out the right one. The jolly fellow, who knew what you were about, held out the radio for all to hear and even threw in a few verbal confirmations for those on the periphery of the circle and the curmudgeon, who was equally aware what you were doing and seemed to resent the fact you were getting a free ride at his expense. I'm not sure these people enjoyed a particularly happy or fulfilling life. I avoided them if I could, but if they were the only option, the opprobrium had to be suffered. *Sports Report* and its 'Out Of The Blue' theme tune were the soundtracks to a Saturday – a comforting bridge between the day's events and the road leading to *Doctor Who*, tea, bed and *Match of the Day*. James Alexander Gordon and Bryon Butler joined my ever-extending list of surrogate uncles as they cemented my introduction to, and entrapment in, the lifelong fate of the sports follower. But if I now had several 'uncles', there was one man who mattered more.

FATHER & SON

Dad was central to all this. The most meaningful and valued shared experiences I owe to sport were certainly with him. And that is all the justification it needs in my eyes. We used to wind each other up playing the generation game – he rather too deliberately expressing his displeasure at current standards and the fact that not everybody was Jackie Milburn or Len Hutton; me wanting to counter every single argument and opinion he gave and hoping deep down that all the England batsmen would play straight as for some reason it always felt like my fault if they didn't when Dad was around. But when he was gone and it was never going to happen again, I realised what a cord it had been between us, how much enjoyment we both got from planning and anticipating (even if the watching itself was rarely easy), critiquing, sharing memories, telling stories and releasing our shared frustrations. The value in this was not just about the sport itself – we would do similar sharing laughs in front of *Morecambe and Wise* and *Rising Damp*, things that were enjoyable enough to watch on our own, but that wasn't the point – I wanted to share the laughter with him as we both knew it was the bond that mattered. So it was with sport.

Although people have been telling me since I was about twelve that I was turning into my father, I have only recently accepted they were right, or at least they are now. Dad always seemed to deal with the triumphs and disasters of our shared sporting experiences with a pretty annoying equanimity (although in reality, I would probably have found it even harder to deal with had he also reacted like a five-year-old – I'm not sure I would have welcomed anyone else stealing my emotional space or implying they might understand in any way what I saw as my own unique brand of suffering). How did he do it, though? Old Trafford and Anderlecht 1977, Highbury 1984, the Ethiad Stadium 2012 – he shrugged these things off and got on with life. I suppose he had to as that was the dad role. He couldn't very well have broken down in tears and sulked for six months. Headmasters just can't do that sort of thing. But if the message to his son was 'it's only a game' and 'there's more important things in life', it singularly failed to have the intended impact. Or perhaps not; perhaps in him I could see some hope… for I realise there was once a time when he too had been me. From being driven to tears by the Australians' domination of the Ashes for nineteen years (plus ça change… he didn't see England win a series until he was twenty), to standing on the Gallowgate terraces at St James' Park and then seeing that other, true United, win the European Cup at Wembley with his Manchester mates. (Not to mention that significant performance of his following the World Cup final.) And as we built our shared experiences, later in life, things seemed to turn full circle to the point where he was almost as wracked as I was as one sporting moment after another crashed and burned. As with any dad, the hobby horses were predictable and annoying, and I have to admit to winding him up on them until we were close to the point of falling out. Bowling too short rather than at the top of off stump. 'These bloody footballers should be marched back ten yards for every bit of chat until they concede a penalty' – the full gamut of reactionary complaints of the ageing sports fan. They would drive me quietly mad. And yes, I am now muttering exactly the same things myself. Of course, I am.

Dad had been there himself, so he understood, and he sparked and encouraged my enthusiasm to do the same. And he was a special man, a far better one than me – a brilliant teacher, and then headmaster, with a burning desire that children should reach their potential and develop their character and that sport had a critical role in that process. He would be out on Friday evenings refereeing, in the classic outfit of the *Lucky Jim* days of school teaching. Woollen socks, baggy shorts, the canvas windcheater and metal whistle around the neck; on Saturdays, when Saints weren't at home, he would be pitchside supporting the school rugby XV. The importance he placed on the sanctity of the game of cricket was evident when his first act as a headmaster was to create 'cricket week' when the whole school either played or watched cricket for a week of the summer term in what seemed like endless sunshine. His headmaster's invitational XI would regularly include ringers of quite breathtaking cheek. But it all rubbed off. I grew up with the message that sport mattered. And that treating triumph and disaster both the same was just as important. I took the first part to heart; the second bit I found a little trickier.

Dad had made the introduction, and the magic of TV and radio had been the vehicle for our first shared experiences. Now it was time to seal the deal.

A GLASS OF CHAMPAGNE

By 1975, I knew the thrill of sport on the TV, and in January, I'd experienced seeing my team and The Dell on it for the first time on *Match of the Day*. Now cricket was to join football at the top of the 'not to be missed on TV' list, thanks to the first Cricket World Cup. The final was probably the first time the idea of the shared experience registered for me. To be allowed to sit all day in the sitting room, with the sun blazing outside, alongside my dad, watching cricket on what I'm pretty sure was our black-and-white TV, was just not the sort of thing Mum usually sanctioned. But here we were together, totally in thrall to the sights and sounds, the West Indian fans dancing and the sound of Red Stripe cans clacking together all day. It all finished after nearly ten hours at 8.43pm – some hour and a bit past bedtime, and I was still there. And though I had no idea at the time, in my first significant day's cricket (if you discount my twelve not out before lunch on the beach at Mewslade Bay), I had seen one of the greatest games ever played and one of the most pivotal in the game's future. This was now something of a theme for these 'firsts' of mine. I didn't realise quite what I was seeing or how lucky I was. And nothing really seemed to go wrong on days whose sights and sounds would live with me forever after, initially on the telly but now through experiencing the real thing – being there.

Two months after turning eight came my first ever trip to live sport. Northlands Road, Southampton, the homely headquarters of Hampshire County Cricket Club, was a genteel place at which to start. In truth, it felt more like one of my parents' parties in the back garden than the overwhelming, slightly intimidating experience my first football match was to be. But I was still agog. I was going to see Australia – those same players I had just seen on the telly in a World Cup final. In the flesh they seemed unreal – not the two-inch-high figures from the screen but huge, scowling, sporting supermen. As they clacked down the steps only feet from me, I knew this was a different world – the real deal. All around, I was picking up cues that the TV just couldn't capture and realised I now felt *part of something* rather than just watching something. Then, for further evidence that my first experiences were touched by a magic I didn't yet understand, the first two batsmen I ever saw walk onto a cricket pitch, representing my provincial club in my home city, were Barry Richards and Gordon Greenidge. To this day, if I'm lying awake picking my all-time world XI, as I often am, I don't get past these two as my openers. Riches indeed.

At lunchtime, whilst I was itching to get the bat and ball out onto the outfield, instead I had to listen to Dad in raptures trying to explain to me what I'd just seen. Richards had been out of the last ball of the morning session, caught at deep midwicket, attempting the boundary that would have given him a hundred before lunch against Thomson, Walker and Hurst. Richards caught Laird, bowled Higgs ninety-six. Of course, my memory is not primarily of the excitement of watching that innings but the hollow, numb feeling I felt when he was out. Not in the plan. Can he come back? Shall we go home now? But Dad was determined to teach me that triumph and disaster thing. From then on, any chance to get to the County Ground was eagerly snapped up. But it would never quite compare with my next debut.

I can see it now, even close my eyes and immediately relive it. Parking the car on Hill Lane, the walk down to the ground in an ever-increasing mass of people, all of whom seemed like giants to me. Vague recollections of language I didn't recognise from home and the tobacco smoke which I did. The first waft of the burger van and frying onions as we turned into Milton Road – an aroma only the sports fan can place in its proper context. Our arrival at the main entrance. I'd been here before, on the outside waiting to catch a glimpse of Mike Channon or Terry Paine after training, red leather autograph book in hand, wondering if anyone would notice if I wrote them in myself if I missed the actual players. But it had always been a citadel I couldn't enter. If this was how exciting it was on the outside, what could possibly be waiting inside?

Into the West Stand Upper with a click of a turnstile twice my height, the walk, in semi-darkness, under the old wooden stand. More crowds. Then up the dozen stairs and suddenly a noise like nothing else before and appearing in front of my eyes a billiard table of the most vivid green I had ever seen. The bluest of blue skies. Heaving masses crammed into a house with no roof. And not a doubt in my mind, 'A Glass of Champagne' by Sailor coming across the tannoy. Where that comes from, I don't know, but it is clear as day. If I ever want to go back to that place, all I have to do is stick that on the iPod and close my eyes. And the telly cameras. Monster trucks with BBC logos all over them. I was thrown by being present at something real that was actually going to be on national TV. Transported to a place of unimagined delight, I found it hard to believe life got any better than this. It was nearly Christmas; I'd made my presents and done my own list; we were playing the best team in the division: the Sunderland players I'd seen in the first division on *The Big Match* the previous year. *Match of the Day* was in town. There was a buzz and an atmosphere I'd never felt before. Here I was with my dad, and it felt like this was all laid on for *me*. Whatever this was, I wanted more of it. And to complete the sense of heaven on earth, the 'seasons in the sun' fairy smiled on me again: we won 4-0. This was easy. In front the TV cameras too so I could enjoy that strange experience for the first time of watching back that night something in which I'd played a part.

The general buzz became a thrilling, concentrated roar as the teams ran out, at which point amidst the rush of excitement, something crept over me which was less expected. In time, it would embed itself within me and never be truly banished. Hello, fear of failure. Just as the Australian cricketers had done before, as the Sunderland players ran out, every one of them looked scary as it dawned on me that they were here with the specific intention of ruining my day. Cowardice took over and I suddenly wanted more than anything for this to be a day when Southampton ran out of the tunnel alone with nobody there that might cause a problem. I realised that if I was going to enjoy sport from now on, I really couldn't like opponents. What they might do worried me. If I thought I had allegiance before, this was now something else, and the days of unconditional enjoyment up to this point were about to cede to something different. As the game started, I leant forward and was suddenly aware my hands were trembling and my feet stamping on the wooden floor without my having played any conscious part in it. There was a knot of something in my stomach. This was where I wanted to be, but it was no longer quite enjoyment. Fortunately, on this particular day, the next lesson learnt was that this purgatory starts abating once you go 3-0 up. If it was a rush of adrenaline I felt when Alec Lindsay scored that goal eighteen months ago, the first goal celebration as part of a crowd – the uncontrollable jump up to try and see, the instant ecstasy and the fact everyone around me felt the same – took me somewhere else, and it happened four times that afternoon. Then I noticed that actually not everyone around me *did* necessarily feel the same. Down below me and to my left – enough distance away that I could observe both clearly and in safety – I was aware of a portion of the crowd standing stock still. Until they decided a better response would be to try to climb the fence. Clearly, these were also 'the enemy'. For the next four years, I would sit in that seat and always keep one eye on the learning experience to my left. People weren't always nice to each other in the real world, it transpired.

Either I passed this audition, or I spent a part of every day afterwards badgering Dad about when we could do it again. Probably both. Whatever made the difference, Saturdays were about to change for the long-term. Waking up on Christmas Day was one of the few moments that could rival that first game for anticipation and nervous excitement. I shared the common eight-year-old take on presents, i.e. size matters. Certainly, your 'main' present should be roughly a minimum of half your own size. So, when I got to my final package and it was the size of my palm and therefore couldn't possibly have been anything I had on the list I had submitted after great thought, and which was now imprinted on my brain, it was Alec Lindsay deflation time again. Even then, I had a sense that it wasn't the done thing to throw a tantrum or burst into tears, so I was desperately trying to fix my face and hide my shock and disappointment. I'm not sure I managed that too well when I opened the parcel to find a small piece of yellow card folded in two, because having allowed themselves a few moments of quiet amusement, Mum and Dad took pity and explained that this underwhelming-looking thing was in fact literally my golden ticket – my first ever season ticket. Admittedly, the fact it was halfway through the season already now makes me wonder whether this was sanctioned because Mum had found another cut-price deal, but at the time, such churlishness wasn't necessary. I was trying to get my head around what this meant. All I had to do was keep this safe and wave it at someone every other Saturday and my own seat at The Dell was assured. And in yet another serendipitous twist, with Christmas always spent at my great auntie's cottage near Oxford, Boxing Day 1975 had Southampton away at Oxford United and there was a ticket for my first ever away game tucked into the wrapping as well. And we won that too. So that was that – no going back. I was now in this for the long haul.

I SECOND THAT EMOTION

For those of us who might want to give our obsession some justification, there is a strong case to be made that sharing experiences with others is what makes life worth the candle and gives it its value. If I find a new artist or album that I love, the real pleasure comes from sharing that with friends whom I think will enjoy it too, whilst of course gaining for myself the reflected glory of the discovery. I've had the same week's holiday in the same valley in the Lake District, with pretty much the same people, every year for half a century. The place is in my bones and my bit of heaven on earth. But I doubt I would take that holiday again if nobody else came to share in it, the value of the experience being in its communal nature. If nothing else, following sport brings us this in buckets. We follow not really for the 'love of sport' but for the emotions and the interactions with others who might share those emotions. Ultimately, on a match day, the game itself is often the least important part; the build-up, the journeys, the time spent with mates are more at the heart of sport than the results themselves. I've explained what this meant to my relationship with Dad, and having shared the experience in our respective youths of knowing how it felt to lose to the Australians at cricket for nearly two decades non-stop, it was not by chance that when England finally won back the Ashes in 2005, forty summers on from our first matches together, the first phone call I made in my state of heady euphoria was to him. When that was done, I jumped in the car with a couple of bottles of Madame Clicquot's finest and drove straight to the family home in the Lakes to share the moment. That part of the memory is as valued as Michael Vaughan with the urn in his hands. Sport occasionally gives us the excuse for such indulgences and to share the happiness. Lord's in 1994 would be just such a moment – outside Southampton's FA Cup final the only time the shared experience was one for the whole family. By then, my job in cricket allowed me to say some thank yous with access to the special places, and my sister and I decided to treat Mum and Dad to a family outing to Lord's. I'd always wanted to share a Lord's day with Dad and assumed I would do so again many times in the future, but it never happened, which is why this one lives with me in a special way. Dad had done similar with his own father back in the day, and I knew for sure he and Mum had shared a courting day there in 1963 against the West Indies, Sobers, Lord Kitchener and all (Dad's idea of how to woo a lady, clearly – another thing I was to inherit). This one was to be for the four of us, and as England Test days at Lord's might be envisaged, this was a classic of the genre. Glorious summer Sunday sunshine and heat, seats in the grandstand, my sister looking every inch the lady in summer dress and straw boater and England collapsing in a heap in pursuit of a victory target against South Africa. All seemed right with the world. From 74-3 to ninety-nine all out rather curtailed our day, but to Mum and Kathryn, this seemed to matter less than the high-class picnic which had been planned to top off the day. Sat in the stands surrounded by Castle Lager-swilling South Africans, whose culinary plans for the day consisted of the odd hot dog to mop up the beer, at the tea interval, we produced from our cool box poached salmon and new potatoes, accompanied by a cold Puligny Montrachet and followed it with strawberries and Chateau d'Yquem. I was feeling at my most self-conscious as I felt we might be guilty of a slight 'overplay' in the environment in which we found ourselves and felt a rush of warmth towards our audience when, at the meal's conclusion, all around us they burst into a spontaneous round of applause. I ought to take the day as a lesson that sport is about the anticipation, the peripheral enjoyment and the aftermath as much as the game itself, and losing seven for twenty-five makes no negative intrusion whatsoever on a special recollection. It's something I'd do well to remember and recreate a little more often today.

The only issue of the live shared experience with Dad, as opposed to that in the TV lounge, was that he did have a habit of making my skin crawl with embarrassment in his interaction with others. You couldn't really take the role he would play of the slightly pompous headmaster out of him, and whilst I had a constant need to radiate cool, Dad would rip it away from me when he opened his mouth. He had a habit of conversing with others he had never met, regardless of their appearance and probable background, as though they would automatically share his sphere of reference, making obscure allusions to things such as Ralph Vaughan Williams' third symphony or the relative merits of the '82 and '83 claret vintages. He didn't seem to mind the nonplussed and rather uncomfortable looks from large Afrikaner cricket fans in such instances in the way I did as I heard every murmured piss-take for the next half hour. Dad would talk to a trainee teenage waitress in a pub dining room as though she was the sommelier at Bibbendum, asking if there was anything she would recommend from the wine list to accompany the dover sole and thereby causing her and the rest of us significant and unnecessary embarrassment. I learnt my lesson around the same time when I employed a similar tactic on a first date. I had a favourite Italian restaurant ten miles from Oldham which I used for such important moments – no second chance to make a first impression and all that. It was generally high class and what I would call proper Italian – marble floors, genuinely Italian owners and waiters – as I had been explaining at length to my companion en route. My disappointment that on this one key occasion my table had been allocated the Saturday girl clearly making her debut in the role didn't stop me. Drawing on all the pomposity I could muster, I asked her if there was a red wine she would recommend with the pasta. A long, contemplative silence was followed by the question, 'd'ya like fizzy?'. Thanks, Dad.

Anyway, I digress… the importance of shared experience runs throughout my sports-following life and doesn't start and end with Dad. Sometimes it creates pragmatic, temporary mateships with people I'd otherwise not have in my sights. These are driven by a shared interest and a preference for companionship when following our teams. During the 1985–86 season which dovetailed with my gap year after school when I had time and money for the first time, away trips became more of an option and attraction, but my closest friends were not that bothered. Travelling and standing on the terraces in a crowd but effectively on my own and having nobody with whom to share the day was a strange and less fulfilling experience. So, throughout Saints' cup run that year, Keith Diamond and I acted as though we had always been the best of friends and travelled the country with a shared objective. And as soon as we lost the semi-final, we went our separate ways, never to reunite. I heard he ended up with one of my more treasured ex-girlfriends which ensured a permanent end to that fleeting comradeship. There were several examples of this sort of marriage of convenience over the years, and they may not have been genuine, but they served their purpose at the time. Sport without interaction loses its meaning.

But it was also a catalyst for real and lasting friendships. When I first arrived at Loughborough with that question in my head of how and with whom I was going to fall in, I had a brief conversation with an unknown fellow sports student who told me later that he knew we had a bond the moment I mentioned my (then) empathy to some degree with Norman Tebbit's 'cricket test' argument, i.e. who do the UK's immigrant population cheer for when England are playing? Not a view to be proud of looking back, and thankfully long since discarded, but for the next three years we were housemates, best buddies, played cricket in our backyard and football for the university. To avoid writing essays we watched sport, sports videos and played a strange baseball board game every spare minute of the day. Without sport, I doubt we would've had much to say to each other, but instead we were joined at the hip.

It has to be said that when I ended up in the privileged position through my work of controlling the allocation of tickets to some special events, including boxes at Lord's and World Cup finals at Twickenham, my list of 'friends' seemed to blossom, but again, some of these days proved that sharing a special occasion, one in which you are similarly emotionally invested, can be the spark for lifelong friendship. Some of my contacts from the business world of sport I now count amongst my most valued friends. Another debt I owe to sport.

HOMETOWN GLORY

I hadn't read the small print on my golden ticket that Christmas just gone. Had I done so, I would've questioned the words 'NOT AVAILABLE FOR CUP TIES'. Not that I was ungrateful, but had I realised the implications of this, I would definitely have seen the hand of my mother involved again; if there were two versions of this thing available, it wasn't likely I was going to be getting the more expensive one. I'll cut my parents enough slack to admit there was no way of knowing that of all the times to take that option with a Southampton season ticket, the coming six months was not the best. My uncanny ability, at that time, to lead my sporting favourites to unforeseen glory like some blissfully ignorant pied piper was about to express itself in a way which remains its most memorable and improbable incarnation to this day. My team's run to the most unexpected FA Cup triumph started as a shared experience with Dad and ended up as one enjoyed with an entire city, gathering an increased sense of belonging as it progressed.

Having opted for the 'no cup ties' ticket, Dad then contradicted himself by buying tickets for the third round, but I wasn't complaining. And by 4.40pm on a cold, dark January afternoon, my team had almost completed their unremarkable exit from the competition at home for the second year running before I discovered the joy and release of an injury-time goal. The even more unremarkable Hughie Fisher bobbled in the only goal I ever saw him score, and although that equaliser was bound to be just a ninety-minute stay of execution, it was a goal and a relief, nonetheless. And yet somehow by the end of March, Saints had won a replay, two more rounds and a quarter-final (against the lowest ranked team left in the competition) and had been drawn against Crystal Palace (the lowest ranked team left in the competition – something was certainly afoot…) which meant my first ever journey to the lights of London and Stamford Bridge on the 3rd of April.

Any football fan knows that semi-finals are horrible, simply not enjoyable, from the stomach pains on the way, to the various pessimistic scenarios you are determined to run through, perhaps in the hope that if you've acknowledged them all in advance, they'll give you due respect and stay away. But this day I needn't have worried. I'd even managed to kick it off that morning with my first ever significant badge of achievement – my twenty-five-metre swimming award from my Saturday morning lesson at the La Sainte Union baths. Another one of my mum's ideas to fill my time and improve me as an all-rounder; I hated everything about those mornings, but unfortunately West London was close enough to home that this regular appointment did not need to be cancelled, and therefore it takes its place rather incongruously in my memory of the day.

From the start of the A33 all the way to Chelsea, I realised we were part of an army – one with a shared goal – and it gave an incredible sense of strength and reassurance. I counted every car with a red-and-white scarf trailing from the window or a car sticker which marked them out as on the same pilgrimage as me. They were everywhere. The Saints *were* marching in. When I saw the stadium – cavernous (if a little down at heel) in comparison with The Dell and the Manor Ground – the whole Shed End was a mass of red and white. I'd never seen such a wall or heard such a noise. The Dell was a quaint place; where had all this lot come from? They were my introduction to the concept of the fair-weather fan. For once in my life, our fans were the dominant force, and I felt a pride which may well have been the thing which keeps the club in my heart to this day. That in itself begs a question about allegiance; I haven't lived in Southampton for more than thirty years; I have no family or friends there, and I am only rarely able to visit the place. I haven't actually been to a home game in most of that time. So why, when Soccer Saturday is coming to a head each Saturday afternoon, do I have a tension in my stomach of a level previously associated with going into an A-Level exam? There is no rhyme or reason to it. What am I trying to prove? Does it really matter to me to know that there might be some reflected glory for the city that formed me? Let's be honest, not too many of the population are going to give a second thought to how Southampton have done, so it's a bit of a waste of emotional energy on my part. Leicester City fans may think they are now somehow elevated in the eyes of others after the events of 2016. I have news for them – they aren't. It was fun for them, but it doesn't mean their city is now rubbing cultural shoulders with Barcelona, Rome, Milan or New York. So why the attachment? The closest I have come to an answer to this came from an unlikely source. When interviewed by Paul Hawksbee about his passion, and that of his entire city, for Newcastle United, Si King – he of Hairy Bikers fame – reflected on Bobby Robson's view on where this lifetime's emotional allegiance comes from:

> 'It's not about the stadium; it's not even about the board of directors; it's about that six-year-old lad, or lass, stood there at their first football game and going, "this is me; this is what I am; this is where I am; this is my people; this is where I'm grounded; this is where I feel I belong", and that's what football fans are about, and that's what it is. It's about that recognition and that attachment to the place that you live and love'.

For a bloke better known for his Yorkshire puddings, that is the most perceptive and sympathetic and succinct insight into this condition I've ever heard. Perhaps days such as these cement themselves more deeply into our consciousnesses than we realise, and, on reflection, my own experience on the 3rd of April, 1976, and the emotions it engendered, were absolutely in tune with those wise words.

As for the game itself, I had that stomach cramp stemming from the knowledge that losing this game would be impossible to bear. When afflicted by this, every minute seems like several hours and only a 4-0 lead by half-time will give you any form of respite. In this case, it was 0-0, which didn't help in the slightest. Then my saviours appeared in the persons of the legends that are Paul Gilchrist and David Peach. Gilchrist hit his screamer right down in front of me and I could see it all the way. Then Mike Channon did his thing. He could glide past defenders with a seemingly effortless and barely discernible change of pace like an Americas Cup yacht heading for home; he also had the habit, on reaching the penalty area, of capsizing in the manner of just such a vessel. And so he did now. It was tenuous at best, but I was perfectly happy to employ those sporting double standards fans use as the need arises, and the penalty put my team in an FA Cup final.

I can't quite recall, looking back, if I knew just how big this was – I think I had a sense of it as we drove back down the motorway in a vast, delirious convoy. I also knew that I would have the whole of tomorrow to bask in the enjoyment and relief as Brian Moore played it all back to us on *The Big Match*, my first experience of the aftermath actually being more enjoyable than the day itself, something which was to escalate over the years to the point where the day itself often couldn't be tolerated.

It's hard to articulate to those not around at the time just what the FA Cup was in the 1970s and what it meant. Certainly, it had unquestioned pre-eminence in the English sporting calendar, but there was something more to it than that, something almost ethereal. The desperate attempts of the BBC to convince itself, as well as the rest of us, that there remains any real equity in one of the few things to which it retains some rights by trotting out the 'magic of the FA Cup' line in every promo, every tortuously lame Lineker programme introduction, has accelerated the devaluation of those words and that concept. But in 1976, it truly existed. This was a time when the FA Cup was *the* prize, *the* day in the calendar when the whole country watched, and now the focus would be on my little team. In Southampton, the run-up felt like we were holding a twenty-seven-day VE day party with a communal happiness and excitement I've not experienced again since. The only slight cloud was the news I was half expecting that I wasn't going. Dad was OK with the semi-final, but a man who bought 'NOT AVAILABLE FOR CUP TIES' season tickets was hardly about to shell out tout prices for the ultimate prize. Never mind, that meant I could take the whole thing in front of the telly for nine hours. I sat impatiently through *Ragtime, On The Move, Champion The Wonder Horse* and finally *Zorro*, which on any other Saturday would've been the highlight of the morning. Today, I couldn't have had less interest in masked vigilantes – I wanted Frank Bough. Not before time at 11.15am, he arrived with Cup final *Grandstand's* David Coleman and all the Davies, Motsons and Gubbas the BBC could muster, and we went through the full 1970's Cup final repertoire from *It's A Knockout* to 'meet the teams' and various other tenuous but riveting time-fillers. This all meant what was to come was the very definition of a shared experience. As Ipswich and Coventry supporters will understand, a provincial city and unfashionable club were about to have their moment in the national consciousness, and for four weeks, the whole place had felt as one – nobody without a smile, strangers forgetting their English upbringing and suddenly talking to each other. If you didn't have something relevant in your window, you didn't belong in the place anymore. The likes of Saints had always had to fight for the odd crumb from the national media table. Twenty minutes as one of the games on *Match of the Day*, which might happen once or twice a season at best, a game on ITV regional Southern TV on a Sunday, which we knew was a cheat because nobody outside a twenty-mile radius was watching or the odd brief mention of Mike Channon being a Southampton player when playing for England perhaps. This was now our time. My weekly *Shoot!* magazine might occasionally have half a page on my team which I would pore over with much pride for the full week; now there were sixteen pages featuring us. It was surreal to see my players – such household names as Mel Blyth, Jim Steele and Nick Holmes – get the full, in-depth focus treatment. The minor concern was the knowledge that we were playing a team which my *Shoot!* magazine's panel of experts had predicted by eighteen to two would stroll past us to victory. I thank Peter Lorimer and Peter Houseman now for their foresight and support. Dad was keen, however, to flag the potential anticlimax, for once with the caring intention of softening the inevitable blow. This pessimism was responsible for one of the poorer family decisions of my early life, which still gnaws at me slightly today. 'Kitgate' part two. My ninth birthday was on Monday the 3rd of May, the final on Saturday the 1st of May. With everything on my list unsurprisingly in some way Saints related, Mum and Dad could see the potential disappointment and devaluation come Monday, opening those presents in the immediate aftermath of a tearful weekend. Most relevant to this were the rumours that a new fashion icon was to be launched at the final, and sure enough, when Saints unzipped their tracksuits to reveal their new state-of-the-art Admiral yellow-and-blue change kit – with sleeve stripes and little badges all over it – even Mr Coleman was willing to give it a shout out. It was going to be the playground statement for the next year, minimum. With the potential anticlimax in mind, an executive decision had been made to move forward to the Saturday an official birthday in the manner of Her Royal Highness, at which point the new kit wasn't yet on sale. At this point, my parents, having made the decision to forward the birthday itself, should, I believe, also have taken responsibility for the call to delay the main present until the following week. What they actually did was to offer me a choice – the current kit on the 1st of May or the new one forty-eight hours later. My decision may now seem odd but try explaining to an eight-year-old with an understandable 'jam today' philosophy that instant gratification may not always be the best option, and they are going to struggle with that concept. So, I unwrapped my bog-standard away kit which was treasured for about four hours before the gobsmacking revelation of the new object of desire in front of me on the TV. Other parents, realising the cruelty of foisting such a situation upon someone without the faculty to make a considered judgement in this most crucial of decisions, may have taken sympathy and purchased the new one the following week anyway in celebration when, after winning the Cup, it was the most sought-after product in Southampton. It was a 'surprise' to which I was primed to react. But to no avail. My attempts to get the jam tomorrow as well as today, hoping my sobbing would encourage the purchase of the new kit regardless, fell on deaf ears, and I can actually still feel somewhere in my psyche the utter deflation when, for the following six months, seemingly everyone in my school was parading the famous, striped-sleeve, cup-winning kit at games, whilst I had to brave the playground again as last year's model, sporting my Bri-Nylon 1975 version, now laughably old-fashioned. My ongoing story of kit disasters had another chapter.

But no matter. The enjoyment of the build-up now gave way to watching the match itself, the torture of which subsequently found a mirror in the first time I walked out to bat in a proper cricket match

– a feeling that from the relative comfort of a friendly dressing room in which nothing could go wrong, I was suddenly out in the middle of the action, a bundle of nerves, with the realisation that there was no way out now and this was the point where it could all fall to pieces. If the first eighty-two minutes – two feet from the TV, curtains closed on the hottest day of the year (although there were one or two more to come that summer) – were uncomfortable, that was nothing compared with the eight that followed our goal. Bobby Stokes (onside, thank you very much) triggered David Coleman's self-conscious trademark 'one-nil'. Madness. Pandemonium. Then my first taste of what was to afflict me forever after – the time v agony graph. Eight minutes. The longest eight minutes of my life to date. Clock-watching by the second, that purgatory which still accompanies the 1-0 lead today, wasn't yet possible as there was no running countdown in the top corner of the screen, only the occasional glimpse of that odd pie chart of a timepiece they used to flash up on the screen, with only the vaguest approximation of how long was left. Why wasn't bloody Coleman telling us the time? Even my perennially disinterested sister was now screaming at every close call, which wound me up even more – what right did she have to care? Where was she when Hughie Fisher scored in January? Alan Brazil once described on his *TalkSport* show the lack of enjoyment he got from Old Firm games as a young Celtic fan, even though he had to be there, saying he was scared to death every time Rangers so much as approached the halfway line. This was my lot now – even Stewart Houston getting the ball at left back many miles from our goal was a moment fraught with terrible possibilities in my eyes. But then Clive Thomas put me out of my misery and a surreal day was complete. This is what you watch sport for, I'm still told. The excitement, the possibility of imminent victory. It didn't feel that way to me and still doesn't. There is no pleasure in that eight-minute experience – not then, not now. In such situations, the final whistle is relief and release from the grip of fear rather than pure elation. So it was now. Southampton, FA Cup winners 1976. Brotherhood of Man win the Eurovision song contest for the UK, then the hottest summer on record. 'Seasons in the sun' for sure. The Pied Piper of 4 Bassett Gardens in his pomp.

I suppose it's my irritating propensity to see the sporting glass as half-empty which makes me wonder now if it was cruel to deliver me such a prize at the end of my very first season. I'm sure I didn't realise then that the sum total of the next forty-five years would be a losing final and two losing semis. In reality, it's a memory (and a video) that has been there to warm me when needed over the years – winning it when it was still just about the biggest thing in world football. And if I needed a lesson to make the most of the good times when they come along, I was to get it just twelve months later.

THE FIRST CUT IS THE DEEPEST

'You cannot accept the beauty of a rose without the accompanying thorns'
JEFFREY G DUARTE

Two years in and already one of the biggest FA Cup upset wins in history in the bag. The obvious conclusion was that sport was going to be a life-enhancing happy experience. (As the sportswriter Emma John also recalled of her early years in a lifelong dedication to English cricket, 'I hadn't yet learnt to be sceptical'.) It was to continue to be so for a while in the most part, but harsh realities were also about to kick in for the first time, a learning experience I hadn't asked for or anticipated. I hadn't had much grief in my life come 1977. I mean proper grief as well as the supposedly less serious sporting kind. The loss of one much-loved grandparent, but after a good innings, and that was it. Cosy childhood, fun school life. It was therefore sport which actually introduced me to the whole concept.

My golden touch was becoming something of a given for me, and I was cocooned comfortably in its embrace. After a summer of basking in both the heatwave and the reflected glow of my team's sudden rise to fame and plaudits, I eagerly awaited the new season and the inevitable sedan chair ride to promotion as opponents bowed down before us. Only, we lost at home to Carlisle on the opening day and by the end of September, my conquering heroes had managed to lose 6-2 to the might of Charlton Athletic and were propping up the whole of the second division. It seemed entirely possible that the quantities of champagne being drunk at Wembley by Messrs Osgood, McCalliog and Steele were still being replicated or surpassed most days after training at The Cowherds Pub. When people suggested we were more of a cup team than a league one, it was perhaps a gentle way of telling us a good chunk of our team were the sort who would happily sacrifice promotion for regular days and nights of hedonism at Windsor Racecourse and that our ratio of Cavaliers to Roundheads was a little askew for the serious business of grinding out points every week. Certainly, there was plentiful evidence that autumn that the likes of Ossie cared not much for the pleasures of the Tuesday night away trip to Plymouth or Blackburn, having been the King of Stamford Bridge, not to mention the Kings Road, for many years. But it has to be said, put the bright lights of a cup tie in front of them and their egos acted as the switches which turned them on. So it was to prove again when I went to my first ever evening match – the atmosphere I loved now enhanced by the floodlights and the fact now I was at the football when I would otherwise have been in bed. This time, the stage for our charming bunch of mavericks was European as well as domestic. The first round of the Cup Winners Cup was another first experience to rank alongside the best. From the floodlights and foreign accents and a distinctly different look to that away crowd down to my left, everything seemed somehow a touch more exotic. I was used to Oldham Athletic. Had I enough knowledge of European football to understand the name Olympique Marseille stood for more than just my toughest challenge so far on Mum's typewriter and actually heralded one of Europe's aristocrats, the fact that we stuffed them out of sight 4-0 would have thrilled me even more than it did. Peter Osgood had decided this was a game finally worthy of both his effort and his finest skills and gave a performance which still makes my top three today. Might perhaps my mental difficulties with following sport in my later years be connected in some way to growing up with possibly the most schizophrenic football team of the era? By Christmas, we had marched into the European quarter-finals, and in January, the two best teams in our division, who we couldn't get near in the league, had been dispatched from the FA Cup as we defended the trophy which had become my birthright. It was all happening again. I sometimes wonder what Dad thought of all this – was he not beginning to get just a little freaked out that since he started taking me to a quaint little second division club eighteen months ago, they had won every one of eight FA Cup ties, won the trophy itself and were seemingly on their way to doing it again, whilst soon to be landing in the last eight in Europe? Was his son some sort of diviner? Unfortunately, March 1977 was to give him his answer. The only complication to the retention and addition of these trophies lay in the upcoming opposition. Whilst it was batting well above our average for a team in the bottom half of Division Two to have consecutive ties coming up against Anderlecht and Manchester United, a couple of bridges too far were homing into view. I was heading for an eighteen-day crash course in crushing disappointment.

I spent the afternoon of the 26th of February, 1977 at the strangest, most exciting, febrile, frightening sports event I had ever been to or have been to since. It was my first dose of cold reality in more ways than one. The Covid lockdowns of 2020 and 2021 were to be a right bag of goodies for us committed nostalgists, to the point where I was asking myself if it might not be better to simply cancel all future sport and make this the norm instead. The warm embraces of Brian Moore and Jim Laker were everywhere as we gorged ourselves on the memory lane programmes filling the schedules left, right and centre. One of the reruns I indulged in was this very Southampton v Man Utd fifth round FA Cup tie, and it reminded me that this game between the previous year's finalists was a major deal, confirmed by the fact that even though Southern TV were doing the highlights, which would normally mean David Bobin or an apprentice Martin Tyler, no less a commentary deity than Brian Moore himself left the LWT catchment area to do the job himself. Brian didn't head for the shires – my shire in particular – for any old game.

The programme was awash with memories. I stared open-mouthed at the screen as the way this had rested in my mind for the past forty-three years was indeed borne out by the pictures. Matches like this really did exist. With someone else sitting in my seat as a result of Mum's 'NOT

AVAILABLE FOR CUP TIES' decision, at nine years old, this was my first ever game on the terraces, and it was some game to pick given the most notoriously vast and violent group of supporters in the country had come to visit. I relived the thrill of the day but also the terror. Pitched battles – adults actually punching each other was not something I had seen before other than on a parentally unsanctioned glimpse of *The Professionals*. Darts in jeans pockets and, outside the ground, *thousands* of fans without tickets who couldn't find a spot in the trees who just stood and listened to the roars without the modern-day option of watching it in the pub. After the pitch invasions, which frequently punctuated the action, fans were simply ushered to stand on the touchline like parents at an under-13s game (although not many of them looked much like my parents). I swear that when Alex Stepney made one save, there was a bloke leaning casually on the other side of the post. And having been used to the safety and the Subbuteo-style view of proceedings I enjoyed in the stands, being front row at pitch level was like a trip to the Coliseum on a day the lions were feeling hungry. It also put me right in the line of fire. I couldn't really see much of the game, but that didn't matter much given my attention was almost solely focused on the fights breaking out everywhere and making sure I was aware of any potential incoming darts or coins. Watching it again, I realised it was also one of the most exciting cup matches I've ever seen and that Saints should have won, Channon's past penalty capsizes coming back to bite him when he was hauled down in the closing minutes, this time for real, and got no penalty, so a replay it was. It would at least mean Saints at Old Trafford.

If United had an aura, then the side we had to play in Europe topped it. With due respect to Liverpool, who weren't to win their first European Cup for another eight weeks, and Bayern Munich, who had won the last three but wouldn't again for a quarter of a century, Anderlecht were probably the best, most exotic side on the whole continent. Packed with a mixture of those Dutch players who had introduced me to the World Cup and transfixed me three years before, and some very handy Belgians alongside them, they were the holders. And having duly put us out of our misery and, by common consent, effectively out of the competition in the first leg in Brussels by winning 2-0, the tie was pretty much done, which was a shame but reduced the stress levels associated with the return. I was still going to see Robbie Rensenbrink and Arie Haan at The Dell, which for thoroughbreds out of context seemed the equivalent to Red Rum or Arkle competing on Southampton Common. It appeared my touch was wearing off, and so it transpired as, within eight days, my team would be getting onto their rollercoaster again. However, this time, it was going to come off the rails and introduce me to that hollow, desperate feeling and the helpless self-delusion in hoping that when you do eventually fall asleep, it won't all come flooding back as reality the next morning.

First, Tuesday night, transistor on the living room mantelpiece, me standing almost attached to it next to Dad's chair, physically incapable of sitting down. United were winning the replay and about to furnish me with another new experience: my team being out of the FA Cup. I stared at Dad with the eyes of the victim who is slipping out of his would-be saviour's grasp on a cliff face, knowing he is to meet his fate but imploring someone to prevent the inevitable. He'd always looked out for me, looked after me. Surely, he wasn't going to sit there and just let my world cave in? But it ended, and I stood there rooted to the spot. If Dad was looking for a sign as to whether I could yet treat triumph and disaster just the same, he got a fairly clear one as I burst into floods of uncontrollable tears. There was definitely a touch of the spoilt child here – I'd been granted an unbelievable start to my supporting life and at the first setback, I felt completely robbed. This just wasn't supposed to happen. It was the gradual realisation I could do nothing about it which stunned me the most. This wasn't Dad's fault, and he couldn't sort it out for me regardless of how much I cried. It was there forever as a life lesson and a mental scar.

If this was fair enough as a law of averages readjustment of my positive and negative experiences, to top it the following week was a little cruel. Get back on the horse, I'd decided, and that horse galloped into town the following Wednesday night to The Dell bursting at the seams and even more electric in its own way than on the day of the United game. The evening kick-off and the violet colours of Anderlecht everywhere, I was back in the safety and comfort of a stand seat. The only fear came from seeing the speed and ability of these blokes in purple who seemed from another planet. Dad's week-long drip, drip attempts to manage my expectations, fearing another burst of tears, seemed well justified now. But with thirteen minutes to go, I'd forgotten every one, and I think Dad had too. We had scored twice; the tie was level; and The Dell was louder than it ever would be again. That noise alone was going to do it now. There was only one winner. Arie Haan didn't look so clever anymore. Chances came to score again. And then... a long ball, a slip from Jimmy Steele – I don't think alcohol-induced on this occasion to be fair – and Francois Van der Elst smashed the ball in with the clinical efficiency of an international forward. There are two types of silence that will always resonate with me. The good one is that of utter calm, the true silence when you find yourself alone in a sheltered spot below the summit of a mountain. It's a silence you can hear. Then there is this one: a sporting crowd that falls in an instant from loud excitement to stunned silence. You know there must be some noise going on, but you can't hear it. Now this helpless, bitter sensation of seeing the ground fall still except for huge cavorting swathes of purple had never been so stark. I've never got used to, or been able to bear with any dignity in my whole sports-watching life, the celebrations of an opposition crowd in such a moment. You hate every one of them. It is the moment that every sports follower will tell you they dread above all others. And there's not one damn thing you can do. (Well, these days turn the telly off, go for a bath and pretend it never happened, but that course wasn't a route open to me here.) My first 'away goal'. Dad explained why it really counted as two, which I would have really had an issue with if I had been listening. The cliff-edge fall from bubbling excitement to complete deflation was a feeling I can still touch. But this time there were no tears – perhaps I had none left – just a numbness. I knew it was done. Two and a half weeks had put a twist on my devotion. OK, it was still intact, but clearly there was going to be more to it now than just days in the sun. March 1977 would go down as a black month and an inevitable, but still no less bearable, first education in the fundamental truth that disappointment is the primary lot of the sports fan.

THE RHYTHM OF LIFE

For the time being, this was to be just a bump in the road. I now had to develop the ability to find the crumbs of comfort in such misery. The lifeline in my case was that although the majority of my early live experiences were at football, I was a sports follower, not just a football fan. This allows me to this day to switch from one sport to another at the times of greatest need. Over the last few years, I've lost count of the number of times I've given up football after a bad day, rationalising that it's a nasty, self-centred, commercially obsessed exercise in which VAR might just be the final straw, and I don't need to be part of it. I can take it or leave it, thanks. Far better to focus on nice sports like cricket and rugby. This is a well-worn tactic which lasts until England lose an Ashes Test or United beat Liverpool with a last-minute winner, at which point I do a U-turn and the cycle continues. Now, in late March, the clocks were about to change. That didn't mean as much to me then as it does now, but I was slowly developing a comfort in the changing seasons as sport became the rhythm of life. My year is measured by the sporting, as well as the Julian, calendar. January: FA Cup third round; the Guinness period (more so these days than as an eleven-year-old) of February: Six Nations; March: Cheltenham; April: The Masters through four consecutive early evenings to late nights of telly and the start of the World Snooker Championship; May: World Snooker and FA Cup finals (and in the good old days, Home Internationals football); June and July: the summer season of Lord's, Wimbledon, The Open Championship, British Grand Prix (perhaps a football World Cup); August: the new football season – complete with sunshine, billiard-table-green pitches, new kits and new signings – and the Oval Test; September and October: possibly a Ryder Cup and European Cup rugby; November: autumn rugby internationals and December: the UK Snooker and, increasingly reluctantly, the Sports Personality of the Year. That is how a year unfolds. It's a calendar around which all other plans are made. When it was unavoidably ripped up in 2020, the weeks and months stretched ahead with an unexpected emptiness as all I had taken for granted disappeared. Of the twelve, the fairest month of all must be May, as snooker at the Crucible and the start of the cricket season-proper herald the arrival of spring, the summer ahead and a lifting of the heart.

I have something of a photographic memory, perhaps not when trying to recall what I've walked into the kitchen for or the names of friends' or relatives' children, but certainly for the sport and music of my youth. That's where you want me in a pub quiz. Events throughout my life are recalled directly through these media. Ask me what I was up to in April 1978, and I'll tell you I was watching Ray Reardon in Sheffield and Ipswich beating West Brom in the Cup semi-final, whilst staying with family friends in Leeds for Easter, reading Roy of the Rovers and waiting on the Top 40 countdown for Gerry Rafferty's 'Baker Street' and 'Follow You Follow Me' by Genesis. (At eleven, my punk cred was not high.) Individually, none of these things really mattered, but as a whole, they paint pictures for me which I still treasure. Sport had become the beating drum which accompanied life. As I looked into 1978, my mental calendar had the year mapped out. Of course, there was the almost ever-present football, but there were other things which guided me through the rhythm of a year.

SUMMER BREEZE

If spring was Easter, the Grand National and the Crucible, synonymous with the holiday, staying with friends and enjoying a time of year bursting with possibilities ahead, memories of summer take me back to a soporific dreamland, with a gentle sporting menagerie played out in seemingly constant sunshine. After the actual curtains-drawn full day of Cup final Saturday came the parochial, and as I came to understand, far from friendly, 'home internationals' to bring the more metaphorical curtain down on the football season. England v Scotland was the only other live game we got and, as such, was a big deal. It also introduced me to the jaw-dropping sight of the Tartan Army and a creeping awareness that that there might be people out there who had an issue with England. This realisation and my resultant future desperation to beat all things Celtic, above all Scotland, was not yet developed fully enough to prevent me supporting them through the next World Cup, but that's another matter.

Thereafter, summer became more genteel. Coming home from school on summer afternoons, with the long summer holiday almost within touching distance, to watch Bjorn Borg, Vitas Geralitus and Jimmy Connors playing a game which now seems only to approximate to tennis, to the gentle accompaniment of Dan Maskell and John Barrett – comfortable bastions of middle England – offered that rare luxury of sport on a school day. Like half of the British public, it also sent me racing out to get a tennis racquet, ideally the one with the futuristic metal frame of Jimmy Connors' rather than my Mum's wooden one from the fifties which, despite being kept all year in a contraption reminiscent of some medieval instrument of torture, still had a head which looked like it could hit the ball in three directions at the same time. Much like my football kits, this was not the thing to be seen with at Southampton Sports Centre. I'm not sure if this is purely a British thing, but the lemming-like need to go out and pretend to be the people you are watching on the telly, strictly for just as long as they remain on the telly, was a feature of these annual staging posts. Today, the cynic in me (me, in other words) sighs when every national sports body makes great play of the standard chorus that success in major events has driven important increases in participation when what they really mean is that success in major sporting events just means a more lucrative TV contract next time around. They know full well that we will take up these sports for just as long as it takes us to realise we are no good at them and all the gear was a complete waste of money.

The urge to play tennis for a fortnight followed the trips with Dad to the snooker club in the weeks around the Crucible. But there were problems with both these pastimes at eleven years old. The snooker table in the club was somewhat bigger than it looked on the telly. The facts that I couldn't see one end of the table from the other, due to distance, smoke and my lifelong stigmatism and that I needed a bunk-up to play every shot meant my efforts were some way short of Alex Higgins'. Potting a ball would usually be both an outrageous fluke and a reason for significant celebration. With the tennis, you started with the annual battle with the inevitable curmudgeonly parks manager to actually get on a court somewhere. These characters seemed to consider the possibility of people below the age of thirty actually using a facility as something to be blocked at all costs. If you want a reason it took seventy-seven years for us to find a British male winner at Wimbledon, just take a look at these miserable bastards. Even if you somehow succeeded in getting on (and you had to settle for a potholed piece of concrete; the dream of the beautiful green lawn your heroes played on was a non-starter. Keep off the grass), a similar problem to that of the snooker was soon apparent. This court was not the size of a TV screen. It was huge; it was hard; and the net was so high the chance of someone of my height getting a ball over it and not also clearing the wire fence around the courts would seem to have to defy the laws of physics.

So, it seemed the sensible solution was to head back to the ease of watching all this on the TV… and in the seventies and early eighties, the most emblematic of all those summer days was the sporting summer Sunday. This was based around the gentle pace of John Player League cricket. It is a seventies memory evocative enough to sit alongside the smell of an empty Tic Tac box or the taste of Top Deck shandy. From 2pm, the voices of Peter West, Jim Laker, Tom Graveney and Tony Lewis would meander through a contest that barely mattered other than in its being there. This was rarely from Lord's or The Oval, rather the ultra-English citadels of Canterbury, Worcester or Hove, all trees, deckchairs and cathedrals. This was the *Antiques Roadshow* of sport; never can professional sport have come closer to representing an English garden party and a village match. That was its charm. Unless Hampshire happened to be on, and they were pretty good at this form of the game since Barry Richards only had to see a TV camera to decide to give the viewers a hundred, this was no-pressure viewing, only ever interrupted by the other icons of summer Sundays: Grand Prix and the final rounds of golf tournaments. If I was still due at school on Monday, the conclusion of any of these would usher in that gathering cloud of anticlimax and disappointment that the weekend was done, and the alarm would go in the morning. But if it happened to be during the holidays and by chance we were not stuck in a tent somewhere, these were luxurious days indeed. Once those long holidays kicked in and we set off on the inevitable camping trips, the summer soundtrack moved to *Test Match Special*, Brian

Johnston, the curse of the shipping forecast, the Radio 3 crackle and that challenge of finding a listenable reception on a campsite in Aberystwyth.

Just such a summer Sunday was the 3rd of September, 1978. Although tinged with the melancholy that the next week would involve the return to school, Hampshire were in with a chance of winning the Sunday trophy. This least glamorous of the one-day pots was frustratingly the only one our theoretically strong side ever seemed to get close to. There was no Barry Richards anymore, the greatest opener I ever saw having finally had enough of the less-than-bright lights of county cricket and headed back to the beaches of Durban, but otherwise this was the classic JPL Sunday. Deckchairs and shimmering sea as a backdrop to the out-ground at Bournemouth. The peace was only interrupted by the crack of Gordon Greenidge's bat as he stepped into the Richards-less breach with five sixes and 122. Oh, the joy of being able to enjoy one of his innings with him on my side rather than the less appreciated hundreds he regularly took off England's hapless bowlers. Our 221 off forty overs was then deemed an almost unassailable target which just reinforces the soporific nature of the whole business. We duly won by twenty-six runs, waited twenty minutes to hear the result of the Somerset game and took the title by virtue of run rate. When combined with Saints' promotion to first division achieved in early May, that summer had been bookended by two successes which maintained the general theme of the happy and victorious days I'd grown used to and which had just become part of the rhythm of my young life.

Something, however, was gradually building which would be the catalyst in the journey from innocence to purgatory: this business of allegiance.

TWO TRIBES

I've asked myself what it is that makes the difference. What makes someone cross the Rubicon and let the drug take control of their life? Whilst I can admire a straight six or a 147 break as much as anyone, I fear I rarely watch for the pure love of the skill on show any more as some claim to; it is about following a *contest*, and from there, it is but a short hop to the thing that changes the whole dynamic: *allegiance*. Once you have this, you are gone. Trapped. Goodbye to rationality, proportion, appreciation and control of your own emotions. Hello annoyance, cantankerousness, schadenfreude, mild panic and endless disappointment. Unless you are a believer in reincarnation and have the conviction that you might get several more chances to come back as Kevin Keegan, you will accept we are on this planet for but a short while. To let the outcome of Southampton's game away at Crystal Palace dictate your level of happiness for *any* of that time is, in the grand scheme of things, preposterous. Is that being a sports fan or something rather stranger? Either way, there are a lot of us about.

If innocent enjoyment, via bitter experience, to pessimistic resignation is the journey, then allegiance is the vehicle which takes us on our way. It's what separates those of us who are sick to the pit of the stomach at crucial moments from those who seem blithely to be able to enjoy it. Where it comes from and why it endures is a mystery. In the early days, it hovers around like a honeybee investigating where the best nectar is to be found. Then, as discoveries are made, some positive and others opening eyes to the possibility of enemies at the gate, allegiances are settled, and they harden like concrete. Where and why they land as they do is likely to be outside your control.

Initially, you seem to be allowed the leeway to experiment, and nobody holds that against you. You don't have to justify your choices as I seem to have had to for the last forty years or so. In his miscellany of sporting reminiscences, *My Sporting Life*, playwright Willis Hall tells of his attempts to encourage his reluctant son to embrace the joys of sport and thereby secure a long-term point of connection between the two of them. He aims to achieve this by urging the bemused boy to find a footballing allegiance. Having settled on Liverpool, his proud Dad buys him a pin badge to wear to school the following day. The boy returns from school having swapped the badge for a plastic stegosaurus and responds to his father's enquiry as to why he deemed the dinosaur more attractive than Kevin Keegan or Stevie Heighway, regardless of how many more millions of years it might have inhabited the earth, by saying he wasn't Liverpool anymore because Harold Bullock in his class said Liverpool were crackers. Although his son then drifted away, never to show an interest in sport again, even for those of us who are serious, there is a formative period when such vacillation can be tolerated. I myself went through Liverpool, via Fulham, for the 1975 Cup final, before nailing my colours to Southampton. But once you have it, you have it.

Now, let's get this one out of the way straight away. I follow Southampton and Manchester United. This always elicits the response, delivered as if there is no way any argument can be brooked, 'you can't have two teams'. But I can, because there is nothing false in my affections and nothing I can do about it. To those who would call me a glory hunter, I say that all it really does is double the potential for disappointment. I was born near Manchester; my dad had his season ticket at Old Trafford and stood on the terraces at the '68 European Cup final; and I grew up in Southampton where I first went to, and fell in love with, football. I now live near Manchester again. I'm done with either apologising for, or feeling I have to justify, this. The fact is, I am almost equally as wracked when either result comes through, with Saints edging the head-to-head games. My antipathy to Liverpool and City these days is as committed as any Stretford-ender's. Hence the contents of this book for those who were getting confused. If it's acceptable for Nick Hornby to flit between Arsenal and Cambridge in *Fever Pitch*, I have a worthy precedent, so you're going to have to accept this from me now. End of story.

John Lennon suggested to us that 'love is the answer'. Well, possibly, John, but not in this context it isn't. Unfortunately, but honestly, hatred and jealousy often play a more significant role in the world of the sports follower. The problem with allegiance is that you become aware that every other team, player and set of supporters are out there specifically to make you unhappy. This gradually makes you a less attractive personality as your hatred for others pulls up alongside your love for your chosen ones and sometimes overtakes it. The DJ and would-be philosopher Chris Evans once espoused the plausible opinion that to envy another and wish them ill simply generates poison inside the perpetrator and causes the target no harm at all. As such, it is not only an unattractive trait but a waste of time and energy, completely self-defeating. On perhaps a more cerebral plane, with due respect to Chris, the German novelist Hermann Hesse endorsed this (although I doubt he heard it on Virgin Radio) when he said, 'if we hate a person…' (and I would add in 'team' here too) '…we hate something in our image of him that lies within ourselves. What is not within ourselves doesn't upset us'. In other words, our antagonism is our problem, nobody else's. I agree with them both, but I still think if you asked him (Chris not Hermann) if he'd take pleasure in Bruno Fernandes missing a last-minute penalty against his beloved Liverpool, he'd be hard pressed to deny it. I may feel some guilt in such a negative emotion, but it's not just fans that suffer from it. Steve Davis has admitted that he hated Stephen Hendry when he was taking his titles and that, consequently, any defeat Hendry suffered, whether at Davis's own hand or not, was a source of pleasure. Davis himself was a similar target for many when he was seeing off Higgins and White with monotonous efficiency. Comedian Johnny Vegas says, 'Steve Davis was not well liked in our house. He'd denied too many of our heroes titles in the past'.

What my experience of allegiance tells me is that its dynamic changes over time in response to your loss of innocence and realisation that others don't reciprocate your initial support. There is also an element of anything for a change and the English trait of wanting to bring the successful back down to earth and a related love of the underdog ahead of true quality. The worst prospect of all these days is playing those who take such an obvious and audible pleasure in beating you that you come to hate them and the thought of any contest which might lead to a defeat. I would have no issue if Southampton never played Portsmouth again, regardless of the fact that we would be favourites to win more often than not. At the time a few years ago when Pompey were threatened with liquidation (having in the opinion of all Saints fans won a tainted FA Cup by spending money they didn't have), a friend of mine made the point that I surely wanted them to survive as they teetered on the precipice as otherwise, I would lose my local derby and the excitement which went with it. He seemed genuinely surprised when my response was that I would happily see them wiped off the face of the earth without a trace. When you get to my level of addiction, ask yourself whether, as a Manchester United fan, you'd prefer them to be knocked out at the group stages of the Champions League or risk playing and losing to Liverpool in a semi-final after an otherwise excellent tournament. There's surely only one answer, and again, you may find yourself asking, *what's the point?* The seventeenth-century English critic William Walsh wrote, 'I can endure my own despair, but not another's hope'. Precisely, even if he wasn't suggesting this in the context of a Champions League tie. In fact, the words come from his *Song: 'Of all the torments, all the cares'* which sounds like it could be an ideal terrace anthem for Southampton fans or the Barmy Army if they want to look it up.

A TOWN CALLED MALICE

'Now hatred is by far the longest pleasure; men love in haste, but they detest at leisure'
LORD BYRON (DON JUAN, 1824)

The balance between love and hate, or at least support and enmity, has shifted the longer I have followed sport, and not in a positive way. It is something I need to reverse. Following the dictum that in trying to determine the difference between involvement and commitment one should consider a plate of ham and eggs, with the chicken being involved and the pig committed, it's clear I have gradually become more pig and less chicken with the concomitant pessimistic outlook. But it didn't start this way. My understanding was that you supported the English teams or individuals, regardless of which ones, because they were one of us, on the same side. I had no appreciation that many of them were very much on the opposite side to those I held most dear. And if England were either no good or not present, then you defaulted to the next British option as a matter of course.

This is how in the late seventies I was to be found supporting Liverpool in Europe, Scotland at the 1978 World Cup and even Wales at rugby given they were clearly the best in the world, and I had no problem with lauding them as such. The fact that, unbeknownst to me, Liverpool would in time come to rival only Portsmouth in my 'anybody but...' category and that those two Celtic nations viewed my own country with a significant amount of vitriol makes this all the more impressive and endearing on reflection. The idea that I could take such a magnanimous approach these days is, sadly, laughable. Throughout the '76–'77 season, I had followed Liverpool in Europe on those Wednesday-night Radio 2 Peter Jonesfests, and they had duly reached the European Cup final in Rome. This was a huge deal for me, and I remember a party on the night of the final at the home of some Norwegian friends (complete with huge Norwegian open prawn sandwiches in the days before Roy Keane took them off the supporter's menu). It felt like a moon-landing-scale event, with even my mum showing an interest. Joy was unconfined when Liverpool won, and over the next five years, I would support in turn Liverpool, Nottingham Forest and Aston Villa as they kept that cup in English hands. I'm sure I would feel more at ease with myself if today I could do something similar with Liverpool, Manchester City or Chelsea, but I can't. Every success they might achieve is a dagger to the heart, their every departure from the competition a reason to relax and celebrate almost as if my own team had won it. This is actually a fair test of allegiance – the British teams in Europe question. There is still the odd purist out there who will profess that if their team isn't involved, they would want Liverpool, Chelsea or whoever to win the Champions League as they are a British team. This stems I think from a misguided belief that it 'reflects well on our football'. In the early eighties perhaps, when teams were made up primarily of British players, but since our teams became versions of the Harlem Globetrotters, with anyone with enough money capable of creating a League of Nations squad, this argument surely loses weight. There was recently a call-in show on *TalkSport* where 'Colin, the Chelsea fan' came on to insist he wanted Liverpool to win the European Cup. The presenters' response was incredulous, and he was advised, 'try something else, Colin, football's clearly not for you'. He was later made 'Numpty of the Week' on the same station. This suggests honesty has now overtaken humbug in relation to such matters, and a desperation for your rivals to be unsuccessful is now an acknowledged and accepted part of most sports fans' make-ups. Similarly, if I watch back today Scotland's infamous World Cup in Argentina in 1978, I can feel a smug amusement as Teófilo Cubillas's goals fly in for Peru and Johnny Rep condemns the Scots to another 'if only' departure. Quite what we would be having to put up with today had Scotland actually achieved what they had confidently promised to doesn't bear thinking about. So, I have to remind myself nowadays that at the time, in the absence of England, they were my team. In 1977 and 1978, unaware that their fans were still going to be throwing their total number of European Cups in our faces forty years later, I was desperate for Liverpool to win their finals; in 2019, I was desperate for them not to. So, what happened? The discovery that the adult world is a far less innocent place, where bitterness and grudges are harboured and the success of others is a threat rather than a reason for applause and appreciation, that's what. I don't quibble with the assessment of the actions of Mr Cromwell in Ireland in the seventeenth century as unpalatable, but what that has to do with Owen Farrell and the current England rugby team in the eyes of the Irish, I am not quite sure. But the inherent nature of the adult sports fan is that if a chip on the shoulder is to be thrust their way, it is going to be sent back with interest. You don't like me? Well, yah boo then, I don't like you either, and I hope you get stuffed. Supremely mature, I'm sure you'll agree, but I cannot exclude myself from that section of the sports-following public. I would love to be the bigger man, the better person, and sometimes I even pretend I can be, but I'm kidding myself. I'm as petty as the rest.

So yes, in 1978, still an eleven-year-old with relatively little exposure to sporting and non-sporting hatred, with no England at the World Cup, I saw Scotland as my team. Perhaps I hadn't registered yet that invading Wembley the year before, cutting up the pitch and smashing up our goalposts was probably an indication that the Scots might not have been so supportive of my country had it been the other way round. These things dawned on me gradually, and slowly, a love for most became a hatred of many. When things get really bad, such as Liverpool winning the Premier League, I pretend I *am* above it. If I show otherwise, I am giving those rivals the extra pleasure they are expecting to squeeze out of the situation. I have no doubt the greatest joy Liverpool fans got from that achievement was not how *they* were feeling, but how United fans would be feeling. Even at the moment of greatest triumph, we see it in terms of others' disappointment, as William Walsh suggested. I have no problem accepting that my part in this is a sign of personal weakness and insecurity, but I'm not alone. That epitome of good grace and magnanimity, Jimmy Connors, admitted, 'I hate to lose more than I love to win. I hate to see the happiness in their faces when they beat me'. I know how he feels. It is how I learnt that one of the most important emotions for the less secure and less generous of us is that of schadenfreude.

TAKE THAT... AND PARTY

Given what was to come across the penalty spots of Europe, it feels right that this emotion should be encapsulated by a German word. A dictionary definition of 'pleasure derived by someone from another person's misfortune' pretty much nails one of the evermore present elements for the less well adjusted of us. You have to be very careful with it as, without doubt, it's going to be your turn soon enough, which is why I tend to enjoy my schadenfreude quietly and without crowing. Racine wrote, 'he who laughs on Friday will cry on Sunday'. (Racine must have had some idea of the Sky Sports weekend schedules to be so presciently accurate). Away from sport, I'd like to think I take pleasure in the success of others. Not only does it then come back the other way, but it also basically makes you a better person. I find it harder when it comes to sport, and this again is on the list of things to try to change in the future. But before we offer ourselves up to too much condemnation, please ask yourself if you can truly say you have never employed it. Be honest, do you never watch the replay of a goal on *Match of the Day* and find yourself watching not the action but the disappointment and reactions of the fans behind the goal who have just conceded? There is a perverse pleasure in this, is there not? Or is this just me? In fact, it is reassuring for me that those whom we hold in some esteem for their wit and intelligence also succumb. TV's Richard Osman, bright enough to make several fortunes creating and presenting cult television formats and writing bestsellers, once said, recalling Peter Ebdon beating Stephen Hendry 18-17 in a World Snooker final, after many years in which Stephen had ruined many of our Easters by traumatising Jimmy White, 'Stephen Hendry... devastated. No one likes to see that', accompanied by a wry grin of pleasure. Offer me Southampton winning another FA Cup in return for Liverpool winning the next three league titles and I would have to think long and hard about it. I don't check BBC Sport online in the morning in any trepidation of the Test score between Pakistan and South Africa, but India winning in Australia is almost more of a pleasure than England beating Sri Lanka. Many things can help cultivate this attitude. Sometimes it is a desire to shut people up. Listening to Glenn McGrath predict the 5-0 whitewashes (especially when he was right) or simply looking at the smug countenance of David Warner makes any Australian defeat that much more enjoyable. One of the highlights of the 2019 Ashes series, which rather compensated for the 2-2 result, was Stuart Broad making Warner look like a lost under-11s schoolboy and dismantling his much-cultivated mean destroyer persona in front of his own eyes. Those, and there are plenty of them, who profess to 'hate' the English, when it comes to sport at least – honourable mentions in dispatches here for the French, Scots, Welsh and Irish and, of course, the Aussies – are opponents I don't want to see beaten by England alone. I want them beaten every time by everybody. This is their own fault as I didn't used to. They started it…

There is one other role for hatred in sport and that is employing it against your own team. When they let you down, you can find it impossible to forgive them, for a while. Or when you feel let down by the people who are developing or managing the teams in which you have invested so much. As a Southampton fan in the world of modern football, you get used to being what seems like the only team in the Premier League not to have bought anybody remotely good enough to improve the team and your own level of anticipation during transfer windows. But it has started happening at United too, and when I see a team supposedly representing what the club used to be about finishing a game in Europe with such an exciting attacking line-up that eight of the ten outfield players are Williams, Shaw, Telles, Bailly, Maguire, Fred, Matic and McTominay, five defenders and three less-than-creative midfielders, I tend towards the reaction Nick Hornby often had for Arsenal in their darker days, namely, 'I hope they get stuffed'. This can be quite a liberating position, as you feel you are making a significant statement, which of course will never be heard and also because it is a shield against potential defeat. So, it always helps to keep a little of the hatred back for such eventualities.

There is also a reverse side to schadenfreude, which for these purposes I shall call *freudeschaden*… it is one thing to take pleasure from another's misfortune, but it is also a human characteristic on occasion to take no pleasure in another's joy. Again, this for me seems to be uniquely confined to sports following. When Jonathan Agnew suggested that even the Australian fans, who had just seen Ben Stokes bring their team to its knees with the innings of his or anyone else's life to win an Ashes Test from nowhere in 2019, would still have enjoyed watching it, it seemed to me an assumption of staggering innocence and naivety, although one which showed Aggers in a far better light than me. Perhaps I should set myself a more attainable target and aim for a middle ground, some form of compromise between the two, and put my addiction into a more sensible place in my remaining time on this earth. To me, *freudeschaden* is a more likely reaction to Aggers' scenario, and it is not the exclusive preserve of the sports fan. In his newspaper column, Jeremy Clarkson once gave an honest appraisal of this. He told of a perfect holiday he thought he was enjoying on the French and Italian Rivieras. From the views to the company and the food and drink, everything was magical… until he heard that back in England, we were enjoying our best summer weather for forty years. This ruined his holiday, given he had spent a small fortune and others were enjoying just as good a time at home. This feeling troubled him and he used it to support his view that, despite well-meaning 'God enthusiasts' telling him that the human being is fundamentally good, it could not be so if we are saddened to hear others are enjoying a bit of luck with the weather. In truth, human beings can at times show that we are not fundamentally nice but fundamentally horrible and that sometimes in our 'ordinary, bitter lives we resent the success, wealth, beauty or even the good fortune of others'. Agreed, this is a rather depressing contention, and some may disagree, but in my experience, it is a default position for the sports fan for a large part of our lives.

The flip side to allegiance is neutrality, which I now consider to be the refuge of the coward. It's another thing which marks out the addict as opposed to the spectator: the inability to achieve this state in any sporting situation. I see people who genuinely watch with indifference to the outcome and realise they are not afflicted in the same way as I am, whereas in my case, I've now reached a point where I find there is no such thing as neutrality, or at least it is extremely rare. The extent of my condition is such that I can be watching something I didn't know was happening and have little interest in and I find that halfway through it, I am desperate for one party to win. I realise I've become attached to one player, or perhaps more likely these days have developed an immediate and probably unwarranted dislike of one who I now really want to lose. This is a strange phenomenon as the outcome won't impact my life at all and will be quickly forgotten in most cases, but I've still taken sides. I find it almost impossible to watch sport without doing so. Take if you will Kevin Anderson against John Isner, Wimbledon semi-final 2018. OK, this did become something rather out of the ordinary finishing as it did 26-24 in the deciding set and, having joined at the start of that fifth set, it became compulsive viewing, but I had no connection to either of these players and would probably never watch a match of theirs again. But an hour in, I suddenly caught myself punching the air every time Anderson hit a winner. Why, I had no idea. I had made no conscious decision to pick a side, but I must have been influenced by something. It disturbed me; where had this come from and what did it say about my ability to enjoy sport? The fact I had to look this up to remember the details just confirms it mattered not a jot, and yet for an hour or so, it seemed to matter more than anything else in the world, and this happens with increasing frequency. Neil Robertson against Yan Bingtao in the snooker. Why do I need a preferred winner? It's a nonsense which simply induces tension where it's not required and by so doing, actually reduces my enjoyment. I've no idea if anyone else out there has suffered from this, but I prefer to dodge any great psychological analysis of it.

Yes, sometimes a seemingly neutral contest will have an indirect bearing somewhere else – if Burnley beat Brighton, it might be slightly more helpful to Southampton's relegation battle, but then again, it might not; if Ronnie O'Sullivan is waiting for his world championship quarter-final opponent, better that it is Dave Gilbert than John Higgins. But sometimes there is absolutely no reason for any allegiance, and yet it happens anyway. I'm not talking here about those teams or individuals you have such an issue with that you would support anybody against them, anytime, anywhere, but even when I have no great interest in the sport itself, I pick sides. I was Ovett, not Coe; I was Hagler not Sugar Ray; I was initially Borg not McEnroe but then McEnroe not Connors. And I am perfectly at liberty to change as the participants do. So, in 1980, I despised McEnroe and wished him a painful and speedy exit from any tournament; by the time he retired, I was desperate for him to win and to regain former glories. *The Times* columnist Giles Smith once drew attention to this arbitrary capacity to change sides. (I was going to say 'willingness' but it's the wrong word – there is rarely a conscious decision made; it just creeps up on you.) He, too, highlights how McEnroe elicited a 180-degree turnaround in public opinion over many years, with many of those who had hated him for his temper and wanted to have him expunged now indulging him as a loveable old rogue. This is how fickle we can be, and there doesn't appear to be much pattern to it. Although, more often than not, a player with real flair and a bit of character will be the favoured one, or I will support the underdog and the changing of the guard, how does that explain my love of Bjorn Borg and my wish to see him win the Wimbledon title every year for as long as he turned up but then take against Sampras and then Federer with a passion. I also feel I can spot from some distance someone who is hamming it a bit, playing the audience, and that is guaranteed to have me plump for the opposition. I prefer genuine character flaws to the more Machiavellian 'nice guy' act every time. This is why, in 1980, during the intense Coe-Ovett rivalry culminating in the Moscow Olympics, I was a committed Ovett man. OK, he was a complex sort of bloke people didn't necessarily warm to, but he was an open book – what you saw was what you got. Coe, on the other hand, seemed just too much the darling of that Middle England type who spends their entire Wimbledon these days swooning and shouting for 'Roger, Roger' in a chant more suited to girls in a school playground. How do these people get admitted rather than committed? Sorry, I digress again. McEnroe and Connors by 1984, same story. One complex but genuine, the other it seemed to me more crafty, showy and more inclined to cheap gamesmanship. The fact that he thought we couldn't detect this and that most of the crowd fell for it simply irritated me even more. McEnroe's dismantling of him in the '84 final in a display as close to tennis genius as anyone ever got therefore remains one of my more treasured sporting memories.

LAND OF MAKE-BELIEVE

In 1978, such negativity hadn't really got off the ground. I was still a besotted youngster without the slightest interest in anything other than sport (with the possible exception of the pop charts and Karen Stewart in the third year). And if real sport was one thing, when you start creating your own fantasy version, you sense you may have a problem. If there were waking hours when no sport was actually happening, all you had to do was pretend. If any further evidence was needed of what my parents saw with increasing concern as my one-track mind, it came from rolling dice. Our closest family friends were my parents' mates from days in Manchester and they, like us, had the nuclear set of one son and one daughter, so the fit was a comfortable one, and I found myself spending most holidays with another sports-obsessed boy two years my senior. Apart from the inevitable self-created cricket pitches on every beach and campsite we visited, when the playing stopped, out came the dice. Every spare moment was filled with virtual Test matches scribbled down into exercise books, the actual scores produced via the roll of dice. Our holiday packing consisted of that old string bag of cricket gear, exercise books, dice and pen. Apart from the odd *Famous Five* book, that could see us through an entire Easter or summer. It was serious stuff with Man of the Match selections, end of season averages calculated, awards pages and often running commentaries, in character, of which Richie Benaud and Jim Laker would've been proud. To be fair, every other young cricket fan in the country was probably up to the same thing. But how many dialled this up a notch by discovering the football equivalent too? I had seen in my *Shoot!* magazine a small black-and-white ad for something called 'Logacta Chart Soccer'. It seemed it might be as good a way of avoiding homework as any and a tap-in Christmas present from Mum and Dad. Forget FIFA 2000, this was a game of genius in its simplicity. Its true value lay in the fact that not much happened in the game itself other than rolling dice and recording scores and points but that thereafter, it was all in the imagination. You could play an entire season of League, Cup and European football and, anally retentive as ever, I not only played the game but acted out the matches and conducted the previews and post-match interviews in my head. I fear I even wrote match reports and dreamed of being Hugh McIlvanney. There was also pleasure to be had in the fact that it was quite a well-kept secret. This was no Waddington's affair. The game was created by one bloke and run from his living room, which in another odd coincidence we discovered was in the next street to our family friends' house in Leeds. We would wander round every Easter to buy our next chart book or points recorder. I believe there are moves afoot in the Logacta underworld to bring back a form of this game. I for one am on the mailing list for any news and fear that, at fifty-four, I could easily slip straight back into this world of dreams. Hello, Mike Baker, your genius made my childhood and nearly cost me my O levels.

Those O levels were going to mean 'big school' in 1979 and an intimidating move from my position as one of the confident opinion formers, playground characters and kiss chase experts in my cosy middle school, to an environment where I was suddenly a very small fish indeed. It may not have helped my confidence in my own security that I had just arrived at a school where my dad was the headmaster and, as such, I was the easiest target of every skinhead bully in the place, not to mention that of the comprehensive school down the road. I remember a daily sense of imminent danger, whether it be in the playground or having to cycle home in the dark across Southampton Common, running the gauntlet of the Bellemoor crews intent on an ambush, in the uniform which gave away my identity as one of the boys from the posh school ripe for the picking. School itself was also more challenging: lessons I found hard for the first time in my life and various extra-curricular activities, none of which gave me any great pleasure. No wonder Sunday nights in front of *To the Manor Born* were filled with foreboding. Take a look at my Mondays... seven lessons, each requiring a hardback textbook I had to lug around in a bag the same size as me, over eight hours whereupon my mates set off for home, many of them across the common together, giving them the strength in numbers to mitigate the dangers of the journey. I, however, went to choir practice until 5pm and then had to wait for a violin lesson. I had zero interest in, and even less talent for, this instrument, and the teacher made no attempts to hide his irritation that we both knew I was wasting his time. The charade was an enforced torture insisted upon by my father who honestly seemed to think if he stuck with this, I would suddenly transform into a classical music protégé. In reality, he wanted me to be Andre Previn whilst I wanted to be Andrei Kanchelskis. It was never going to end happily.

If I thought that sport would be my release from all this, I was to be disappointed. For once, it was part of the problem rather than the solution, at least in its active schoolboy incarnation. Firstly, my dad was presiding over a school which didn't play football. That in itself was bad enough, but it meant that the compulsory sport in the dark days of winter was rugby. Now, given I was about seven stone wet through and that a lot of the other kids had come via prep schools where they had apparently been playing this brutal game since they were about three, meant it wasn't a game at which I was going to shine. In fact, the goal on being introduced to its physical challenges was to spend most of the time trying to stay out of harm's way. This was made considerably more difficult when, on considering my size and cowardice would not be great attributes in the open spaces of the backs, the master in charge decided I would be playing at hooker. That of course meant being slap bang in the middle of a scrum of fifteen other boys twice my size and with twice my self-belief. My understanding was that my job was to wait for the ball to come in and hook it back before the whole thing collapsed on me. I was willing to give that a go… until I found out that my opposite number, having given me some verbals straight from the Joe Marler handbook, was not interested in the ball himself and simply used the cover of the scrum to kick seven bells out of my shins whilst trying to stick his fingers in my eyes. This was nothing like being the best player in the Hollybrook playground with the tennis ball, and every Friday night, Junior House Evening was a matter of utter dread, and the crowning glory of the misery of school first-year rugby was unfortunately 'kitgate' part three.

Being in the right uniform or kit was a big deal at our school, and I still have suspicions that my dad had recruited some extra help to police this.

Our family dog regularly joined Dad in his study and would sit quietly on the deep windowsill looking out of the large window which overlooked the front concourse of the school. Quietly, that is, until he saw anyone not wearing a blazer, at which point he would start barking at the moon. To this day, he retains the title of the school's only ever canine prefect. Nobody was going to get away with not being in the right gear. The school had two shops from which uniforms, sports gear and the like could be purchased. One was a proper one which sold new products, neatly folded in polythene wrappers. The other had the ominous name of the OBNO shop, the acronym standing for 'Outgrown But Not Outworn'. Second hand, in other words. I may by now have painted a clear enough picture of my mother for you to understand that this was manna from heaven for her. Notwithstanding the fact that it was my own dad's school which required pupils to have all these various products, and, as the head's son, I was not in great need of anything else which would make me stand out from the crowd, Mum decided the OBNO was the place for us. As every other first year, it seemed to me, had all the requisite new gear, my kitbag was to be made up of stuff at a quarter of the price, regardless of unimportant matters like fit.

The requirement for rugby was two shirts: one white, one navy. There was good reason for this other than just to mark out which side you were on. They were smart tops which at least gave the wearer a passable likeness of an England or Scotland international. My mother had, however, discovered her holy grail at the OBNO in the form of a home-made, second-hand, *reversible* shirt – navy on one side and a kind of off-white, bearing the legacy of several years' mud, on the other. As an expression of parsimony, this was the ultimate product. Of course, Mum would have liked it had this shirt been last worn by a similar-sized first year, but she sure as hell wasn't going to miss out on the bargain for such a minor detail. I therefore took to the pitch, conscious of the sniggers all around, in a shirt which was at least two sizes too big, at least twice as heavy as anyone else's and with no buttons on a V-neck which almost made it to my navel. It's safe to say neither was it a DuPont garment, made as it was from a material that seemed to soak up and retain any element of moisture in the atmosphere. I wasn't blessed with the most searing change of pace to start with, but dragging this thing around in my wake must have made me look as if I was going backwards compared to everyone else. It was on about the fourth time I was forced to don it that I discovered the major flaw. On one particularly foul-weathered Wednesday afternoon two-hour games session, even the sergeant major persona of our rugby master took pity on us halfway through. We were dispatched to the changing rooms to replace our sodden tops with our fresh, dry ones. See the problem? As my mates pulled on their dry, clean second shirts, I took mine off, turned it inside out and put it back on again. I can see why my rugby career never really took off; I can also see why I retain a small mental scar to this day, along with a chest covered with hair, which is no doubt an evolutionary by-product of a twelve-year-old frontage left open to the elements.

In such an environment, it was no great surprise that I should seek further solace and protection in my imaginary sporting world. In addition to my dice, I was now given a helping hand when my latest football magazine got in on the act. I had recently made a radical decision to substitute my previously sacrosanct *Shoot!* Magazine with a new kid on the block called *Scoop*. Apparently, this was part of a rivalry between IPC and DC Thomson in the publishing world, but all I knew was that this new addition was the marriage I needed between the one hundred per cent factual *Shoot!* and the more fictional *Roy of the Rovers*. Such gritty weekly storylines as *Stark – Matchwinner for Hire* (a quite ridiculous concept in which the hero seemed to mix the world-saving antics of James Bond with the match-saving abilities of James Beattie) and *This Goalie's Got Guts* were a short-term highlight of Thursday mornings at the breakfast table. My favourite feature, however, was something called *The Intercity Super League*, billing itself as 'computer soccer' in which it seemed the magazine had stolen and enhanced my typewriter-based fantasy results and Logacta dice and turned them national. Fictional teams created from arbitrary geographical regions were made up by a mix of players selected from real teams within those regions. So it was that the 'computer' (yes, of course) played out matches between Glasgow Wanderers, Eastern Town and Pool City, amongst others. Southampton players appeared for South Coast City. Unfortunately, given they could only be supplemented with players from the likes of Brighton and Portsmouth, the computer didn't rate SCC very highly and regularly had them battling relegation. The fact remains that I was genuinely nervous about the outcome of these games and immediately flicked to *The Intercity Super League* page each Thursday with actual excitement created by this nonsense.

Another reality I was having to get used to alongside that of proper school was that, since Saints had been promoted, I no longer had my season ticket, Mum reasoning the hike in price for Division One to be too great and Dad conscious he needed the headmaster's son to show some willing to get involved in school sport on a Saturday. My last game in my own seat had therefore been the home match with Tottenham in 1978 which had clinched promotion. Any tickets in the future would need to be queued up for and delivered only a spot on the terraces. The excitement of being in the real, seething mass of the crowd and singing the songs was rather offset by only being able to see about a third of the pitch and therefore the game.

The land of make-believe was all very well and filled a valuable role in my attempts to cosset myself away from these new challenges, but there is no substitute for real heroes and, fortunately, the start of the eighties was to deliver them in the form, above all, of a certain Keegan, Thompson, Botham and Higgins.

HEROES

The strange evolution of my Southampton team from cosy also-rans to national consciousness was about to reach its zenith, or at least to enjoy the moment which would ensure there was to be a zenith. There was a certain irony that this was to happen on one of those very same depressing winter Monday schooldays usually reserved for nothing but misery, but the Monday of the 11th of February took a rather different turn once the choir and violin were out of the way. Returning home, I saw the front page of our *Southern Evening Echo* and read it two or three times before I believed it. Kevin Keegan, European Footballer of the Year, biggest name in football and hero since that '74 Cup final, was signing for Southampton. Dear old Lawrie McMenemy had built something of a reputation for enticing 'names' down to Saints over the previous couple of years, but he'd surpassed himself this time. Now we were serious news and serious contenders. For the next two years, I'd queue up on Friday nights to get my precious ticket, with school sport now firmly off the agenda, and watch the sort of football we had no right to expect at The Dell. Two years in a row, we were in the mix to win the title. Heady, heady days. Suddenly, the grind of school didn't seem to matter if we had this to look forward to each weekend. Keegan, Channon, Ball, Watson, Charlie George. We may not have been Liverpool, but we were the most exciting team in the country by a distance. There was one game in particular on Saturday the 5th of December which embodied this whole period: Saints against Manchester United again. This was the glamorous United of the equally glamorous, in his own estimation at least, Big Ron Atkinson. They had Robson, Wilkins, Stapleton, Moses and more besides. For the first time in three and a half years, Dad and I were back in the stands... or, more accurately, the directors' box. Through the school, Dad had a contact with the chairman which finally paid off with this invitation. It was my first time in an inner sanctum of plush carpets and drinks at half-time, and Big Ron himself, all jewellery, expensive aftershave and champagne post-match. It was a treat to recount on Monday morning, for sure. A performance inspired by a Keegan at his most effervescent produced a 3-2 win in front of the cameras, probably best remembered for the best disallowed goal of all time. Keegan's overhead kick from outside the area defied gravity and several other rules of my O-level physics course but happened whilst David Armstrong was minding his own business in an offside position a good forty yards away. The culprit partly made amends with the winner shortly afterwards, but it remains one of the more churlish refereeing decisions I had to cope with over the years. Five games later, we headed the first division for the first time in our history after another Keegan goal at Middlesbrough. My pied-piping really couldn't have taken us any higher.

Three weeks to the day before Kevin made his Saints debut, a guy called Daley Thompson appeared on my TV screen. The behind-the-Iron-Curtain TV production gave the Moscow Olympics their own unique feel. The previous games in 1976 had seen British athletics at a low point, with a single bronze medal for Brendan Foster, giving him the status of national hero. This time, there seemed to be a few more possibilities. Having spent the last year swapping world records seemingly at will, it was assumed the Coe and Ovett show would carve up the middle-distance golds, and from nowhere, a Scot (or as is necessary in such cases, a Brit) had just won the hundred metres, Britain's first since the *Chariots of Fire* days of 1924. Then there was this young Londoner, not yet part of my sports-watching consciousness, taking part in an event I'd never heard of. Daley Thompson was not to be what I was used to as an English supporter. For a start, he said he was going to win, and then he did so (and topped it off by whistling the national anthem on the podium when he retained his gold four years later). The guy transfixed me over two days as he took on two German supermen and beat them hands down, event after event. Here was a new type of sporting hero. He wasn't going to play the demur, self-effacing role of the English sporting honest trier; he wasn't going to behave in a manner to please the British sporting establishment and he wasn't going to apologise for being England's first born and raised black sporting superstar at a time when footballers all over the country were still having to kick bananas off the pitches they played on. This bloke was a walking piece of charisma, fitness personified, a human tracksuit. If an awards dinner requested black tie, Daley would show up in his three stripe T-shirt or not bother showing up at all. Here was an English guy who wanted to mentally destroy his opponents, who would do anything to get an edge. Christmas Day was famously a training day as he knew nobody else would be. He had the looks, too, which hardly lessened his boundless and infectious self-confidence. A sort of 1980s John Pienaar with muscles. The historian Dominic Sandbrook said in his political and social history of the 1980s that Daley wasn't just a sporting hero but a standard bearer for a gradual but real change to a more tolerant society. He had an impact over and above his sport on the social development of his nation. And he had the perfect profile for a new type of sporting hero for me: iconoclastic, charismatic, not always the darling of the establishment and above all, a winner to boot. Where he led Ian Botham and Alex Higgins were set to follow.

The impression Daley made on me made it all the more surreal that almost twenty years later I was playing left back to his left-sided centre-half in the annual adidas Marketing v Sales match. In order to counter the greater youthfulness and fitness of our Sales opponents (the player I marked being the previous year's leading goal scorer in the League of Ireland – I was cordially invited to meet him and shake his hand at half-time, having not got anywhere near him for forty-five minutes), this was the sort of ringer our marketing connections allowed us to bring in. It was a chance to witness close-up several elements of Daley's character: intense competitiveness, of course (these games were by no means friendlies, and Daley didn't turn up to anything to lose); his innate sporting ability as he showed why he had a potential football contract on the table before athletics took over; his relentless positivity and complete disinterest in anyone who didn't share his view of how to make the most of one's talent and one's life; and above all, his generosity and willingness to just be one of the group. As an inspirational brand ambassador, I could see why his adidas contract well outlasted his athletics career. The idea, watching the grainy pictures of the new hero that summer, that one day I'd be a sporting teammate of this guy was preposterous but goes to show the turns that life can take and the doors that sport would open up.

Next up, Ian Botham. There is little point in recounting too much of the detail of 'Botham's Ashes', the series during the still iconic summer of 1981 – if you don't know the story by now I can't really help you – but as Keegan and Southampton were making a faltering but entertaining attempt at the first-division title in that winter and spring, Botham as England captain was leading a similarly faltering, but less entertaining, effort to stave off the West Indies with a modicum of dignity. In fact, given what was to follow against those opponents for the rest of the decade, Beefy could, and does, argue that his attempt was one of the better ones. But my cricketing hero, who bestrode the world from his arrival four years earlier, was a forlorn and careworn figure, and it appeared many had lost belief. I wasn't one of them. Still every innings had the potential for greatness and to turn things around. How desperate I was for him to shut everyone up. Which he duly did, of course, by then winning the Ashes single-handed from several points of complete hopelessness and cementing his English sporting legend status for all time, regardless of what came next (which was considerable, if a little more sporadic). The significance of his heroics was not simply in their performance, however. Those who lived through it, especially as part of their teenage years, will never forget that English summer. Many would nominate the victorious battle for the Falklands the following spring as the pivotal moment, not only in the career of a certain Margaret Thatcher but also in the renewal of the country's spirit and self-belief after years of industrial and economic decline. Fourteen-year-olds tend to be shielded from the worst of such things and certainly, I lived through it more with a comfortably distanced interest than any sense it was negatively impacting my existence. But I would make the case that the passage from gloom to optimism actually began that previous summer, and with Beefy being one of three key elements, here was another strange case of art imitating life. Some might see it as pure coincidence but the Ashes, and Ian in particular, were, in my eyes, a clear contributory factor in the change of atmosphere, from the nadir of the inner-city riots and burning buildings to the patriotic outpouring of the royal wedding.

On the 2nd of July, the second Ashes Test began at Lord's with England 1-0 down after losing an uninspiring game they should have won in Nottingham. Brixton had already exploded in April and the grey, rain-interrupted match seemed to fit with the general air of solemnity. First day at Lord's, England captain Botham lbw, Lawson nought. The next day, the Toxteth L8 area of Liverpool erupted in the same way, for many of the same reasons of distrust and futility as had Brixton. Last day at Lord's, Ian Botham bowled, Bright nought. A pair; a resignation; our hero a depressed shadow of the previous bundle of positivity. The next day, Moss Side, Manchester, joined the list of inner-city suburbs up in flames. I wouldn't suggest people were throwing petrol bombs and looting in protest at Beefy's dismissals, but there was an odd synergy to the timing of each, and it appeared just a steady stream of bad news, of a nation going to the dogs both on and off the field.

By the time, a fortnight later, we had reached the wedding of Prince Charles and Lady Diana Spencer, which the Great British Public seized upon as a release and reason to forget the first half of the summer, Ian had already performed his first miracle at Headingley, transfixing the nation, including a good percentage who had rarely watched cricket before, and rescuing the Ashes series. Perhaps a miracle of regeneration was yet possible. That the second consecutive Test match he had pulled from the fire began in Birmingham the day after the pomp of the flag-waving, Rule, Britannia-singing street parties which accompanied the royal nuptials was serendipity again. It played to packed houses at a raucous Edgbaston under the blue skies and in the searing heat which had replaced the grey and cold of June and early July. Another miraculous win and England were back in business. I honestly believe that, subconsciously or otherwise, the reason Botham's Ashes remains as iconic a memory as there is in English sporting history is the circumstances in which it happened and what it meant in the wider context of British self-evaluation. Sport having the power to change lives, I suppose.

The main issue with having a hero such as Botham was in the inability to watch even the most spectacular innings with any enjoyment whilst it was in progress, given the possibility that it could end at any moment. Therefore, as with much of sport, the finest part of the day would be the anticipation that Botham was still to come rather than the innings itself, knowing well the total anticlimax that would follow his departure. In his paean to lost English cricketing summers, *A Last English Summer*, Duncan Hamilton articulated the same difficulty when he went to see Mark Ramprakash bat with an opportunity to see him score his hundredth hundred. He recalled he felt nervous for Ramprakash and nervous for himself – he wanted to be able to tell people he had been there at the historic moment. Hamilton also recounted the problem the cricket writer Neville Cardus had watching his heroes (a reassurance for me that such things afflict wiser men than me). The object of his affection was the Lancashire batsman Reggie Spooner, and by all accounts, Cardus could barely bring himself to watch a single ball he faced. Cardus is quoted as saying, 'a boy looks upon his heroes with emotions terribly mixed' and that he felt 'they were going to get out every ball'. Exactly. For me, the Botham experience was to be the first incarnation of a problem in watching in real time which was to evolve to the ridiculous level it has reached today. In fact, Neville had it worse than me, as I have the safety net of the highlights should my cowardice lead me to miss something special; his decision to turn away was final. He also employed numerous superstitions before and during Spooner's innings, believing, according to Hamilton, that he was 'protecting Spooner against the miseries of failure and also protecting himself from witnessing them'. This is something I return to on occasion to this day. At Loughborough, when watching major sporting moments, we used something called a 'ziggy' if we wanted either to ensure a positive outcome to a specific moment or more often to jinx an opponent into the required mistake. This piece of voodoo involved standing with arms outstretched, pointing at the screen, waggling fingers and humming 'ziggy' continually until the conclusion. The myth we built up around this was that it actually worked, especially if you stuck to the rules, which included not going to the well too often. Once per game was deemed acceptable. I do still employ these methods in moments of greatest panic, despite the mounting evidence that they are not the transportable, mind-bending witch doctor spells I would like them to be. And if they don't work, at least I can say I did my bit; I tried everything.

There was one more slightly flawed hero yet to come. The Falklands conflict had been underway for four weeks by the time the World Snooker Championship began in 1982. One may now be deemed somewhat more important than the other but, fascinated as I was by the first British conflict of my lifetime, in truth I think I felt more excited about the Crucible than San Carlos Water. I'd had five years to get into this sport, this tournament and the role it played, straddling my birthday as it did and generally signifying a time of much annual happiness. By 1982, I was at the height of my obsession with it, getting as many frames on the telly in as possible before Mum sensed it was time for some sort of activity or a return to homework. (Dad was happy to join in with the excuse to spend weekends in the armchair.) Since I'd started with snooker, there was one player, one character, that stood out and perfectly fitted my hero template. Alex Hurricane Higgins was my favoured one from the start. The year before, he had been beaten in the second round by a youngster called Steve Davis, who was to prove the polar opposite to Higgins in playing style, character and level of success over the years to come, severely irritating the Hurricane in the process. This had rather undermined my tournament in the same way that early departures for White and O'Sullivan would do in the years to come. So, by '82, I was even more desperate for my walking hard-luck story to join my growing list of successful favourites. It turned out to be one of those sporting stories much loved by the media who picked up on the latest state of play in Higgins' tempestuous relationships in his personal life. *The Guardian* later sketched a contrast between the two beings which seemed to exist within the one person: The Hurricane and Alex Higgins. The former was the possessor of the erratic genius that allowed him to play the game like no other and be the darling of the public. Alex Higgins was the troubled soul riddled with self-doubt which he looked to manage via various vices.

The Guardian noted that by the end of 1981, The Hurricane was as popular as ever but was becoming ever more distant from Alex Higgins, exhausted from a relentless schedule of exhibitions and lonely hotel rooms, an alcoholic and now saddled with a drug problem. But by early '82, he was also a new father and relatively new husband. By all accounts, he still broke promises to his family regularly, but he was clear they were to be the thing that would turn his life around. Now, we all love a story, and this one was very much in the public consciousness. We Brits also love an underdog, which is precisely what he was at the start of the fortnight. The redemption story, which was to end in famous tears and embraces at the end of the final, was one his fans and his press were willing to happen, amidst concern he would find a way to turn it into tragedy. But he didn't. On that Sunday night, he topped off a 18-15 win with an archetypal Hurricane clearance of 135, and the emotion knew no bounds. The nature of snooker, where one small error can leave you sat in your chair unable to prevent disaster, creates huge tension for the pessimistic fan. With players such as Higgins, and later White, the fact that this can happen at any moment, no matter how well they are playing, and usually does, means following them is an experience of almost constant concern. Give your affections to Davis or Hendry, then sit back and enjoy. But as I said, allegiance unfortunately doesn't work like that. In fact, looking back and seeing that in the semi-final, Higgins had beaten the debutant Jimmy White, given what was to come over the next thirteen years, we might not have been so ecstatic at the outcome. In a first to sixteen match, Jimmy was 15-13 up, and 15-14 and 59-0 up. As good as in the final. And he missed, and his opponent made one of the greatest clearances of all time, won the decider and put him out. Sound familiar? For Jimmy, 1992 and 1994 may have been more painful, but the seeds of those unhappy moments may well have been sewn by our favourite that night, little did we know.

My mid-teens were therefore producing a string of special favourites and their special moments, which reinforced my charmed life and my innocent belief that this was the joy of sport. There is, however, another kind of hero who can impact your enjoyment in a very different way.

DO YOU REALLY WANT TO HURT ME?

There's this thing about heroes. Ideally, they need to be on your side. Keegan was Saints and England; Botham was England; and Daley and Alex were individuals, so you had made your own choice to support them and take the consequences. So, pretty straightforward. What I struggled with was the problem of fantastic players, and great personalities, playing for the other side. How were you supposed to handle that? I was to learn that great opposition players are better, and far easier to love, when they're gone.

What experience are we really after? Are many of us truly sports fans anymore, i.e. fans of sport for its own sake and those who perform it best? We used to watch and admire great individuals regardless of their teams or nations. From Keith Miller to George Best. Nowadays, it feels like anyone who might threaten our chance to win are wished nothing but failure. I respect those who can still resist this, although I find it hard to emulate. A good, cricket-loving friend of mine was desperate to watch Sachin Tendulkar score a hundred against England when he went to a game in India. He wanted to see the great man bat and to have one of his more special days. Good for him, but personally, I wanted him out first ball. He wanted to watch one of the greats in action whilst he had the chance; I was happy not to see him at all.

This conflicting love and hate relationship with the best players has caused me no end of mental wrestling and contradictions. My favourite cricketers of all time include Viv Richards, Malcolm Marshall and Shane Warne, all of them genuine greats of the game. I also had a personal love of Carl Hooper who seemed so effortless and graceful whilst always maintaining his West Indian gunslinger cool. When he was at the crease, I was torn between the quality I was watching and the concern that an hour of him could stuff England right out of sight. When I saw Shane or Viv or a Carl Hooper cameo, I knew I was watching greatness and should *enjoy* it rather than just appreciate it. I tried and, shamefully, I often failed, but that is my problem and my loss, not theirs. If you grew up, as I did, as an English cricket lover in the eighties, you may recognise the struggle I had in trying to enjoy the exploits of some undoubted greats of the game who were regularly engaged in dealing out thrashings to England. Of course, once they had retired and they could inflict no further damage, I could be big enough to miss them. At the time, however, there was this terrible dichotomy; they were lighting up the game and yet they were ruining my summers. Now these players have packed up, I can genuinely enjoy them. I now watch back the documentaries and replays of old matches and appreciate how special they were. In fact, *appreciate* is the wrong word – I could *appreciate* them *at the time*; I just couldn't *enjoy* them. I congratulate myself on my magnanimity in conceding nowadays how good they were. Unfortunately, whilst they were actually playing against, and destroying, England, I was too shallow to take such an approach. What compounds the confusion is discovering post-career what good blokes they are and therefore probably always were. It was something of a disappointment to have to like Glenn McGrath when he joined the TMS commentary team and came across as the epitome of charm, good humour and balanced analysis. Having spent the previous decade seeing him as public enemy number one, this was hard to accept. Warne is a humorous, equally generous and fascinating talker on the game (God knows what the Ashes scores would've been if the Aussies had ever had the good sense to make him captain); Viv was just Viv and in retirement, the occasionally bombastic, glowering presence gave way to a smiling West Indian with a voice like treacle, giving every impression of comfort in and agreement with his status as one of the greatest of all time. Even now that one-day cricket has supposedly been taken to several other levels by new shots and attacking mindsets, the greatest ODI innings of all time remains his 189 not out against England at Old Trafford in 1984. I watch it back at least once a year in awe and fascination, looking forward to seeing it every time. I can clearly remember on the day itself, however, sitting in front of the TV, getting very excited that West Indies had collapsed to 166 for nine. The innings was as good as over, and perhaps this was to be the summer we would take it to the best team in the history of the game after all. My growing frustration as the last wicket then added 106, 93 of them from Richards' bat splattered to all parts of Manchester, remains with me. I was watching genius that would light up my DVD trips down memory lane for years to come, and I hated every ball.

Then there was Malcolm Marshall who was one of the nicest sportsmen I ever came across in my thirty years in sport. At least with Maco there was some relief that if I struggled when he was splintering England, I could enjoy him on my side as part of my Hampshire team. For a young Hampshire and England fan, one of the benefits of South Africa's absence from the international game was being able to enjoy Barry Richards safe in the knowledge he could cause me no real pain. Malcolm Marshall was somehow different. There was a certain ghoulish fascination, sadistic and masochistic in almost equal measure, in watching him dismantle my favourite batting line-ups, not to mention Gatt's nose. How could a man inflict such physical and mental torture on my England heroes and still become my favourite cricketer? He *was* a phenomenal player and the closest I got to actually enjoying his greatness whilst it was still happening.

I thank all these guys now for enriching my sporting experience and memories and apologise for being such a narrow-minded individual. But, as I say, my loss, nobody else's.

ANOTHER PLANET

It's one thing being beaten by the good guys. If Viv Richards or Shane Warne is too good for you, it's time to hold your hands up and accept that defeat is not so bad. A less palatable realisation creeping up on me was that the bad guys often win too. To date, I hadn't really experienced that horrible, lingering taste which comes with the opposition winning when they clearly don't deserve to, but this lesson was to begin with the 1982 World Cup.

The 'España '82' World Cup remains for me the definitive example of the breed. Perhaps it was its timing, situated at the apex of my teenage football obsession as a just turned fifteen-year-old. But I don't think that has encouraged an over-rosy recollection of the teams, players and matches that adorned those few weeks of summer afternoon and evening viewing. It didn't do any harm that for the first time in my sphere of memory, England were involved nor that they began their tournament with the fastest ever World Cup goal when Bryan Robson scored against France after twenty-seven seconds. I'd barely got my packet of Malted Milk opened on my return from school. A 3-1 win against that French team was all the more impressive as their true quality became apparent.

But the real joy of the tournament were the teams and players I had hitherto never seen from Brazil and France. One of the reasons World Cups were such fiestas for us in those days was this opportunity for unveiling the best players in the world you barely knew existed. Quite honestly, today, watching a load of Liverpool and Chelsea players you see every week play against similar from United and City gives these tournaments the feel of just a few more games. Back then, every one was to be treasured and every one had the potential to reveal something or someone new and exciting. So it was in 1982. The first game I watched introduced if not the best then probably the most fluid, skilful and carefree football team I've ever seen. The Germans (as we were to find out shortly) were a more ruthless victory machine; Barcelona 2009–15 may well have been even prettier on the eye, although were something of a cheat given ninety per cent of this was delivered in the form of one player, but the '82 Brazil team better fitted my template because of their flaws. These not only took the very visible form of a centre forward called Serginho, who was so incongruous in the company of the rest of this team that you half wondered if he'd won a competition on a packet of Brazilian Shredded Wheat to play with them, but also their tragic, yet somehow endearing, ability to throw away a trophy that by rights should have just been handed to them by default anyway. From the moment Socrates and Eder scored wonder goals in the first game against the Soviet Union, I was smitten. (Eder being the source of one of my uncle's better ad libs – he knew little about football and was showing scant interest in the game, but when the commentator shouted out 'Eder!', he jumped in immediately without looking up from his book with the addition, 'you with the stars in your eyes' well before Uncle Albert appropriated this joke on *Only Fools and Horses* some years later. Like Eder, my uncle was clearly ahead of his time.)

Zico, Falcao, Junior plus Socrates, Eder and more – they seemed to be playing with a different ball, one that had that bit more life and which zipped about as if via radar from boot to boot. To that point, I had never been as crestfallen watching something which in theory should have been 'neutral' as the day they threw it all away against a previously very ordinary Italy side and had to head for home. That also denied us the chance of the final that should've been: these artists against Michel Platini's France. Now, France were doing a passable impression of a European version of Brazil based on a midfield three which still runs straight off the tongue today: Platini, Giresse, Tigana. And if Brazil's departure before even the semi-finals seemed wrong somehow, France's experience was about to exceed it and give me my first taste of totally undeserved and bitter defeat.

Even before their semi-final kicked off, all right-thinking people were willing this team of flair and invention to knock out the seemingly ever-present, functional West Germany. An avoidance of stereotyping would be desirable here but honestly, here laid before us was the embodiment of German efficiency and a sense that win at all costs was uppermost in their thoughts. So it was to prove. It is hard to explain now how much better France were in the match and how much more pleasure they were giving me as I watched. Quite how they didn't win it remains a mystery to this day. Infamously, at 1-1 after an hour, the German goalkeeper prevented what seemed a certain goal in a one-on-one with France's Patrick Battiston which would have given them the lead they so deserved. He did not achieve this, however, by dint of a save, rather a flying feet-first assault which had the Frenchman being carried from the pitch with two missing teeth, two cracked ribs and damaged vertebrae. Quite what

Mohammed Salah and the like would have made of this these days one can only imagine. Unfortunately for the poleaxed Battiston, he was in no state to roll around milking it, unable to move as he was. And surely, he had no need of this anyway. Today, Harald Schumacher may well have been fighting a prison sentence, certainly a good six-month ban. This night, there was no red card. In fact, there was no free kick. Schumacher immediately took his place at the head of my hated sportsmen list, and I couldn't wait to employ my schadenfreude on him come his imminent defeat. In injury time, France then hit the crossbar. We should have known what was coming. Happily, the justice I unquestioningly expected sport to deliver appeared to be on its way as France went 3-1 up in extra time. Then the Germans did their German thing and somehow equalised. That meant my first ever World Cup sudden death penalty shoot-out. The utter purgatory of this innovation was of course going to stalk me for years to come, but this was the first time the stomach-churning tension they induce had been forced upon me. It may not have been England yet, but I couldn't have been more committed if it had been. And, of course, the Germans won, with the final penalty saved by the keeper who should by then have been helping the Spanish police with their enquiries. I was dumbstruck for quite some time afterwards. Why would West Germany be allowed to play a final they didn't deserve to be in? Given they clearly cheated their way there, surely the sporting bodies could step in and right this wrong? I was to learn that sport doesn't work that way. The Italians did us all a favour and allowed us that schadenfreude after all by comfortably beating the Germans in the final, but not only had a lesson been served up about having to deal somehow with the injustices of sport, but a new enemy had been created. That enmity was to fester for another eight years before it erupted with a vengeance.

THE HURTING

Gradually, my almost constant upwards graph of happy sporting successes was beginning to fluctuate in the same way as my adolescent hormones as I headed towards official adulthood. There were still sunny days, but increasingly, I was having to deal with the downside too. The hurting began in a phone call with my Geordie grandmother. Grandma still lived in Whitley Bay, which wasn't exactly 'popping round' distance from Bassett Gardens, Southampton, so instead, the dutiful grandson would make regular calls, partly because he actually liked Grandma but also to ensure the Christmas tenner was never at the slightest risk. Normally, these were standard affairs covering the 'how are you?'s and 'what are you doing at school?'s. This one, however, was never to be forgotten for the bombshell it delivered. Halfway through a call in early August '82 (the fact it only came halfway through subsequently irritated the hell out of me, showing as it did her complete failure to grasp the seriousness of the situation), Grandma said, with a casual air scarcely appropriate as I mentioned the new football season, "Ooh, Kevin Keegan's signed for Newcastle…"

I laughed. I actually laughed. Whether this was because I assumed Grandma was having another of her increasingly frequent away-with-the-fairies moments, or it was an involuntary reflex reaction to news I could neither believe nor accept, I'm not sure. "No, Grandma, that can't be right," came my patronising response. "Keegan plays for Southampton, and we've just nearly won the league. Newcastle are in Division Two."

"Well, it's here in the paper," she assured me. By now, significant palpitations were assailing me. I had to get off the phone and check this out. This was before Google, websites or even Ceefax, so I had to wait for the TV news to confirm the cataclysmic truth. Kevin had had a row with Lawrie and had his pride injured, which in Kevin's case meant no way back – he was done with Southampton; he was off. These days, a fan of a team like Saints knows and is resigned to the fact that if any one of your players starts playing anything like, they are liable to be off to the next step up the ladder without a moment's thought. (In fact, I once got to the stage with James Beattie, hardly Barcelona material, that when we were safe from relegation that year, I actually wanted him to stop scoring. I knew if his tally went above twenty in the Premier League he was as good as sold.) But that day, I couldn't quite compute it. What would happen now?

Well, what happened now was that my previously ever-improving, title-chasing team lost their hard-earned place in the UEFA Cup in the first round to some Swedish part-timers and, by the end of September, were in the relegation zone following such impressive results as 6-0 against Spurs, 5-0 against Liverpool and 4-1 (at home) against newly promoted Watford. Defeats, by the way, not wins. This wasn't how it was supposed to be. Things gradually improved but were never quite the same post-Kevin. With him went our place towards the top of the national media's priority list and our sense of impending glory.

I said there were sunny days, and in fact, the following season, Big Lawrie had built an ever-better team, if far less glamourous. This one actually finished second in the league, without ever really threatening to win it, but not bad for my lot nonetheless – the ship had clearly been righted. And as if to emphasise the new rough-with-the-smooth outcomes I was having to get used to, they went on an FA Cup run, which was the best of times and the worst of times.

This delivered, alongside Ole Gunnar Solskjaer in Barcelona fifteen years later, my most treasured goal ever. Saints had been drawn away to Portsmouth in the fourth round of the cup. This was always a horrible draw as, not having had to play them in the league for years, we had been spared any possibility of the unimaginable consequences of defeat. But now not only were we favourites, but it was to be at Fratton Park, an absolute bear pit of a place into which any Southampton fan ought really to fear to tread. *TalkSport's* Paul Hawksbee, a lifelong Tottenham fan, says that he absolutely hates derby games. He just wants them over with and out of the way. They aren't in anyway enjoyable other than in the aftermath if you've won. This was precisely my take on this game. My perennially half-empty glass suggested what might be coming. Despite the very real dangers of entering even the outskirts of the city, never mind the stadium, a huge swathe of braver Saints fans than me had taken over the away end at Fratton, and I was eternally thankful to every one of them for defending the pride of our club without my needing to get involved. Consequently, the atmosphere was like no other away game I can recall. Getting out with lives intact seemed as improbable as a win. Sure enough, for eighty-nine minutes, Pompey battered us – posts, crossbars, Peter Shilton and wild misses from the never-to-be-thanked-enough Alan Biley had, incredibly, kept the scoreline blank. We were within seconds of getting a draw and of my benefitting for once from just the sort of unjustified outcome I had been so outraged by eighteen months before. In injury time, we summoned our first breakaway attack of the match and that sweet, beautiful little goal machine of the previous couple of years, Steve Moran, tucked the ball in the net in front of the Southampton fans. I had never seen an away end explode the way it did in that moment, and this probably remains, alongside Freddie's over to Ponting in 2005, my most YouTubed moment in sporting history when times get tough. Aside from Hughie Fisher, Aston Villa and 1976, I hadn't really experienced that unique rush and release that comes with the last-minute goal going the right way. There is nothing to beat it. And Hugh's didn't really rate against this, given it wasn't expected and it wasn't Portsmouth.

Now we had a portent – the last time we had scored a last-minute goal in the FA Cup, we won the thing. And by the time we reached the semi-final against Everton at Highbury, we were in the unaccustomed position of being favourites to do so again. Given we had won every round away from home at increasingly tough places, we deserved it this time. Highbury was positively genteel compared to Fratton, so I duly set off with Dad to stand on the terraces that April day. We were given the clock end, the traditional away end, whilst Everton got the vast north bank opposite. This meant that, although we were once again well represented, the impression was that Everton fans were everywhere. I suddenly really despised every blue scarf and top hat, every individual and the whole mass of them. I couldn't watch this lot celebrate at my expense. I've said any semi-finals are horrible – FA Cup semi-finals are even worse; winning them is the only way to survive them; I certainly wouldn't recommend losing one and especially not as favourites. Unbeknownst to us, Everton were then just setting out on their path to championship and European glory and, looking back, this was a real 'name on the cup' job. It was a truly awful game made worse by the unbearable tension. Saints had their moments but were off their game. The last minute of extra time arrived at 0-0 and with a goal looking unlikely if we played until Tuesday. Everton corner, ball swung in low and there, in clear vision but far enough away at the other end of the pitch to make it look almost slow motion and unreal, the ball popped up in front of Adrian Heath, the smallest guy on the pitch, who nodded it in. I can still close my eyes and see that net move. It seemed to take a moment at the clock end for us to register both the goal and the eruption of the blue bank behind it. We saw that bouncing wave of celebrating away fans, that moment which turns your heart to stone, fractionally before the wave of sound hit us. It is a strange phenomenon to be in a ground where one end erupts in sudden, violent noise and the other is in total silence, something only the football supporter, I suspect, recognises. And here it was. I hated that north bank; I hated their euphoria; I envied their unconstrained celebration. This was a new and very real level of sporting disappointment. The first goal we had conceded in the entire competition, stretching for nine and a half hours, had knocked us out without the time to respond. Clearly, a large number of those standing with me on the terrace felt the same thing and were more inclined to find a way to dissipate their frustration. I take pause when I think that the subsequent pitched battle, rolling from one end to the other in cavalry charges of fans dodging frighteningly large police horses, was the catalyst for the erection of fences at all semi-finals. They may have been coming anyway, but what was to happen five years later at Hillsborough would put the disappointment which accompanied this one into its proper place.

One of the consequences of this day was my first attempt to lessen the pain through rationalisation. We weren't good enough; we didn't really deserve it; it had been a frustrating and unenjoyable experience and therefore I could live with the loss. Dad agreed, impressed and somewhat surprised at my response. The fact that he endorsed my position on this only made it worse. Because, of course, I didn't mean a word of it when I looked deeper inside myself. Rationalisation of this sort is a good attempt, but no matter how much you want to believe it and want it to work, it simply can't compete with gut feeling. Gut-wrenching feeling. I was trying to make myself feel better and I still try it to this day. And I'm still kidding myself every time thirty-seven years on. The sense of emptiness I felt would have been even greater had I known I had just attended a football match for the last time ever with my dad.

We were to make another semi-final two years later, and we lost that too. I spent most of the day trying to avoid a rain of bottles from the great, good-humoured Liverpool fans we had heard so much about and should have been equally as despondent. But whether it was because it was a Liverpool team who everyone knew in their hearts was going to win, or whether it was my slight shift in life perspective, this one washed over me in a very different way. And by now, past my eighteenth birthday and into official manhood, there were increasingly other ways of placing sporting outcomes in less elevated positions in the list of factors determining my life's enjoyment.

INTERREGNUM

1986–1988

GIRLS, GIRLS, GIRLS

There comes a time in the affairs of men when females start to enter the picture. I had actually been an early starter in this regard – what was seen by others, I discovered, as a confident line of chat and an unexpected ability to make girls laugh, and not just in my swimming trunks, making up for any shortfall in the looks department. Hollybrook Middle School had been a non-stop playground merry-go-round of 'he loves her' and 'she fancies him'. This was taken on a level by the advent of the phenomenon that was the Lordswood Disco. This was actually a format for kids' parties at houses on the local Lordswood housing estate, which was a rather different place to my base in leafy Bassett. And rather different things happened. A social snob at eleven I wasn't, and anything which had a chance of ending in a smooch with my favourite girl from school was not something to be ignored. For these were not kids' parties of the jelly, ice cream and pass the parcel variety, rather a lounge with chairs moved to the edge of the room, starting as these things should with boys along one wall and girls the other. As things started to chill out, so the mixing began, until the record player reached The Bee Gees' 'Too Much Heaven' or 'We Do It' by R&J Stone and the close clutching could begin. I can still remember the first one as a personal day of triumph – an afternoon at Saints v Blackpool, 3-3 (Channon hat-trick), followed by an evening ending with Angela Hafey in my clutches to the sound of 'Under the Moon of Love'. Not a classic tear-jerker, I'll grant you, but it served its purpose. Anyway, the point of this is to indicate that I had my male antennae twitching from an early age with reasonable success as, for some reason, one of the more acceptable boys in the girls' estimation. That status was to vanish come big school, but I would make hay whilst I could. At that stage, though, these affairs of the heart (or whichever organ was instigating them) were not deemed worthy of supplanting sport in my own hierarchy of needs.

My very own Peter Osgood was once quoted as saying, 'women are around all the time, but World Cups come only every four years'. I'm afraid not only this would be deemed unacceptable today under the misogyny banner, but from what I remember, it isn't a very accurate reflection of how Peter had categorised the relative importance of the two things over the course of his career and was perhaps an attempt to revise his personal history somewhat. But it does raise the question of whether an addiction to sport and an interest in the opposite sex can happily coexist, how that relationship can work and which should take priority at any given time…

In my experience, ignoring sport can be done, which is helpful to know when things get bad and require ignoring. My occasional self-delusion that I can take sport or leave it as I please may have its origins in the fact there were days gone by when a love life took precedence. It is only with the arrival of the long-term commitment relationship – with all its unswappable pleasures, but without the need to eschew everything else for the thrill of the chase – that the sports obsession can take over again full-time. One month into my relationship with my then new girlfriend, now wife, I actually chose a trip to York races over the now iconic England v Scotland game at Euro '96, spending the afternoon playing Rockefeller, buying champagne in the sunshine of the county enclosure and paying not the blindest bit of attention to the match which riveted the nation. In fact, it may have been this day that subconsciously planted the thought that this could be the way to survive the most unbearably tense events in the future – it was a blissfully chilled way of getting through it and getting the right result to be enjoyed later. A couple of decades on, however, this order of priorities is a thing of the past and we have, contentedly or otherwise, reached the domestic settlement of two television rooms and the tacit understanding that *Match of the Day* is going to be the closest thing my midlife gets to late Saturday night excitement… it's something of a relief to be honest.

But this focus on other pastimes can often just be a mask, used tactically at times of greatest need or, rather, lowest sporting achievement. In *Fever Pitch*, Nick Hornby admits to himself that his own diversion away from Arsenal for a period was actually nothing to do with other more lofty, artistic, or less lofty carnal, interests, as he had tried to convince himself – it was all to do with the ineptitude of Arsenal's strike force at that particular time.

There is always the possibility that your chosen one, temporary or permanent, might share your love of sport. My first true heartbreaker, a holiday romance at fifteen, wrote to me all the way through the '82 World Snooker Championship, sharing my devotion to Alex Higgins. This might seem ideal marriage material, but in fact, there is something that just doesn't feel right about it. My relationships were supposed to be a release, a shield and diversion from sport when the need arose. I realised I had no great desire to share my passion (in this particular regard) with a girlfriend. Far better to be with someone who had not the slightest interest and could therefore draw you away.

At the age of almost sixteen, the idea that I would miss an England international for such an attraction was far-fetched, and yet, come March '83 and a European Championship qualifier between England and Greece at Wembley (no, I didn't have to look it up), the lure of a house party, which offered me the opportunity of a third date with Christine without having to think where the hell to take her, meant that come 8pm, I was ensconced on a sofa in the darkest corner we could find, seeing if there was a chance of beating my then personal best. I didn't even ask once if I could check the score – I completely forgot it was happening. I felt this made me cleverer than everyone else for not being bothered anymore, whilst others were getting upset. On discovering afterwards that it had been an excruciating goalless draw followed by the usual TV inquests, I began to see the sense in this shift in priorities.

Such a shift was probably given an extra shove by the inspirational decision of my father to admit girls to the sixth form in autumn 1983 for the first time in 430 years of history. Ahead of his time in enlightenment and diversity? Or trying to give his son, who entered the sixth form (unfortunately and not for the want of trying, not in that sense… grow up) that very same year, the best possible opportunity of finding a nice girl? Thirteen girls amidst a hundred plus boys meant a large amount of jockeying for position, and he who would put the Saints result or David

Gower's cover drive above this quest would be nowhere. As it turned out, I was pretty much nowhere anyway, that lack of presence on a rugby field and my embarrassing attempts to become a bass guitarist on the school stage one lunchtime leaving me hurdles too significant to overcome. So, although I managed to offset this occasionally with increasingly productive liaisons after turning my attentions to the all-girls' school over the road, thereby improving the odds simply by dint of the numbers, and just beginning to devote a little more emotion to these than sporting outcomes at that time, I had to wait until A-levels and school were done before this approach reached its apotheosis.

THE BOYS OF SUMMER

Having left school in the summer of '85, now officially an adult and officially clueless as to what would happen next, my close group of friends and I navigated the following winter and spring in a variety of ways as we looked to delay any major decisions. There was firm agreement that living day to day for a while was the way to go. Several took the round-the-world-trip route, ending up developing their social educations and contacts, as well as their understanding of mild narcotics, in salubrious places such as Penrod's Bar in Fort Lauderdale and the beach bars of Bondi. I, on the other hand, as befitting my less adventurous nature, decided on staying put and working in a local bookshop. This put money (and a swathe of sporting autobiographies) in my pocket for the first time. By the time March '86 arrived, I was ready to reward myself for this endeavour, given the good times I understood my mates to be enjoying around the globe. I followed the trend of the group by becoming the third to purchase the one thing which defined our cabal more than anything else: a second-hand Triumph Spitfire. Now, admittedly, I was no mechanic, and what I purchased for the money I had was unlikely to ever make Le Mans. It could do about thirty or so miles in a trip before the odds on it breaking down for some reason or other became too short to make it wise to continue. The doors only opened from the outside on the driver's side and the inside on the passenger's which, given it was a two-door car, meant entering and exiting the vehicle had the look of a clown's routine. I should really have kept a bucket of shredded silver paper in it for maximum effect. But it was red; it was convertible; and it was a sports car, and it was the passport to the summer of my life. By May, the wanderers had returned, complete with tans, bleached mullets and the second status symbol beloved of the group: Marlboro soft tops. These, allied to our three sports cars, gave us the tools to take all before us in a long, if only occasionally hot, summer. Their new look may have been more *Baywatch* than my pallid, all winter in the UK version, but by keeping my cool, long-sleeved shirt on for as many hours of the day as possible, eschewing shorts when I could and ensuring I placed my new car keys in visible locations wherever we went, I played my full part. Fortunately, my Spitty's thirty-mile range was just enough to cruise in convoy to the beaches of Christchurch and Mudeford which we therefore did almost every day. As long as we spent enough time sunning ourselves and checking out the beach bars, my pride and joy would have just about recovered enough for the trip home. If there was any doubt at all about this, the option of a night's stopover in the bars and on the beach could be triggered.

Our attempts to create a south coast version of the O'Toole/Harris/Reed school, with a bit of Georgie Best thrown in, were enhanced by two more strokes of good fortune. Firstly, the alpha male in the tribe – the inevitable one with the looks, the body and the imminent officer training position with the marines – topped off his list of attributes with a set of parents who owned the trendiest restaurant-cum-bar in the city. The refuge of many a footballer and local celebrity, the glitterati must have been surprised when a group of six fairly uncouth lads rocked up like they owned the place and started chatting up the female clientele with more success than they'd had. A little further down the road was a rather different establishment called The Frog and Frigate. This spit-and-sawdust bar, replete with acoustic guitarist leading the throng in raucous renditions of the singalong standards in the days before karaoke ruined things, was quite deservedly legendary in Southampton amongst those in the know – it was still a pretty well-kept secret. It had the additional benefit of location, location, location, standing as it did half a mile from the residential area used by the nurses of Southampton General hospital and, as a consequence, being their preferred joint for letting their hair down on a Friday night. Saturday mornings weren't always full of life, wherever and with whomsoever you might be waking up, given that the sardine-packed nature of the bar and the Friday singalongs meant pint glasses were out of the question, hence my introduction to the only drink you could retain in the melee thanks to its bottle design: Newcastle Brown Ale. Happy nurses, Newky brown and the select few heading back to a free lock-in at Pepper Joe's was the pattern of the summer. My favourite broadcaster, Danny Baker, once said the secret to life is to have no money and live like you've got £20 million – a great trick if you can do it. That is a good approximation of what we were getting up to.

All this, as you might imagine, was enough to move me further and further away from the sporting obsession. If there was ever going to be a moment for a more permanent divorce, this was it. England losing Test series at home to New Zealand (for the first time ever) and India in the same summer mattered not; even the Mexico World Cup, whilst picked up at its more crucial moments, generally washed over me in a way that would've been unthinkable four years before. Yes, Maradona was a cheating bastard, but it hardly ruined my summer as it surely would these days. In fact, England's disastrous first two games were completely ignored in the haze of a boys' trip to Newcastle that, surprisingly, was slightly less disastrous than England's on-field efforts. This had nothing to do with our new penchant for the city's biggest export – we had a mate at university there and the Baja Beach Club was something we'd heard everyone had to do at least once in their lives.

I'd therefore had an entire summer in 1986 when the chasing of a good time took precedence. I wouldn't say that that summer was completely 'in my control'; in fact, it was pretty much out of control, but I'd realised that enjoyment was better secured through things in which I had some actual involvement and where my own decisions and actions could have a direct bearing on the outcome, than relying on the likes of Tim Robinson and Terry Fenwick to arrange it for me. I'd seen Southampton lose their FA Cup semi-final in April and that was it until I left for Loughborough in October. In-between times, not much came before seeking the pleasures of the grape, the grain and the flesh. I stored away the newly acquired knowledge that this realignment of priorities could be re-employed sporadically over the following dozen or so years. Nine summers on, I almost missed Dominic Cork's Test hat-trick against the West Indies, having opted for a late 'lie-in' on a first weekend away with a new friend. I say almost. To my shame, the TV in the room *was* on in the background, and when the third wicket was confirmed, my explosive reaction was probably something my companion had been expecting me to experience in other ways. The relationship didn't last. Nor did the innocence (and debauchery) of the summer of '86.

THE END OF THE INNOCENCE

There were no more ways to delay the long-feared step into reality. In one of the more drink-induced moments of optimism during the summer, I had suggested to Dad that another year of contemplation to avoid any rash decisions might be a good idea and that having missed out on the hedonistic global tour the year before, I might consider joining one of my mates, who had enjoyed the first one rather too much, in a sequel. I have rarely been disabused of an idea more swiftly or emphatically – my assumption that my new adulthood allowed me the leeway to make such decisions was apparently well wide of the mark, and furthermore, my additional assumption that I might continue to have a roof over my head before I set off was equally erroneous. Having done rather well to have talked my way to an unconditional offer to study Sports Science at Loughborough – something much sought after and unattained by far more capable athletes than myself – my father didn't quite see the benefit of turning this down in favour of backpacks and spliffs. Strange man. At the time, I was livid, but thank God for the intervention. Although it's still my ambition to spend my reincarnation as a surfer dude beach bum, reckoning I've done my sensible corporate thing in this current life, what I would have missed out on by walking through the wrong sliding doors at that moment doesn't bear thinking about. So, having avoided one of the worst decisions of my life, I promptly replaced it with another. That dressing down from Dad had clearly overplayed in my head the need for a change of attitude and to start being sensible and practical. So, I decided a Spitfire was not the thing to get me to and around Loughborough (somewhat more than thirty miles away), but I still felt wheels would give me an early advantage when I got there, so I traded in my beautiful red companion for... a bright orange Skoda. I can only think the summer's excess had finally taken its toll.

I say I paid relatively little attention to the '86 World Cup, but even I wasn't so detached that England in a quarter-final meant nothing to me; let's face it, compared to previous attempts I'd been aware of – two 'did not qualifies' and one group exit with a whimper – this was if not the summit of Everest then at least the Hilary Step. No need to recount the detail of what, or rather who, happened in that game against Argentina, but if the previous tournament had introduced me to the concept of undeserved defeat, this was different gravy. 'The hand of God' seems to some to have become more iconic than fury-inducing over time, which irritates me. This was the worst piece of cheating (or best, depending on your point of view) and the worst piece of linesmanship (regardless of your point of view) and it now being granted an asterisk that says it was followed by one of the greatest goals of all time, from one of the greatest players, is annoying in the extreme, to me at least. The fact that England were on the end of it obviously wouldn't help me to let it go even if I wanted to. But here was evidence that cheats can prosper even on the most important of days, and the news that Maradona's countrymen – indeed the whole of South America – were lauding him, and still do, for a clever piece of skill and 'trickery' simply reinforced my question of myself and of sport at the end of my festival summer: what's the point?

If I needed an appropriate metaphor to mark the end of the first, happy phase of my sports-following existence and a portent for the less ingenuous real world which lay ahead, this could not have been bettered. This was the end of the innocence.

Or perhaps I've gone three years too early. Maradona may have bookended one part of my life very appropriately, but perhaps the 1989 Ashes have an equal claim to being the most apposite harbinger of the harsher realities of life, coming as they did at the end of my interregnum at university. The three years at Loughborough may have looked more sensible when compared to the summer just gone, but they could hardly yet be called the 'real world'. They did extend that period when sports watching was not as intense a matter as it had been before and was to be again, this time less because of the opposite sex, although that was not something to jettison completely. Now it was because most of those around me were more concerned with doing than watching. We were privileged enough to be at one of the world's leading sports colleges, being tutored and trained by coaches most of whom were way too good to be wasting their time on the likes of me. The football club was not only my way of getting some exercise four to five times a week, but it was my social home which formed friendships so strong that reunions go on to this day – sadly less frequently based around active participation as the oldest team in the annual six-a-side tournament and more often now straight to the post-match revelry. After a successful couple of years at left back and midfield in the sixth form at school, at which point football was finally permitted, any pretensions I had to making my mark as part of the all-conquering Loughborough first team were managed via my first chat with my hall social sec, also on the football club board, who took me through the current first team midfield. Captain of British Students, captain of the RAF team, the son of a former Manchester United manager now himself on the books at Old Trafford and a wide man who had played in the first division for Middlesbrough. Suddenly, my man of the match award against Cricklade College seemed rather inadequate as a playing CV. No matter, I settled in as a committed dirt-tracker and then upped my game considerably at about 5pm every Wednesday and Saturday, leaning on my training from my previous summer to boost my credibility through significant Purple Nasty consumption, and sometimes even retention, and rarely failing to make it to the dancefloor at Sammy's for the warm down. We weren't disinterested in sport outside the Loughborough bubble – we still retained our club allegiances, national allegiances when the Six Nations came around, and were happy to settle down to VHSs of England's winter Ashes win in Australia and laugh uncontrollably at our Scouse housemate when Michael Thomas's last-minute goal went in to win Arsenal the title at Anfield. But the bottom line was that winning and retaining the UAU title was simply more important now than the FA

Cup final. Failing to make the top echelons of the football hierarchy did have its compensations. My best mate was an all-round sportsman on a different plane to me (fly half for Nottingham schools, football for Notts County academy and England schools cricket tourist to Barbados with the likes of Atherton, Hussain and Ramprakash. I did remind him that he was the only one of that squad not to play first-class cricket, but that was really a sop to my own inadequacies rather than much of a stick to beat him with). By the start of our third year in the late summer of 1988, he had seen off some significant competition, by dint of his determination, to secure his place in the first XI defence. Another good mate was now installed as first choice keeper. Loughborough were a popular choice as pre-season opponents for the various Midlands professional clubs which, unsurprisingly, drew a bit more of a crowd to the first-team pitch. I was in position to watch Tom and Andy take on Derby County one afternoon at the end of that summer. I will own up to a tinge of envy, which dissipated within about five seconds of kick-off. Now, these clubs would normally bring a collection of trialists, reserves hoping to be noticed and occasionally a new signing or two for an initial run-out, but the unspoken understanding was that too strong a side might defeat the objective of a competitive game. However, that this was an occasion when these formalities had been stretched a little became apparent as County kicked off and a guy took the ball from the centre circle, utterly skinned Tom and from about fifty yards, sent a shot so hard against the crossbar that not only did Andy fail to move, or even give any indication that he'd seen it, but the ball rebounded so far that it counted as the first time we'd made it into Derby's half. When I had regained my composure and feet and stemmed the tears of mirth, I enquired of one of the Derby staff who the player was. The answer was Lubos Kubik, a Czech international who had just returned from starring in that summer's European Championships. It was a long afternoon and confirmed to me once and for all that my own future lay in spectating.

PART TWO
THE REAL LIFE
1989–2002

NEW DAWN FADES

Three years at university were coming to an end. The PGCE/Masters options to avoid the real world for a little longer had to be considered, and there were certainly some role models at Loughborough – those who seemed to have turned up as freshers and never have left, some of them now looking closer to retirement than the world of employment. I was never quite sure how they did it or managed to finance it. I knew pretty quickly that this wasn't for me – despite the attractions of the sense of freedom, lack of any real pressure and regular 'ballooning' behaviour with a fellow bunch of student footballers who also refused to grow up, the hand-to-mouth existence began to wear thin. It was time for my own new dawn, although I had zero idea of what that might bring. I had vague ambitions to become the next Christopher Martin-Jenkins or Hugh McIlvanney but wasn't sure I fancied years at journalism college (the fact this was based in Portsmouth seemed to be telling me it wasn't for me) or a couple of years on the Argus somewhere in the provinces. My idea was to do a month writing articles for *The Cricketer* before being welcomed onto the *Test Match Special* team and spending the rest of my life watching cricket for money. But as with the sporting new dawns, what the vision was and what actually transpired were rather different.

The illusory concept of the new dawn in sport is one all sports followers will recognise. It comes into play when your team has been rubbish for an extended period. They aren't actually getting any better in terms of results, so another way needs to be found to create that hope that sustains us no matter how tenuous. And we, of course, fall for it every time because we have to. Delusion is better than reality at such moments. There is an accepted pattern to the sporting new dawn. Change the personnel involved; ideally bring in people who have some past and romantic connection with the club or team; change your kit; talk about a new 'project' and a return to playing with style and passion. Unfortunately, there is also an accepted pattern to what happens next. A month of hope, sometimes even a couple of positive results to enhance the illusion, and then a descent back into defeat, rancour and various further departures. The saddest thing about the new dawn is that once the fairy story has been shown up for what it is and you are back where you started, you actually feel worse than before the whole thing started.

The summer of 1989 as I left Loughborough ended up as the demonstration of the new dawn par excellence and yet again, the sport I was watching eerily paralleled and reflected my own stage of life.

Since their Ashes win in Australia in the winter of 1986/87, England's cricket team had been rehearsing quite effectively for how they intended to play throughout the nineties – namely regularly disintegrating against both vastly superior and supposedly inferior opposition. In their quest to arrest this, the tactic often seemed to be to stick pins into the county scorecards to find the next Ian Botham. When that ended up being Derek Pringle or David Capel, with due respect, you can see the problem. It often seemed to be last man standing. What made things worse for us supporters was that this often seemed to be self-inflicted by crass, on-the-hoof decision-making by those at the top. This began with the decision to jettison the captain, who had recently retained the Ashes on foreign soil, because he'd had a barmaid in his hotel room eighteen months later. Regardless of the protestations of innocence, even if it did occur, then, given this was Gatt, not necessarily everyone's idea of the incarnation of a lady-killer, my own reaction was one of both surprise and congratulations to both the skipper and the said barmaid who had been willing to take the job on. This creeping progression towards Roundhead-ism and holier-than-thou pontification only served to further antagonise us lovers of the beautiful summer game, who, as worshippers at the altar of Gower, could see what might be coming (and duly transpired a few years later). It was deemed the problem was too much fun, too much flair and too much enjoyment for the watching public. The era of the sergeant major and hair-shirt approach was upon us, and as the results got worse, rather than stop digging, the men in charge seemed to want to maximise the use of their JCB. As an England sports fan, this is just about the most maddening cycle you can go through, and with us, it seems as predictable and regular as the sunrise across all our sports. Gooch not Gower, Ron Greenwood not Brian Clough, Sam Allardyce not Harry Redknapp, sack Terry Venables, Stuart Lancaster not Wayne Smith. Now we as a breed are fairly phlegmatic that England are going to lose quite often, and historically, they have rarely let us down, new dawn or not. The issue is not losing, it is achieving those defeats with a sense of joylessness and a willingness to deny the watching public the entertainers they are willing to pay to see. So it was by the end of 1988 following a 4-0 home defeat by the West Indies, the sense of optimism that now was our time, with no Holding or Garner anymore, rather deflated by the arrival of Ambrose and co. False dawn. In the process, we had been treated to twenty-three players and four captains, and when the music stopped, the parcel was in the lap of Graham Gooch – fantastic batsman but rapidly morphing from Cavalier to Roundhead and no longer anybody's idea of someone to extol the virtues of swashbuckling the way to victory.

Fortunately, the lack of a tour that winter allowed for an unusual opportunity to draw breath. It was the classic breeding ground for a new dawn. Sure enough, by the start of the summer of '89, the Cavaliers were back in force and in charge. If you wanted maverick nostalgia and romanticism, as well it transpired, unfortunately as a rather alarming lack of a connection to planet earth, putting Ted Dexter in charge of things ticked all the boxes. Add to Lord Ted the return of David Gower as captain and the stirring words from them both and everything suddenly seemed set for England to take on the world, rather conveniently forgetting the fact that nothing had actually happened on the field of play to support this optimism since the latest nadir the previous summer.

As with many new dawns, we were drawn in further by the way it started. The Australians had arrived for an Ashes summer, with pretty much the same personnel we had strolled past two winters ago. There was a fantastic one-day series and Gower, almost without a run since the summer began, then hit a serene double hundred against the tourists in the county match. All was set fair. We were in for a comfortable and enjoyable summer. England then made over four hundred in the first innings of the first Test. All still on track. Then our bowlers went all round Headingley as Australia scored over six hundred – with a rather alarming level of ease and confidence as well an aggressive, confrontational attitude which completely threw us all – somehow won the Test and within four weeks had walked off with the Ashes. By September, Gower was gone; Ted was irretrievably damaged; Gooch was back; and it was to be a diet of Roundheads for the next decade at least…

Meanwhile, as the Ashes were being surrendered at Old Trafford cricket ground, across the road at the Theatre of Dreams would you believe a new dawn was on the horizon? Again, I would point out a connection as I had just arrived in Oldham and was shortly to reconfirm my Pied Piper faculty by seeing Manchester United win their first title in twenty years. In the summer of '89, however, before my rescue mission had had chance to take effect, I arrived in the north-west to find the once mighty United in a bad place and losing money year on year. Fergie was on the brink of being shown the door; there were few signs of revival as Arsenal had now joined Liverpool in the title stakes. This was new dawn time if ever there was one, and again, I feel my arrival somehow had something to do with it.

Not only did United spend money on half a new team with the likes of Ince, Webb and Wallace coming in, but some may recall a saviour had arrived in the form of businessman Michael Knighton. Having convinced the United board to allow him to buy the club for £10 million, he announced himself by upstaging the new arrivals, performing keepy-uppies in front of the Stretford End, who promptly hailed him as the conquering hero who would deliver the better future. We all fell for the new dawn line again hook, line and sinker. Such flamboyance gave the United hierarchy second thoughts and pressure, and a PR machine gradually sidelined him. Knighton argues, quite convincingly, that the new dawn which *was* eventually to transpire over the following decade was based on his vision. I, of course, would suggest instead that it was my arrival and more lasting presence which made the real difference.

The final confirmation that this was the end of the days of wine and roses (although the wine was to make something of a comeback) was the fact that having surrendered the Ashes in Manchester when we assumed the nadir had been reached, England actually managed to lower the bar even further over the following three days of the series. Given this was my last weekend of freedom before moving away to start my new life, I guess I can be forgiven for seeing in it another parallel. On the 10th of August, day one of the fifth Test, surely the pressure and the shackles would be off England and we could make something of a comeback. By the end of the day, Australia were 301-0. Not a single wicket in over six hours of cricket. A day and a half later, they had passed six hundred yet again, and England, happy surely that they could bat on such a proven road of a pitch, were 14-3. Fortunately, Dad was nowhere to be seen that day as I didn't really need his aggravated confirmation that playing across dead straight balls with bats coming down from around second slip was not the best way to negate Terry Alderman. The game was duly lost by an innings and plenty to go 4-0 down. The symbolism was complete.

Two new dawns, two demonstrations of desperate fan gullibility and two complete disasters. Not great portents for my own fresh start.

LIFE IN A NORTHERN TOWN

If a temporary term-time sojourn halfway up the country in Loughborough was one thing, the next move was rather more significant and just as unexpected. Whilst my mates from home either remained in the bosom of their families in leafy Hampshire or made the short trip to West London to ride Maggie's new wave as fledgling property developers, I set off alone to a northern mill town – the decision made to move to Oldham previously explained. It hit home that this was a real departure, not just pretend, when my father arrived in my bedroom as the last new shirt and tie went into the last suitcase to advise me to be sensitive as my mum was downstairs in a state of some emotion, and the goodbyes might be slightly tearful. It was a fine attempt at a father-son stiff-upper-lipped farewell, only undermined when, halfway through his warning, he burst into tears. This was a significant farewell – the real thing, the real world for sure.

I was to demonstrate almost immediately my continuing role as an angel of good sporting fortune. Oldham Athletic were, and had forever been, an unfashionable and largely unsuccessful team making their way in the darker lower reaches of the football pyramid and without even a sniff of a significant trophy. Within eight months of my arrival, they had played in a League Cup final at Wembley and two mighty FA Cup semi-final games with Manchester United, the first of which they were within minutes of winning. The whole town was abuzz with football fever as never before. In a manner reminiscent of my Southampton team fourteen years earlier, the players became local heroes and retain that status to this day. Rarely has a Latics team tripped off the tongue, but I am not in need of any research to rattle off Hallworth, Irwin, Barlow, Redfearn, Barrett, Adams, Milligan, Henry, Holden, Ritchie, Marshall and subs Warhurst and Palmer.

I have to admit, I didn't share in the love for my new hometown club and their exploits, partly because I had watched them knock Saints out in the League Cup quarter-final replay, partly because of their ludicrous plastic pitch but above all, because of the hypocrisy I could see from my close yet detached position. When I arrived in August, Oldham's home games were half-empty, with the majority of the town's football followers the owners of Manchester United replica shirts. By March, the ground was heaving and reverberated to the sound of locals explaining how they had always been Oldham and not United. Of course, once the party was over five years later and Oldham made their way back down whence they had come, these people reversed their journey, claiming they'd always been red through and through. The fickle nature of the floating supporter. I may have had two teams myself, but at least they were permanent relationships.

Any initial reservations I had as to whether I had just made the maddest call of my life to date (and there were plenty as I struggled through the streets of Oldham pre-sat nav and considered whether this place was actually in the same country as the city I had just left) eased within a month of my arrival at work when I got what I hoped I had moved up there for: my first taste of working with my heroes. The MD at our small sports company was a genial Irishman with a glint in his eye and more than a touch of the Barry Hearns about him. I got the impression from my interview onwards – when his first question, designed to test my reactions, I suppose, was a now rather suspect 'are you a rapist?' – that he was not averse to the unconventional. A month in, he advised we had signed up a certain David Gower to endorse our cricket brand (done at the start of the summer as new dawn England captain; now looking slightly less like the deal of the century) and that David needed to visit HQ but had just had his shoulder op so needed to be driven up and back. Would I be willing to take the role of chauffeur? Well yes, but the slightly beaten-up Nissan Micra Mum had passed on to me for my new life was unlikely to meet David's well-known penchant for the finer things in life. "No," he said, "you take my car." (A new Jaguar XJS complete with revolutionary car phone and the rest – just a shame that it stopped short of a Dom Perignon compartment in the back.) Well, this wasn't a bad start to professional life…

"When's he coming?"

"Next Friday."

"So, I'd need to drop him back to Leicester Friday night?"

"Correct."

At this point, a plan formed in my head, and before I could check myself and consider whether this might lead to the shortest employment in the company's history, I explained (untruthfully, but plans could soon be amended) that I was due back in Loughborough that same weekend and it would seem mad to drive to Leicester, eight miles away, return to Oldham and go straight back down again, so might I keep the car over the weekend? Fortunately, I had picked the right bloke – his initial gobsmacked look eased into something approaching a knowing grin at the effrontery. Looking back, I get the impression he thought it was exactly what he would have asked, given the same circumstances. "Get me a pool car by Thursday and you can have it," he said.

This had two consequences. Firstly, as a very impressionable and still nervous twenty-two-year-old new recruit, I found myself sitting next to one of my greatest sporting heroes for five hours all told, during which time he had no means of escape. I would love to say that I handled this in a cool, urbane and professional manner and thus in a charming and understated way built a level of respect and interaction which would eventually form the basis of a lasting friendship. I'd love to, but unfortunately, I can't. In truth, I was too young and starry-eyed to carry out the operation in the way I had visualised the night before, and if by some miracle Mr Gower is reading this now, I can only apologise (for the journey, not the book). My rather tongue-tied attempts at casual conversation, whilst also getting over the fact that he was so important to my early sports-watching years that I knew more about most of his innings than he did, was only topped for awkwardness when I made first use of the car phone to call Dad whilst David was secured in the passenger seat. I guess this was my attempt to show Dad I had arrived with style in my new profession, but I was regretting it as Dad genuflected. His thank you to David for giving him many years of pleasure was genuine and heartfelt but must simply have confirmed to our England legend that he was in the company of two overgrown schoolboys. David, of course, bore it with all the charm he could muster, but given he had just been beaten 4-0 by Australia, lost the England captaincy and had a painful operation, he was understandably in the terser zone of his mood spectrum. In the end, I did get some inside stories of Ashes trips, all the confirmation I had hoped for of the reality of touring with Beefy and ultimately a memorable day. Perhaps not as memorable as that night, though.

Having secured the car and dropped 'Lubo', as I now embarrassingly felt I could call him, back in Leicester, I cruised down the A6 and proceeded to seek out as many ex-girlfriends as possible to offer them a lift in my new motor. I also delivered my mates to the Union bar – about nine of them piling out – the implication being that after one month, I was already a powerful young executive of whom they could be proud and, more importantly, jealous.

It was one of two sports-related car journeys seared into my memory from those early days in my supposed real world. Actually, these were about as unreal as it gets. If the first one was serene, the next one was anything but. A few years on, post-Italia '90, I had signed a deal with Gazza, as had everyone else at that time. That gave me my first taste of agents to the superstars as they negotiated a deal to wear shin guards as if it were their contract at Lazio. We had done a deal, but six months in, we still hadn't met with Gazza or even managed to track him down. He was in his injured early days at Lazio and, needing an image or two of the great man with our product, I ended up with a pretty tenuous trip all the way to Rome with a pair of shin guards in my pocket purely for this purpose.

Paul's reputation for elusiveness and suspect reliability was already established, and I assumed correctly that a man bearing shin guards might not be top of his priority list when set against a day by the pool in his palatial villa. So it was that after forty-five minutes of standing at the side of a road on the outskirts of the airport waiting for the pick-up I had been advised would be waiting for me, I was starting to run through the scenario of returning from an expensive round trip to the eternal city without having so much as set eyes on the quarry and imagining how well that would go down at the office. I was also expecting an Italian driver in a suit and a Mercedes. What actually came screaming round the corner was a red Ferrari driven by what I recognised to be Gazza's mate and general factotum, Jimmy 'Five Bellies' Gardiner. "You Ben?" he shouted, barely slowing enough for me to catch the words. "Jump in." We then set off on what I can only describe as my first and only Formula One race. The first minute of the journey was spent desperately searching for a seat belt, but one was not forthcoming. Thus, as the big man weaved through Italian juggernauts at speeds well into three figures, I clung on for my life. Somehow arriving in one piece, Gazza and I did our best to pretend he knew what Sondico shin guards were and that he even remotely cared and, job done, I closed my eyes again and took the return journey. I may have been seeking life in the fast lane, but this was a bit too literal for me.

IN TOO DEEP

By now, I'd managed to extricate myself from my product role of scrutinising price lists and sticking Velcro onto goalkeepers' gloves and sidled into what I'd envisaged in the first place: signing and marketing players, looking after the likes of Gower, Lineker, Bryan Robson and Malcolm Marshall. This was more like it. It did, however, add a new dimension to my sports watching, which was to remain a complication for the next thirty years. Now came the realisation that sport, results and performances mattered not because they mattered but because, all of a sudden, my professional life depended on them. This hardly lessened the tension of watching. It was one thing getting uptight about Southampton, the England cricket team or Jimmy White – I was used to the nerves which compromised the enjoyment. Now I had individuals that were important professionally to get worried about, as well as my own personal allegiances. From this point on, very few sports events allowed me to be relaxed without some sort of vested interest which the glass half-fullers would have seen as a benefit, simply adding to the interest of otherwise unremarkable games. In reality, it just gave me fewer chances to enjoy sport with the detached and dispassionate air of the neutral. What's more, this could also actually detract from moments which should have been pure successes. In the years to come, if England beat Australia but neither Pietersen or Bell had got any runs, or Broad had gone round the park, or England beat Wales in the Six Nations but George Ford had a nightmare and was subbed at half-time, I couldn't fully enjoy the moment. I needed Ben Youngs in his three stripes to keep Danny Care in his Nikes out of the side. Every team selection was a moment of truth to see what percentage of my guys made it. Then, the first ten minutes of any game was spent checking if they were in the right product to save me from questions from up the chain of command. I was also now in an environment where it has been deemed necessary rather than a matter of choice to discuss and therefore elongate the pain of every sporting moment. No longer could the worst moments be compartmentalised and ignored as if they never happened.

I got my first experience of this through those goalkeepers I had signed up to Sondico. There rarely seemed to be a game in the early nineties which I could watch without praying for a performance from one and wishing disaster on another dependent on their respective sports brand sponsors. The result of these games didn't matter, but these details did instead. Again, the first check would be for what they were wearing. The odds of this ever being perfect were heavily reduced by the products I was challenged to get them to wear. At one time, we marketed a glove with heavy plastic spines down the back of the fingers, the idea being to reduce finger injuries. This was fine for little Johnny playing at school on a Wednesday afternoon who either didn't much like the idea of catching the ball or was just plain petrified of it. It wasn't, however, something that overly concerned international goalkeepers, all of whom had apparently got this far in their careers without the help of such a groundbreaking innovation.

With Chris Woods, the England keeper, now signed up, I had to devote adrenaline to games involving bloody Sheffield Wednesday of all teams and hope that his rival David Seaman had shockers for Arsenal. And, of course, from the moment Chris came on board, his form seemed to fall apart whilst Safe Hands lived up to his name and stole his England position, never to relinquish it. By the time Seaman had his 'Nayim from the halfway line' moment, it was too late. From now on, I would form totally unjustified dislikes of certain players just because of what they had on their hands and feet.

Occasionally, the professional and personal vectors would intersect. If the two elements required different outcomes, of course the personal won the day. Even once I had joined adidas in 1996, I could never subscribe to the good company man view that I should want Bayern Munich to beat Manchester United in the Champions League final just because they wore a certain kit, for example. Be serious. Then, on other days, both things required the same result, which made things less conflicted with regard to company contracts but simply increased the need for the right outcome for me. So it was in September 1991 when Hampshire made their first ever final of the Nat West Trophy. Gower and my favourite Malcolm Marshall were both playing for my team that day. Not only were they both heroes (and given 'Maco' was not playing for the West Indies, I could for once be right behind him), but both were endorsing our cricket gear. After what seemed like decades of trying, Hampshire had finally won their first ever one-day trophy in 1988, but Gower was not yet with them, and Marshall missed it whilst on tour with the West Indies. The latter was genuinely emotional that he'd missed that historic day with his adopted family and was desperate that he should be on the winning side now. Almost as desperate as I was. For my part, I was in theory at Lord's on business, having secured the tickets through my contracted players and with the simple task of delivering Maco's bat to him for the upcoming World Cup. He was setting off for Australia via Barbados straight after the match and this rather important piece of equipment needed to be passed on to him at some point during the day. Admittedly, the wise thing to do would have been to drop it off first thing before heading up to the Compton Stand rather than sitting there all day with a bat in my hand looking to everyone else like someone taking the game rather too seriously by bringing my kit – the cricketing equivalent of turning up at Old Trafford to watch United in full replica strip with a ball under my arm. But this was not the course I chose, keen as I was to get to my seat. My business demeanour from this point gradually ebbed away as I sat in the sun with a mate, in the uncovered stand, keeping sensibly hydrated via a conveyor belt of warm beer. My 'buoyant' mood was enhanced as the sun slipped down around eight hours later and Hampshire won a nail biter in the last over. What followed was not acceptable business behaviour but was a form of release from the tension of the last hour. Setting off on a mission to get the bat to the pavilion, I was apparently diverted instead into haring over the Lord's turf waving the said piece of willow over my head. It was next seen at St Pancras station, where my similarly giddy mate and I had half an hour to kill before boarding our train. Chris, a former Derbyshire professional, was first to point out we had a bat (about £500's worth of bat for that matter) but no ball. A conversation ensued with a rather confused lady (Caribbean, just to round off the theme of the day nicely) at the fruit stand being asked what she had 'for a game of cricket'. Settling on an orange as our best bet (the colour at least reducing the chance of having to come off for bad light), we duly moved an estimated twenty-two yards apart along the platform and I got ready to purvey the off spin which had served me well through school. In agreeing to bowl first, I was in no state to have thought through the decision in terms of my chances in this contest. Firstly, an orange isn't blessed with a particularly prominent seam; secondly, a tarmac platform is hardly a raging Bunsen of a pitch; and finally, the fact I was bowling to a guy with a first-class century to his name didn't put the odds in my favour. In fact, the straight drive that met my first delivery sent orange pips far and wide halfway to King's Cross and left pith and an ugly, if sweet-smelling, mark in the middle of the

World Cup bat. We nearly didn't make it to the train; the bat definitely never made it to Australia. I don't recall how often Maco batted in that tournament or with what.

At times, it feels like that was where the fun stopped when it came to the sporting experience of the 1990s. This was to be the era which defined what it means to be an English sports fan, challenged our ability to stick the course and had us questioning what the hell this stuff was doing ruining our lives.

IT'S GONNA HAPPEN

> *'Pessimism, when you get used to it, is just as agreeable as optimism'*
> ARNOLD BENNETT, ENGLISH DRAMATIST

The next ten years or so, although occasionally punctuated by the odd moment of relief, served up a pretty constant diet of dire defeat and acute disappointment, and this was gradually to develop in me certain traits to be found in a lot of my kind. This was when sport chose to reflect my own current life experience that reality can be tough, and success isn't a matter of right.

The first of the characteristics to blossom and then remain ingrained forevermore was a default state of pessimism, which was as much an insurance against the level of pain ultimate defeat might bring as a genuine prediction of the outcome. It dawned on me that there could be real benefits in pessimism. Now we are in an era of rather greater success, I severely irritate friends with my constant assertions that anything that can go wrong is about to, regardless of the actual odds. I'm hoping it's not too late to change me now. My mindset is a product of those 1990's disasters – a kind of sports-watching post-traumatic stress disorder, which I would campaign to have recognised as a genuine condition. It becomes a more comfortable default position than hopefulness. George Bernard Shaw suggested, 'he who has never hoped can never despair'.

Now I accept that is a fairly negative take on anything and can understand why it would drive other people nuts, but it is my comfortable cocoon. I'm not saying it is a position that's easy to maintain – somehow the hope keeps coming to sit on your shoulder and whisper in your ear. But at least the pessimist's view gives you the chance to offset your mood when it all goes wrong by saying 'I told you so' and therefore acts as a defence mechanism. It's a simple system. Botham will always be out next ball – if he isn't you can breathe again; if he is, you are an insightful analyst of the game. It endears you to nobody but that's not the point.

There is also something about the English and sport where the next best thing to victory is complete disaster. Far better something which will allow us to unload our frustration and hold an inquest. There have certainly been times when United were so bad under Van Gaal that I was almost willing them to lose 7-0 once they were 2-0 down. This is a strange way to behave but somehow the chance to rant to mates, the radio or the newspapers is more therapeutic than a close 1-0 defeat in a half decent contest. Churchill once said of the British, 'they are the only people who like to be told how bad things are – who like to be told the worst'. Admittedly, this may have been said in a rather different context, but there is an element of national characteristic here which I have come across in the English supporter. And if this is true, we were about to be told, and experience, the worst for some time to come, because the reality is that through the 1990s, my pessimism seemed to become a self-fulfilling prophecy. Or to put it another way, it was regularly completely justified. One after another, the let-downs queued up to test our patience and our true level of addiction.

I VOW TO THEE MY COUNTRY

In the summer just gone, an article by the Archbishop of York, Stephen Cottrell (another unlikely contributor to this story), called for 'a vision of what it means to be English as part of the United Kingdom' and, against a background of apparent flagellation of the English by our own metropolitan elite, suggested the average English person's 'heartfelt cry to be heard is often disregarded, wilfully misunderstood or patronised as being backwardly xenophobic'.

There was, and is, an element of this in how I feel about supporting England, particularly in contests with our nearest neighbours. What follows, I can assure you, is not a xenophobic rant – I have some Scottish blood; I'm married into an Irish family; and two of my favourite rugby players – indeed people anywhere in the world of sport – are Welshmen; it is more of a plea not to be categorised unfairly as an England fan in relation to others and to drop the idea that where other fans are passionate and patriotic, we are arrogant and nationalistic.

The Six Nations is often a good illustration of this. Let's be honest, there is an undertone of England not being liked very much by at least four of their opponents in this competition. This irritates the English enough to reciprocate which is a shame but, in my experience, a reality. The most tiresome manifestation of this mainly manufactured animosity is the insinuation that any victory by the French or our Celtic cousins over the Red Rose was a righting of everybody's wrongs and an answer to any number of historical injustices. The idea that the other competing nations were less arrogant than England and what came over as an assumed monopoly on the right to be passionate about their sport and their country grated with me. Is this oversensitive, a paranoia relating to something which just doesn't exist? Comments like those of Gareth Bale in advance of an England v Wales game at Euro 2016 might suggest not. Bale unburdened himself in the *Daily Telegraph*, referring to England, where he had made his name, as 'the enemy', offering the opinion that 'we've got a lot more pride and passion about us than them. If you're Welsh, look at the rugby, we feel more pride and passion than anyone else'. I completely understand the pride and passion of Gareth and the Welsh nation and support their right to enjoy it, but there is a reason I have a slight problem with this, namely that there is no copyright on passion and what was this if not a form of the arrogance alleged against me? Imagine those comments from an Englishman and the howls of protest they would elicit. Look at the rugby indeed. Does anybody else recall the humility of the Welsh invincibles and their public before any rugby game against England in the seventies and eighties? Hubris is not an exclusive preserve of the English; a reminder here of the Scottish football team and nation's confidence in their prospects for that 1978 World Cup and the fact that they went on a tour of the country of the open-top bus variety *before* they left for the tournament. Hmmm.

To the accusations of arrogance and historic oppression, I would say two things: firstly, that I have just laid down in some detail my ingrained pessimistic approach to sport and ability to see a superior foe in just about anyone, and therefore, it is not only annoying but completely unjust to label me, by dint of being an England supporter, as arrogant; secondly, I can say with confidence that I personally did not rape the land of Ireland in the seventeenth century, that I didn't close any steelworks in South Wales or buy a second home in Aberystwyth and that I didn't impose the poll tax on anybody, so this artificial creation of some sort of crusade against the oppression of the Celts rings a little hollow. And I don't begin to understand what we've done to so upset the French, unless it is the more recent oppression of their front row by Brian Moore that they are still struggling to accept. In between Waterloo and fishing quotas, there were a couple of significant conflicts in which we surely played a positive role? To me, these things seem more a badge of convenience designed to create an additional hostility on the pitch and in the stands to improve the odds of victory, that's all. This is why, far from entering every Six Nations expecting England to win it as everyone else believes we do, I for one would argue it's harder for England to win it than anyone bar Italy, given their opponents see the match against them as their one to get up for above all others, in some cases, winning that game alone being the mark of a satisfactory tournament. This antagonism wasn't always so strident, so when and how did it come to pass? Well, possibly in the year of my birth (so yet again a paranoid version of myself might see some mystical parallel, even if I might be deemed to be stretching my theme a little here). The historian Peter Clarke, in *Hope and Glory*, his political and social history of Britain in the twentieth century, identifies 1967 as a significant moment in the development of a new salient cultural nationalism in Scotland and Wales in particular. The increased support for the SNP and Plaid Cymru was seen in by-election upsets, notably in Hamilton, Lanarkshire and in Rhondda West and in the passage of the

Welsh Language Act that year. So, the moment I landed on the planet coincided with a significant rise in a nationalist, anti-English, culture in the nations against whom I was going to have to suffer rugby matches twenty years hence. I'm just saying…

I have come to realise over the years that there is a list of ingredients which dictate just how much importance and emotional energy I attach to any sporting event. If you can apply the majority of these elements to a particular contest, you stand to maximise the angst, and English sport in the 1990s seemed to have the recipe for most of the decade. The base ingredient is often a long period of failure against the same opposition. For evidence, see Ashes cricket 1989–2003. Losing to the same people for fourteen years is bound to increase both your antipathy towards them and your desire to eventually stuff them out of sight. If this monopoly gives that opposition an air of arrogant condescension, it simply adds to the desperation to wipe the smug grins off their faces. And we aren't just talking about the teams themselves here – it is their supporters, sometimes even the entire population of their countries, who seem to be laughing at you, too comfortable by half. Into this envelope I could put, fairly or otherwise, not just the Aussies at cricket but German international football, the USA Ryder Cup team (plus entourage, fans and country), Arsenal FC in the early 2000s – Wenger, Keown et al – and individuals such as Hendry, Sampras and so on. To be fair to these last few, it's really just that they were too good and rather boringly so, but it was easier to pigeonhole them as arrogant for my own purposes. In the face of constant defeats, the Englishman's one consolation was that we had better supporters (with the dishonourable exception of our lovely national football supporters partly for the boorish thuggery but mainly because of that bloody band). Ashes series could still deliver some enjoyment in watching the risible attempts of the Australians to ape the Barmy Army of which they seemed so envious. They couldn't seem to comprehend the black humour and the unconquerable cheerfulness in the face of on-field humiliation and actually making an ironic virtue of it. Not really the Australian way. But as their irritation grew at us pretending not to care, so they felt they had to have a bash at it too, especially when they started to rack up the defeats themselves, but they simply aren't cut out for such behaviour. For a start, The Fanatics is the sort of name which you get at those forced jollity corporate team-building exercises I've been made to suffer on occasion. And the canary yellow get-up doesn't particularly add to their credibility. German football fans, with a national stereotyping about their difficulty with the concept of humour, particularly of the self-deprecating variety, have a similar issue. I was allocated the seat next to a senior adidas executive – German, Bayern Munich and football to his core – at the Euro '96 final. He couldn't comprehend how, England having been kept out of the final by Germany four days previously, the stadium was full of England supporters singing 'Three Lions' as passionately as at any time in the tournament. It's our statement, I suppose – you can beat us as often and as painfully as you like, but we're still here.

Stephen Fry defined the difference between patriotism and nationalism as the former being 'I love my country' and the latter 'I hate everybody else's country'. This is a very fine line for the sports supporter, especially in the face of constant defeat. 1990 was to be a year dedicated to three national teams that delivered us an annus horribilis two years ahead of Her Majesty's. It gave us four defeats of varying anguish but all in the 'significant' category. Two were fully deserved; two were made worse by the feeling of being cheated of our just desserts. The first three all left me with long-term 'what might have beens'. And having now made the step into a full-time sporting occupation, avoiding any of them was not an option even if I'd wanted to.

The fun began on the 17th of March, 1990 (and ran on and off until the penultimate day of the year). Scotland v England rugby, Murrayfield Stadium, Edinburgh. Now I love the Six Nations as I did the Five Nations before it. My balance of the love of sport for what it brings us regardless of results versus the inappropriate levels of misery caused by defeats may have become a little maladjusted, but I like to think I can still see the value in the bigger picture in moments of greater maturity. I've given a nod to the role the tournament plays in kicking off the sporting calendar and getting me through winter weekends. When moments like the 17th of March, 1990 come along, you try very hard to remind yourself of this. Who would want to lose the weekends this tournament affords us? Travelling as a group for long weekends, savouring the varied delights of some of Europe's finest and most hospitable capital cities; the welcome, the interaction and the banter is, on the whole, good natured and forged of a shared understanding of the value of the experience and that the match itself, if not quite incidental, is just a part of the overall tapestry (probably the least enjoyable part in many cases). One of my favourite sports trip memories of all is of a weekend in Marseille for the quarter-finals of the 2007 Rugby World Cup. For sure, the fact that England knocked out Australia and shortly afterwards France did the same to the All Blacks did no harm in creating the atmosphere of general bonhomie, but it was the three days based around the Old Port square in the city, talking rugby, watching rugby, ordering Kronenbergs by the trayful, all with like-minded souls in a plethora of different national jerseys which made the lasting impression. It's this stuff you have to keep drumming into yourself every time you begin slipping to the wrong side of Mr Fry's two definitions. Unfortunately for me, for the Six Nations to endure and retain its value, one has to accept that it needs sides other than England to win. This is a difficult one. Let's face it, losing to Wales is not a happy occasion for an Englishman, but *never* losing to Wales would be worse in the long-term. It's the same with cricket and the West Indies – losing to them for twenty-two years through the seventies and eighties got a little tedious, but it was somehow more of a pleasure to play, and get stuffed by, a team of such quality and which played such a part the cultural story and integration of its islands' countrymen than it was to win seven Tests in a year against them in 2004 as they slipped into an international wilderness. These sports are nothing without serious opponents. Accept this, and you do have the benefit of a comfort blanket against the losses. Although eaten up inside, on the outside you can profess your appreciation for the wider health of the game with as much false sincerity as possible in an attempt to prick the bubble of your conqueror's self-satisfaction. Let the bastard know you are accepting defeat magnanimously for the greater good.

This was the context in which I was going to take in what was then the Five Nations in 1990. It should also be said that, other than the blip of an isolated Grand Slam success ten years before, England had been getting turned over by just about everyone for a long time. Wales had taken their 1970's domination on through the eighties and not lost to England since the first year of that decade. I remember having to sit and take the taunts of the Welsh contingent within the Loughborough first XV in 1988, sat as we were in front of Adrian Hadley's two tries which condemned England to another home defeat. A year later, a still emerging, if not quite resurgent, England had higher hopes but crumbled again in the cauldron of Cardiff Arms Park in a match the media had certainly defined in terms of mutual animosity. But England *were* emerging, and the country was suddenly aware of its rugby team again and its potential. Our optimism (even mine) grew through a 23-0 win over Ireland, a record win over France in Paris which announced something special was going on and another record win over Wales to settle a few scores, even though as former All Black captain Graham Mourie once pointed out, nobody beats Wales at rugby, they just score more points. The wins were only half the story – the world-renowned stodgy, forward power and penalty-goal-obsessed English had just racked up eleven tries in three potentially awkward games. Scotland alone stood between us and a Grand Slam. England Rugby was correspondingly now at the top of my list of 'must-see, must-win' sport, and the Scotland game which would deliver the Grand Slam couldn't come quickly enough. The Scots had made their own progress, though less spectacular and, to their own irritation, less trumpeted, to three wins from three. For the first time in living memory, Scotland would play England with everything on the line. The build-up was unsurprisingly full-on, and the anticipation had steadily grown for what was clearly going to be one of my more important sporting contests. What became steadily more apparent and more irritating, however, was that it appeared the whole Scottish nation had been whipped into a fervour and convinced this rugby match should represent some sort of payback for everything from Culloden onwards. This broiling sense of anti-Englishness was by no means unconnected to Scottish resentment at being used, as they saw it, as guinea pigs for Mrs Thatcher's poll tax experiment the year before. Now, on that spring Saturday, it seemed Scotland wanted to shift the emphasis of the match from a rugby result which would decide a trophy, to a nationalist statement. The manufactured elements kept coming: the bagpipe-led slow march onto the field, the fact someone had found from somewhere a tune, which would avoid the need for the Scots' team to sing the national anthem, called 'Flower of Scotland'; that the words to this little ditty were an uncomplicated celebration of Robert The Bruce's victory over the English at Bannockburn simply reinforced the feeling that events from more than six hundred years previously were somehow deemed both relevant and beneficial as a potential tool of victory in a rugby match.

Accusations of sour grapes might be flung at this point. I don't deny for a moment that it all made for great theatre which is still remembered to this day; what it also did was heighten the stakes and increase significantly my desire not to lose this rugby match above all others and consequently have to suffer a triumphalism of epic proportions and a supposed justification of every tactic which had been employed.

The good news was that most good judges could see only an England victory, in which case all the air would go out of this balloon; all would be forgotten; and we'd move on. All England had to do was turn up. Only, of course, they didn't turn up. To my horror, they let me down – they fell for all this nonsense and were completely thrown by it. It was clear where this day was going long before the final whistle, and all would not be forgotten after all, and I would certainly not be able to move on. If it took England a long time to get this out of their system, it took me considerably longer – I'm not sure I have to this day. It wasn't losing to Scotland in a Grand Slam game which hurt as much as losing to this contrived anti-Englishness. Unfortunately, the strategy's success led to annual attempts to replicate the approach to the same end from the Welsh and, in time, the Irish, as well as the Scots. This made every Six Nations game thereafter a matter of national pride with an added dimension – I didn't want to lose these games at any cost to the point that the enjoyment of watching them was somewhat compromised.

Twenty-five years on, in a BBC Sport retrospective watch-along of the game, the then England captain Will Carling, the ideal hate figure and personification of English privilege for Scotland that day, recalled an encounter with a Scottish journalist before the 1995 match at Twickenham, which was another Grand Slam decider. (The 'England as hated oppressor' horse was still being flogged, reaching new heights that year with the much-promoted viewing of the Scotland team the night before the game of the new film *Braveheart,* a somewhat loose retelling of the story of Scottish hero William Wallace and his treatment at the hands of the English, culminating in a rather graphic portrayal of his being hung, drawn and quartered. Well, it didn't work for them this time (and wouldn't at Twickenham for another twenty-six years). 'I could tell he wasn't fond of me at all', said Carling. 'It got to the end of the interview, and he said: "How do you take the fact the whole of Scotland hates you?" I said: "That's fine, because I hate you too." He dropped his pen and said: "You can't say that!" I said: "Hang on – you can hate us, but we can't hate you back?" That's what frustrates me about being English'. And that, in a nutshell, is what used to frustrate me too.

To offer some balance, when Scotland recently won at Twickenham for the first time in thirty-eight years, the England performance was so dire that I had no issue with the Scots or their deserved and gleeful celebrations. It is just how I recall the rugby in the nineties and how the media, and as a result the various publics, wanted to turn the tournament into a platform for tiresome pseudo-nationalism (as opposed to patriotism). It just made the watching that much tougher. The posturing eventually just got too boring. But I'm pleased that today, probably as a result of my job in which I have spent seven weeks with a Lions squad on tour, I have experienced seeing four nations' players come together in a common cause and been able to get to know and like any number of them, which has made it slightly easier to take when they turn England over. Don't get me wrong, losing to anyone in the Six Nations remains something to cloud the weekend, and it gets no less irritating having to suffer those purportedly lyrical pre-match Dylan Thomas impressions of Eddie Butler's, but the balance has been adjusted. I can almost now see and be grateful for the game being the thing. At least in 1990 it couldn't be argued that England had been hard done by – that they were well beaten was beyond doubt. That couldn't be said of the next twist of the knife just six days later.

I hadn't even begun to get up off the canvas. But the nature of sport is that there's almost always something just around the corner and that the hope fairy settles on your shoulder again ready to raise you up before the count of ten. England rugby had let me down. At the same time, on the other hand, England's cricketers had been turning the world upside down. As potential pick-me-ups go, pinning my hopes on an England tour of the West Indies was not the safest of bets. The last time England had won so much as one Test match, there I was still awaiting Alec Lindsay at Wembley. The last three series having finished in an aggregate of 14-0 to the West Indies didn't bode too well either. And, of course, the new dawn of the previous summer, Dexter, Gower and all had been less than an unbridled success. What was the answer? What was England's best chance? A new dawn apparently. We were told a new broom would sort this out. There would be no more Gower or Botham, considerably less fun and a squad of young, fast bowlers, regardless of record or proven quality, to beat the Windies at their own game. Now forgive me for being less than convinced and saying I had heard this one before. And then, blow me, at the end of February 1990, England turned up in Jamaica and blew the world champions of the last fifteen years away. They didn't just win, they won by nine wickets without ever looking like it might go wrong. Devon Malcolm had Viv Richards as his bunny. I must admit to sitting up and taking notice – perhaps it was time to fall in love with our cricket team again. The only concern for glass-half-empty man was that we had tweaked the lion's tail. Upsetting Curtly Ambrose seemed bound to have its consequences. Even after Sabina Park, the idea of actually winning the series was still the height of optimism.

The series was historic for a reason other than England's first Test match win against this team in sixteen years. As the football World Cup was soon to confirm, 1990 may have been the start of a *decennium horribilis* for English sport, but it was also a pivotal moment for sport as a whole. It didn't feel that way at the time, but looking back, sport and, above all, its consumption by the likes of me, was never to be the same again. To a degree, it could be argued that this was another step towards the end of the innocence. The man who had taken over setting much of the world's media agenda and was to become the darling and kingmaker of successive UK governments had decided the best vehicle to advance his empire was an England cricket tour. The object of Rupert Murdoch's affections may have seemed an incongruous one but not when you recall that this tour was the very first significant English sporting event to which his newly merged

BSkyB company had secured exclusive rights. Nothing would ever be the same again. The age of Charles Colville and Richard Keys was upon us, for better or for worse. Although the coverage felt rather amateurish compared to today's slick, if self-important, version, it allowed us to watch a tour from abroad live for the first time. Not even Ashes tours yet afforded us that. These were riches indeed and made the experience of seeing England go 1-0 ahead even more unreal. So it was that just six days after the pain of Murrayfield, I was able to distract myself by clambering behind the sofa to watch the West Indian response to the English effrontery. Then it started happening again, and by halfway through the match, I was truly starting to dream. This was on. Hope over experience. This was one of dear old Devon Malcolm's two career tours de force, taking ten wickets as England ratcheted up our levels both of astonishment and nervousness. England had dominated, and the West Indies seemed even more astonished than we were. Just a month before, I'd woken up to news of the greatest sporting upset of my lifetime: the invincible monster of a fighter that was Mike Tyson having lost his crown and his senses to a punch from journeyman Buster Douglas that he never saw coming, suffering a defeat that likewise nobody ever saw coming. The odds quoted against were 42-1. Now England were taking the Douglas role, probably at similar odds, and the West Indies were doing a fair impression of Tyson, seemingly stunned and confused, having never seen this coming.

Trinidad is certainly a beautiful place, but it is not without a reputation for a considerable amount of rainfall, and the match had been interrupted a sufficient number of times to be taken into the final day despite the low scores. Under clear skies, no match of 846 runs would have even come close to a draw. There was some irony, admittedly, in our praying for the rain to stay away after a decade of praying for our batsmen to be able to watch it from the safety of the dressing room. But after years when it wouldn't save us at Old Trafford and Headingley, for it to deny us out in these beautiful islands would be a cruelty hard to bear. But despite the time lost, there didn't appear to be any danger of time running out on England at 73-1 on that last day. Chasing just 151 to go 2-0 up, and with the customary abandonment to come in Guyana that meant at least a share of the series, they were just seventy-eight away.

Bad things come in threes, apparently, and so here was our proof. First, the captain and batting rock Graham Gooch had his hand broken by the malevolent fast bowling presence that was Ezra Moseley; then the rain arrived to wipe out the entire afternoon session and bring my innate pessimism right back into the equation; and finally, the West Indies, having seen their opportunity, proceeded with one of the most notorious demonstrations of gamesmanship (some would say cheating) the sport had ever seen. Aware of the potential for more rain, and with enough local knowledge to know that the light would fade fast at a point in proceedings not too far distant, the stand-in captain Haynes managed somehow to dupe the umpires into allowing his team to bowl 16.5 overs in a few minutes shy of two hours. Sure enough, the bad light came, and England were stranded thirty-one short. As anticlimaxes go, this would be right up there with any so far in my sports-watching canon, but somehow, this was made worse by the fact that it was the West Indies who had perpetrated such an act. Now, let's be honest, there aren't many teams in this day and age who wouldn't aim to do similar, but at the time, it was something of a shock to see the 'win by fair means or foul' mentality and still worse that it should succeed, the umpires thereby responsible for a far-reaching negative impact on the game which might have been quashed at birth. But despite the years of drubbings at their hands, the West Indies team represented something to me. Not the patronising cliche of the 'calypso cricketers' which so irritated Clive Lloyd but the fact they played the game with flair and panache. Haynes himself was a hero, a status not diminished when I was later lucky enough to meet and spend time with him. This somehow seemed dirtier than it otherwise would have been, coming from them. A little bit of the love for them disappeared that day and took a long time to revive. This had echoes of my own experience as the kid who, for a long time, had got everything they wanted and when something went against them simply threw the biggest tantrum they could muster. Was 14-0 not sufficient for them? Could they not allow us our moment?

Just to confirm my reaction wasn't another case of personal sour grapes, no less a West Indian legend than Brian Lara was to refer to this moment in his 2017 MCC Spirit of Cricket lecture, expressing emotions that matched my own. Recalling seeing his heroes behave in such a manner, he said, 'as a West Indian, I was truly embarrassed. As a young cricketer who looked up to a lot of the individuals in the team, it was one of the saddest moments in the world'.

England, having sensed they'd had their chance snatched from them, duly and more understandably than usual had to bend the knee in the remaining two Tests to lose a series they shouldn't have done.

In another case of life parallels, the West Indies weren't done with me yet. Gooch and England weren't alone in suffering at the hands of Ezra Moseley. In my youth, cricket had been my sport, as far as any sport had been mine. Those days being Gordon Greenidge on the sand at Mewslade Bay had not been entirely wasted. Loughborough hadn't been conducive to continuing my amateur career as the temptations of the tables outside the Union bar on sunny summer days were too strong to be ignored in favour of eight hours on the cricket pitch. But on arrival in the north-west, resurrecting my off spin in the local leagues had seemed a good way of making new contacts and getting myself a social scene. My gentle Hampshire upbringing didn't include much knowledge of league cricket in the north, and my assumption that facing seventeen-year-old fast bowlers on well-kept, fast school pitches would stand me in good stead proved to be somewhat wide of the mark. Somehow, that summer I found myself involved in a fixture against Oldham whose professional that year was a certain… Ezra Moseley. It came as something of a shock when one of my teammates explained who was on the opposition side as whites went on in the changing room. The general atmosphere of apprehension didn't bode well if these guys were used to playing here and were still perturbed. Where did that leave me? I negotiated my way down the order in a plan to only make it to the crease once Ezra had retired to the outfield. Unfortunately, my timing was awry, and I arrived shortly after he began his second spell. Now, this was a guy who had proved too much for the England captain and one of our greatest ever players of fast bowling. What the hell was I doing here? I heard the first ball he bowled to me, but I damn sure never saw it. Somehow escaping with my life, the innings was short and my league cricket experiment not much longer.

It wasn't quite the end of my cricket career or the decision-making process by which I decided it was time to wind it up. By '91, I'd moved to lodge with a mate in his cottage on the outskirts of Huddersfield, and a summer playing occasionally for Upper Hopton Cricket Club seemed more the ticket. They had a beautiful ground in the countryside with the classic pub overlooking the pitch. Here I was in a chapter from *England, Their England*. All we were missing was a blacksmith coming in at number four. Sitting in the sun, chatting amiably and waiting for a bat felt far more civilised than the previous summer's experience. I was confident enough this time, as I saw the opposition's ageing opening bowler coming in off about five paces, looking as though travelling any further might end his career, that my past ability level and experience should allow me to enjoy myself. Once again, however, my life was to be blighted by the curse of kit. This time, it was the complete reverse of my mum's make-do-and-mend embarrassments – my kit was *too* good. A new summer meant a fresh raid on the company warehouse to update my gear, which included trousers and shirt bearing the David Gower autograph of our clothing range. As I walked to the wicket, I was positively gleaming, wearing brand spanking new pads and gloves and carrying a virgin piece of Test-match-quality willow. Add to this the fact that some had heard I was not of northern, never mind good Yorkshire, stock, and the reception that greeted me at the wicket was, most kindly put, disparaging. Yorkies are not known for their sufferance of fools or southerners and play their cricket hard. My taking of a guard was accompanied by non-stop derisory sledging. I half-expected to turn round and see Steve Waugh crouching at second slip. The Ashes could not have been more hostile. No matter, this bowler wasn't Ezra, and I'd soon shut them up. Each of the six balls he then bowled to me came down at a speed not much greater than my own off breaks. Every one hit the black sticky dog of a wicket and nipped smartly past my outside edge into the keepers' gloves. At the end of the over, my bat was no less virgin than it had been on its arrival with me at the wicket. Cue further hilarity behind the stumps. I think I managed a few runs but not enough to offset the humiliation. I sensed it was time to put away the gear and go back to offering my expert opinions whilst watching on the telly.

Anyway, at the end of England's tour, for the second time already that year, a tantalising glimpse of success had turned to cold reality. Unfortunately, it was not to be the last. For me, here, alongside 'the hand of God', was the most blatant example yet that undeserved defeat is so much harder to take than a beating fair and square. As the clouds began to part at the start of the following decade, it was the thing which tipped me over from a desire to see England win to an absolute desperation that they must. 2003, 2005, 2019 – these would all fit into that envelope. Oh, and July 1990.

WORLD IN MOTION

Where to start with this one? Over thirty years on, it still gnaws away. To head off the finger-pointing at the English making a big deal out of losing a semi-final (a perfectly valid accusation come 2018), this particular one has to be placed in context. If the West Indies tour had been a pleasant surprise and an unexpected outcome, albeit with a sad end, in which an extremely unpromising starting point was turned into something altogether more exciting, England's 1990 World Cup did something similar but on a far greater public stage.

England generally did not feel like a happy place, with much sense of self-worth, in the spring of 1990. Poll tax riots were presenting us nightly with scenes we normally associated with revolution against Central American dictatorships, heralding the death throes of the Margaret Thatcher era and the imminent arrival of economic crisis, negative equity and other such joys not conducive to generating a party spirit that summer. The prophets of doom were plentiful. Football itself, and English football in particular, seemed to be reflective of that downbeat prognosis, by now a pretty sordid and uninspiring affair. The tabloid newspaper war of the 1980s was still raging and had instilled in its combatants a set of ethics based on a policy of 'anything goes' or, more specifically, 'anything that sells papers to a prurient public justifies the means'. The resultant tactics and stories (many of them just that) further engendered a sense of conflict and mistrust. If this was true of society as a whole, football – as the staple of the back and sometimes front pages, was one of the main battlefields selected by the editors. The almost constant negativity around the England football team, often personally abusive to individuals, not only helped widen the divide between the institution and its public but gave the team the impression, I would guess not erroneously, that half the English press would prefer them to crash and burn rather than win the World Cup.

Two weeks after the worst of the London riots came the first anniversary of Hillsborough, and the sense of shame and revulsion still hung over the game. Maggie had no interest in football, nor possibly any understanding of its social impact, but every interest in crushing the associated culture of violence which had become an increasing embarrassment in how England was perceived overseas and in creating a culture of nihilism and anarchy which was beginning to evade any control. It felt like the country, and its football, needed a fresh start. Youth culture too had been in one of its fallow phases for several years and was in similar need of regeneration. The late eighties, as if holding its hands up that the Lawson boom feel good days had in the end been a temporary release and the party was over, had not been an explosion of creativity – certainly not at a level resonating with the general public. Stock, Aitken and Waterman seemed to be bent on destroying Britain's reputation for musical talent and innovation and we were drowning in a sea of daytime soap stars performing what sounded suspiciously like the same song with the odd lyric and key change. But a little further down the scale of national consciousness, things had been stirring. House music, and the things that went with it, was driving a new rave scene, whilst independent record labels such as Factory were giving a leg-up to a new generation of creative music artists and creating a new club culture in England's major cities. Here was a way out of the torpor of the last few years. Given my recent arrival in the north-west, it seemed to me that my ability to bring cultural success and rebirth just by my very presence was now extending from sport into music and youth culture too. Fanciful? The year I arrived in Oldham was the year The Stones Roses released their eponymous first album and New Order had their first ever UK number one album. I rest my case. The latter were about to play a significant part, although with little intention of doing so, in the watershed year of English football.

There was certainly no optimism that England were set for a tournament which would contribute to a lifting of the national mood. More likely, something akin to the European Championships two years previously, in which England had contrived to lose all three games whilst their followers smashed up various German town squares. Four months later, a scoreline of Saudi Arabia v England 1-1, and an accompanying headline urging the beleaguered manager to 'in the name of Allah, go!', didn't suggest much progress. But for us fans, certainly for myself, the results were just a by-product of something more depressing: the ongoing insistence of the England hierarchy that our national team should serve us up football of utter joylessness. At the top, Graham Kelly was the personification of this descriptive noun, Bert Millichip the ultimate mandarin who did the same job for 'incompetence'. Between them, these two had delivered a string of managers to set the heart arresting rather than racing, the criteria apparently being a lack of skeletons in cupboards and potential to rock the boat rather than an ability to create exciting and successful teams. So instead of Mercer, we got Revie; instead of Clough, we got Greenwood; now, love him as we did eventually, we had Bobby Robson. Safe pair of hands. Meantime, a succession of mercurial, if maverick, entertainers from Hudson, Osgood and Bowles through now to Glenn Hoddle had been misunderstood, mistrusted and misused. There is a fallacy that we England fans will happily take results in whatever way they might be achieved. In my experience, it's simply not true. We're on this planet a pretty short time in the grand scheme of things and we're unlikely to see England win a huge number of major football tournaments in that time (my total to date in fifty-three years numbering... zero). So, we'd prefer a bit of entertainment, some enjoyment, wherever that may take us. Admittedly, we'd not yet reached the Graham Taylor-inspired apotheosis of being represented by Carlton Palmer and Keith Curle, but give me Hoddle; give me Tony Currie; give me (above all) Matt Le Tissier, and let's see how we get on – you never know, watching England might even become a pleasurable experience. Now, Robson and England were doing their best to downplay the emergence of another maverick talent named Paul Gascoigne. That he was ultimately to defy all their attempts to ignore him through his sheer brilliance on the field was to prove one of the defining factors in the change that was on the way.

The other, and even more well founded, lack of optimism was centred around a certain percentage of the England supporters being able to behave in a way that wouldn't shame the country, the players and everyone one of us who wanted to be proud of England. If that sounds pompous, remind yourself what a bunch of thick, one-dimensional ambassadors for our country and our people these morons were. In his definitive book on Italia '90 from an English perspective, *All Played Out*, journalist Pete Davies writes of a set of encounters with some of the purest examples of the species in Cagliari. Without a hint of irony, they suggested the locals were looking for a fight by staring at them and 'always talking Italian'. 'This ain't a flower show. It's the fucking World Cup', one 'fan' offered as an explanation of his approach. This is the other reason – a more significant one than lack of success and flair, and narrowly more significant than that self-appointed band playing *The Great Escape* theme non-stop at every England game all over the world – why following and remaining in love with England football is so difficult. How can I put myself in a position where these people represent me, when we are both cheering for the same outcome? You know the victory you crave would ultimately just put more air in their tyres and offer them a platform. They couldn't get rid of them whatever they did, but if the England team could achieve enough on the pitch to put this lot in the shade for a while, that in itself might deem the tournament a success. In this context, it was long odds that Italia '90 would become one of the most iconic, uplifting and ultimately deflating moments in English sport, but it did. So, what happened? Three things: England started playing good football; the Germans and penalties got in the way; and football bonded with club and youth culture in a way which would change the game forever.

The actor, sometime nineties hell-raiser and long-time totem of England team support, Keith Allen, co-wrote the song that was to begin the process and to change the vibe. He says of 'World in Motion', 'the idea of New Order doing anything football related was ludicrous, never mind England. But the tune became anthemic'. There had certainly never been anything like this before to accompany a departing World Cup squad.

'Back Home' in 1970, 'This Time (We'll Get It Right)' in 1982 and 'We've Got the Whole World at our Feet' in '86 (so memorable I had to look it up) were all not only factually incorrect but of the 'squad stands on stage grinning self-consciously and failing to mime properly' variety. Now, John Barnes was one of just six players asked to turn up to a studio, and he recalls he had no idea one of Britain's foremost indie bands was going to be waiting for them. Allen again: 'it was this perfect storm of New Order, club culture and football and that particular World Cup, 1990. It was the biggest watershed in football 1990 – that's where everything changed… *everything* changed'. This was where the correlation began between football, music and culture that grew through the Premier League, Britpop, Posh & Becks and ultimately sat the footballers of the future at the top table of the Blair era of celebrity culture. And more than just the song, which was good enough, the accompanying video did more to reconnect with fans than a Barnes free kick. Barnes looked like that rare beast – a footballer who looked cool without consciously trying to. Perhaps it might be wishful thinking that having a player of Jamaican heritage as front and centre, mixing with Sumner, Hook, Allen and the rest, performing a rap which didn't make the skin crawl, looking cool, comfortable and very much part of the gang, might have made an impression on the meathead brigade and even given them cause to reassess their world view slightly, but regardless, suddenly I wanted this team to do well – the song deserved it. It felt like something might be changing.

A decent song, however, as 1996 was to confirm, doesn't actually win you the thing. The football we played was unfortunately going to have more to do with it. And there remained this stale approach: rigid, restrictive and almost designed to ensure some very talented individuals consistently underperformed. Those individuals took the flak, but it was the mindset and the system that should've done so. Then, probably fair to say by accident, strange things started to happen. Firstly, amidst the mealy mouthed mistrust of flair – seen in England at least by the people who picked and coached the team as some sort of luxury which could only weaken the whole – a young, less than fully mature Geordie called Paul Gascoigne had emerged, and there was a fan clamour that he must make the squad. Looking back now, it is hard to fathom that come the 25th of

April, there was still considerable doubt whether Gascoigne would indeed be included (although breaking his forearm taking a swing at someone in a match Robson was watching from the stands a couple of months earlier may throw a little light on that). But that night, a month before 'World in Motion' was released, was to be another moment at which things started to change. I can remember the sense of awakening and the thrill in watching Gascoigne's performance against Czechoslovakia which forced the management to take him whether they liked it or not. It was as eye-opening as the first sight of Maradona on the same pitch nine years earlier, but this guy was ours. He went past people; he tried things; he didn't seem to care much about 4-4-2…

And systems were the other hot topic. The Dutch had played a different game to England at the Euros two years before. Ever since, the charge was that England were wedded to worshipping at the Charlie Hughes altar of an archaic 4-4-2 formation, which stifled the life out of the few players we had who might cause the opposition any serious problems. Many in the media, notably the calm and perceptive Patrick Barclay, extolled the virtues of the sweeper used by every team that had won a major tournament since England's in '66 (excepting Brazil in 1970 whose players all could, and did, play in just about every position on the pitch). We supporters were keen to at least see it tried – something different, something new. Robson's defence was his defence… his insistence that if they had been the only team who had qualified without conceding a single goal, they hardly needed to be more defensive, was a worry to those of us who saw this as an attacking option to free our more gifted players rather than the too literal 'another defender' assessment. His suggestion that it worked for the Dutch because they had better technical players than we did was an even greater concern coming from the man charged with winning us the trophy.

So it was that England began in Cagliari, initially amidst a renewed hope in my heart (if not head) against Jack Charlton's more-English-than-England Ireland team. Hope which was then once again conquered by experience within ninety minutes as a turgid, safety-first match petered out in stalemate. It had been maybe the ultimate expression of 4-4-2 and why nobody wanted to watch it or saw it winning anything anymore.

Holland were next. The question now was more who we might support in the knockout stages once England had returned home.

Suggest then that four of England's next five fixtures would produce arguably the best four games of the tournament, getting that bit better every time, and the carabinieri would come looking for you. They might do similar if you were dogmatic enough to claim that this had nothing to do with the sweeper system which suddenly appeared against the Dutch. Gary Lineker is adamant this was not a change brought on by player power, rather the result of a broad consultation between senior players and management, but you can sense where his vote lay when he says, 'we *always* played 4-4-2, rigid and regimented, and we were always overrun in midfield. All of a sudden, *we* had three in midfield'. And one of those three was Gascoigne who that night announced himself to the football world. Suddenly, we were playing *football* – the sort you enjoyed watching – and we were matching the best. In all my time watching England, this was the game which drew back the curtains and showed me a different view, one in which we might actually do something and enjoy it on the way. (Holland were often good patsies for this, the only game which comes close being the 4-1 win against them six years later.) No going back now, surely?

A scrappy win against Egypt and we were in the second round. A great game against Belgium, partly because it *was* a great game and partly because we so didn't deserve to get through it. So much for enjoying the ride… once you get to this stage in a World Cup, watching is hard enough, but watching when the other team is creating chance after chance is hell. Extra time is hell. Penalties are hell, although, as we'd never been through them before, we weren't yet aware just what hell. We were surely about to find out. And the rationalisation of my best mate's girlfriend that as we didn't really deserve to still be in it anyway, those penalties were surely just a free hit, didn't cut much ice. We knew this was going to be truly horrible and, as if chained in the Tower peeking out at our gallows, we awaited our fate. Then, with twenty seconds left, a Gazza free kick, an unbelievable volley from Platt – absolute ecstasy. There is nothing quite like the rush of a goal at that point in such a game – not just a goal but the sure knowledge that they've no time to spoil it. Lineker says, 'the Platt goal was one of my favourite moments ever in football', realising at the same time as the rest of us we'd just been spared a fate worse than death. For now.

Quarter-final. Blimey. The negativity, the gloom, the vitriolic press, the dour football, suddenly all receding as, for the first time, I felt the 'country as one' thing. I'd had it in my city when Saints won the Cup, but this was another level. England being England, we first of all saw the assignment against Cameroon as the easiest available path of progression, relying on the then still widely held perception that African football provided plucky but naive, faintly amusing nations there to support FIFA's ambitions of global reach, rather the evidence of our own eyes that they could really play. And play they did – considerably better than England who duly put us through another 120 minutes of torture, trailing until Lineker's penalties came to the rescue. Many of the team say to this day that they shouldn't have won that game. But they did. And we, Gazza and all, were somewhere I had never been: a World Cup semi-final.

We know what happened next, and it remains one of the greatest 'what might have beens' of my sporting life. England and Germany had history, certainly, particularly at World Cups, but here the story of penalties began. What was it that made this one so different, so hard to shake for years afterwards? It is hard even now to watch the anniversary reruns without hoping it might somehow end differently, and the eyes and words of those players doing the talking heads belie the idea that any of them have truly been able to put this to bed. Maybe it was the fact that this team was perhaps the last really good one, the last time you could run off the line-up in your head without a second thought, perhaps that this time we were actually playing exciting football worthy of the stage or that we had the discovery of the tournament in Gascoigne. It somehow seemed that all this and the bravery to change the system *needed* to be rewarded with success – I worried that it was the only way of keeping the footballing curmudgeons from dragging us back in the other direction. It is a strange and frustrating phenomenon that when occasionally we reach such heights, somehow within six months, everything has almost imperceptibly drifted back to where it started – the positivity and the things that had taken us there in the first place seemingly forgotten. How we got from here to the depression of the Graham Taylor era European Championships two years later being the prime example which still feels like something of a mystery.

But the real reason for the lingering hurt? The truth is the sports follower can take the justifiable defeat (Euro '88 didn't cause lasting pain because England were terrible), but losing when you don't deserve to never really gets out of your system. The idea England might make a World Cup semi-final was one thing; that they might then actually deserve to win it and not do so still feels so wrong. Sport would be so much easier to bear if the gods decreed that outcomes be fair.

It was probably worse that for all the England-Germany rivalry, this was based not on genuine dislike of the German/Dutch variety but on a mutual respect. The players and the fans knew we were the two best teams at the tournament and that in truth this *was* the final. The respectful and emollient words of the Germans afterwards were of no help. Sod your magnanimity; we should be in that final. It was a flip-of-the-coin job, and someone called wrong on our behalf. If only the outrageous fluke of a deflection which gave Brehme his goal had come off Paul Parker at a marginally different angle, if Waddle's shot had been a quarter of an inch further to the left, if it had gone in off the post rather than screaming straight back at him like some sort of metaphorical arrow to the heart. Far better for our long-term mental health for Brehme to have beaten Shilton with the free kick of the World Cup and Waddle to have hit the corner flag.

So, it wasn't the losing to Germany, even losing a semi-final, but the manner of it. This was the start of what the journalist Henry Winter refers to as 'England's brutal relationship with penalties'. It's all very well enjoying the drama of this endgame when you're not directly involved; I never had been before and therefore didn't know the true hell of it. In *All Played Out*, Pete Davies refers to 'the stupid, heartless bingo of penalties – a heartless piece of ersatz TV drama irrelevant to the game of football'. Certainly is if you lose, Pete. As this one began, it was as if I was almost one of the team. Davies suggests that the issue with football supporting is 'at football you don't just watch, you take part' and that 'every bit of me was frozen apart from the heart that beat'. Never had that felt more accurate than now. It's not the greatest theatre of conflict for the glass half-empty man, and this time, I felt even more justification for my indomitable pessimism than usual. If we were going to win this, why would Waddle's shot not have gone in? What's the point in a hard-luck story if it doesn't end in hard luck? At least I wasn't alone. England captain Terry Butcher said years later, 'I just had this horrible feeling in the back of my mind that it was not going to happen'. So, not just me then. Terry, I've every sympathy, but this is what I go through *all the time*.

The system for penalties seems designed to bring the natural pessimist to the brink of self-harm on the maximum number of occasions. Like the work of sadistic genius which is the tennis tiebreak, it is a constant rally between relief and despondency, between hope and concern. You want to go first, as England did. It's the safety net that you can miss and still be in it. The relief of 1-0, 2-1 and 3-2 up. Every time, surely the pressure would increase on the next German until one was bound to miss and give you the luxury of breathing space. But the Germans didn't seem to realise this. One of the greatest keepers of all time went the right way every time and didn't stop a single one – the frustration was total. Then Pearce and Waddle and all over.

As Pete Davies put it, 'the black pit of loss opened wide'. I sat there, trying to compute the fact it was over, and it shouldn't have been. Butcher remembers 'the feeling immediately after the penalties was – we've lost… but how have we lost?'. Lineker's summation spoke for me: 'it felt like the end of the world – I know, context and perspective and all that, but at the time, it's just desolation'. Which would probably work as an ongoing mantra for any of the sports fans I know.

Then there was the empathy. We had lived this adventure with the team and the manager, and it was done before its time. The emotional outpouring and love for Gazza when his world caved in and the tears came were not for everyone. But this was the guy who had delivered for us, given us some true joy over the last few weeks and represented every one of us who dreamt of playing out their boyhood fantasy. Gazza had played that way and lived the whole tournament that way. The heart bled for him, and there was an anger in me that this should happen to one of the good guys. Those who give so much pleasure deserve pleasure in return.

The legacies from Italia '90 were many and varied. The genuine pride in being English which emanated from Bobby Robson in such an endearing, straightforward way had infected the public mood when it showed no sign of emanating from anywhere else. The whole thing changed our relationship with football. Gazzamania became the first example of how celebrity and personality would take over from the ability to score twenty goals a season. Football became an acceptable branch of the arts, a new hobby for the great and the good and was now wedded to club and youth culture. And it laid the ground, for better or for worse, for more of Rupert Murdoch and something called the Premier League.

But ultimately, and this is why it resonates and still vaguely gnaws at me today, Italia '90 is, for those of us prone to nostalgia, the most evocative sporting moment of all. 'World in Motion', *Nessun Dorma*, sounds that immediately transport you back to a moment when the English sporting world shook and changed. Shilton says that hearing that aria today can still bring tears to his eyes – he hadn't realised how special it was until it was over. And the English opera singer Sean Ruane recounts how it changed his life. Growing up in Bacup, there was 'just nothing', then along came Italia '90, and he heard Pavarotti for the first time. 'It lit a spark in me'. Indeed, the whole thing lit a spark in many of us – one not yet fully extinguished. Leaving the last words on the matter to Gary Lineker, 'I think Italia '90 was an incredibly important moment for English football, a watershed, a moment for good. If only… *if only*'.

A losing semi-final as the seminal moment in English sport – somehow appropriate? Yes. Apologies? Not a chance.

ASHES TO ASHES

Had 1990 finished with me yet? Not quite. After Murrayfield, Trinidad and Turin, there was a need for some sort of balm and England's Tests against India in a summer of sun were doing their best to provide it. Personally, seeing an England batman make a Test score of 333 was something of a fillip; professionally, I had been waiting all summer for the clamour for the return of David Gower to have its desired effect. Since our trips up and down the motorway, David had not yet stepped onto an international pitch with our bat in his hand, which was something of a problem. Not only was the latent twelve-year-old in me yearning for the return of my favourite, but it was also now something of a professional necessity. Having been made, not for the last time, to serve a period of penitence, for what we are not quite sure (possibly failing to laud to the skies the virtue of shuttle runs), back he came midsummer for the India games. The problem now was that he also had to make a success of them which made watching the six innings he was to be afforded my most tortuous cricket experience so far. There was a sense for us worshippers, convinced as we were that we were crusading for the righteous against the Gooch/Stewart forces of darkness, that those forces were trying to give our man just enough rope to hang himself. Despite fifteen Test match hundreds to date, many of them playing a key part in previous Ashes series, it was deemed necessary that young David score some runs in these three Tests to earn a place on another upcoming tour to Australia. There was also a sense that they wouldn't have been too unhappy had he failed to do so, which made me all the more desperate he should shove it to them. From being around him at the time, I got the feeling that whether or not he saw this as the insult to him that I did, he had never been more determined to take his chance and, it transpired, never more nervous. From that point, every single run, every cover drive for the ages and every ball that passed without him flashing Kapil Dev to gully were to assume the utmost importance. Making seventy-two runs for once out in the first Test seems now to have been a reasonable start. The only issue was that in that game, England made 925 runs for the loss of eight wickets, so eight per cent of those runs coming from the man that mattered didn't quite make the necessary impression, especially whilst his sergeant major was setting a world record of 456 runs in the match. A total of sixty-two runs across innings three, four and five gave us all visions of his Qantas ticket floating away on the wind. It wasn't even guaranteed he would get a shot at innings number six – the last of the summer – especially whilst England's openers were putting on 176 for the first wicket of that second innings, seemingly wanting to deny him that crucial final opportunity. Never before had I wanted an England wicket so desperately, Chris

Tavare possibly notwithstanding. Why wouldn't one of the buggers get out? When they did, what followed remains one of my favourite innings of all time. Given the pressure, the situation and the fact that this was the last chance saloon, he served me up a performance of quite breathtaking insouciance. It saved the game, the series and his Test career, for now. They couldn't leave him behind now. All was set fair for a tour I could now genuinely look forward to, with Gower back where he should have been by right and which would put right the aberration of the summer of '89 and bring home the Ashes – a final jewel in the Gower crown. And a chance for us to sell some bloody bats.

Only, it didn't quite turn out that way. Hope over reality again. By the penultimate day of this sporting year from hell, England were 2-0 down and duly gave up the Ashes again in the first week of the new year. Looking back with the hindsight of what was to come over the next dozen years, two things stand out. Firstly, this was a pretty innocuous Australian side to be trampled by compared with what came later, and this was only number two of eight successive thrashings which were to take us all the way through the '90s and beyond; secondly, the confirmation that even the most dismal of experiences can find some redemption in performances of true class, in this case the debacle of the tour having the saving grace of two sublime Test hundreds from Gower, looking at least one level above any other Englishman. So, the deflation of the tour was offset by the fact that we were now assured of a few more years of divine pleasure watching this guy play. Weren't we?

IT AIN'T WHAT YOU DO IT'S THE WAY THAT YOU DO IT

One of the things that in my experience irritates England sports fans more than any other is our sense that those in charge of our games, and some of those who play them, don't understand us, why we watch and what we want. We were about to suffer a decade of almost constant defeat and disappointment. As I've indicated, my view is that if you are going to go through that, it would be some compensation if you went down with all guns blazing. Lose by all means, but please lose in style. Give us something to hang on to, some reason not to walk away from the whole sorry business. We fans want style and excitement. We hate being the country that is scared of maverick talent which would walk into a Brazil or West Indies side. They don't get that. James Agate wrote, 'the English instinctively admire any man who has no talent and is modest about it'. Ron Greenwood, Roy Hodgson and Ian Branfoot must've been fans. The England Rugby legend that is Martin Johnson, a man whom I got to know and like immensely, once perplexed me when I read his contention (admittedly, at a time when he was under some media pressure as the then England coach for some dour performances) that the crowd at Twickenham would be happy to see England win every game 9-3 if it meant they were successful. I can assure him that is not the case. Sometimes it's worth the risk to give us a little flair and excitement – we win rarely enough anyway for god's sake. Hudson please, not Trevor Cherry, Gower not Rob Bailey, Hoddle not Peter Reid, Le Tissier not Carlton Palmer, Cipriani not Paul Grayson. Life's too short. People follow Ronnie O'Sullivan, Jimmy White, Alex Higgins. Nobody gets giddy about Stephen Hendry, Mark Williams and John Higgins. To my mind, it is the duty of the people responsible for putting sportspeople in front of us for our paid entertainment to make the outlay worthwhile and give us something we want to watch. Not to do this, especially when the necessary tools are staring them in the face, is a dereliction for which they should be held accountable.

This has me arriving at the much-quoted words of Danny Blanchflower when captain of an exciting Spurs side, that the great fallacy is that football (for my purposes here, read sport in general) is about winning when, in fact, it is about *glory* and doing things in style and not forcing those watching to die of boredom. Oft repeated but no less a bullseye for that. Partisan though I am in my sports watching, I still agree with this, and it could be my anthem to articulate my single greatest frustration as an English fan. Why have I been saddled with a sporting nation so sceptical of flair and talent and whose people in the pivotal roles so fail to understand what matters to us? England fans across our major sports have been treated to years of conservative tactics, nervous negative selection and a distrust of skill and personality. We want to see the maverick player, lose our worldwide reputation for caution and pragmatism. Give the damn thing a go and to hell with the consequences. Given the Phil Neal, Paul Mariner, Mick Mills brigades managed to get us to a sum total of no World Cups for twelve years, might it not have been more fun, and no less successful, to have gone a Hail Mary route of Bowles, Worthington, Osgood, Cunningham, Currie and the like? OK, they might've had to fish them out of the pubs and betting shops of north London to get them onto the Wembley pitch, but what the hell – it would've been a lot more entertaining. It's a national sporting disgrace that the genius of a footballer that was Matthew Le Tissier did not have an England team built around him for a decade. Yes, it's a Southampton fan talking, but that just means I've seen more of him and therefore better appreciate the scale of this scandal. And look what happens when we do it differently. Clive Woodward's approach with England's rugby, Vaughan and the 2005 Ashes, Eoin Morgan, Trevor Bayliss and the 2019 World Cup. Del Boy was right all along – he who dares, wins.

For all the wasting of the maverick talents of our footballers, the two bits of mismanagement which leave me genuinely angry to this day are the province of our cricket authorities and concern two players by the names of Gower and Pietersen.

DON'T TAKE AWAY THE MUSIC

I profess to having a personal interest here. In both cases, I ended up working with these world-class cricketers and getting to know them, if not closely then well enough to learn a little about what mattered to them. The first chapter of Gower's autobiography (the first one that is… that wine cellar doesn't pay for itself) is entitled 'Fun, Style and Excellence', referring to an award from a national newspaper on being named International Cricketer of the Year in 1983. In it, he explains that the plaque he received bearing these words means more to him than any other award or medal. 'In many ways I am happy to forget the statistics of a career in cricket and to remember the fun of it as well as feeling that I have given spectators a little pleasure too'. I can assure him that is a typical understatement. It shows a philosophy that endured 'despite the fact that it torpedoed me in the end'. The fact that it did is to the ever-lasting shame of those who were responsible as far as I'm concerned. But David's contribution to my enjoyment will be remembered far longer than that of those philistines. It is a clear theme of his book, however, that whatever the caricature that may have been perpetuated, he cared deeply. England truly mattered to him. Having been around in the summer of that innings against India, I have my own evidence of that. It is a matter of prolonged vexation that the whims of certain people couldn't see the light-hearted side of a cavalier moment in a Tiger Moth biplane or accept that it wasn't always the wisest policy to insist on force-fitting all characters and dissenting voices into a particular regime. I resent the fact that their blinkers robbed me of his presence and cost me potentially two to three years of watching the sort of talent you're lucky to see once in a generation. Cricketers are ten a penny; David Gower isn't. His subsequent omission from my next three years of watching from 1992 to 1994 produced successive losses of 2-1 at home to Pakistan, 3-0 away to India, 4-1 at home to Australia and 3-1 away to West Indies, so his omission was clearly a raging success and the act of vandalism, which scuppered any chance of some light relief through watching the guy bat, wasn't exactly validated. That this drove Gower out of the game completely I'm sure left a sour taste for him for a while; personally, I can still taste it. Jonathan Swift was right: 'when a true genius appears in the world you may know him by this sign, that the dunces are all in confederacy against him'.

And then the same damn thing happened again. Now, here is where my opinion will differ from others who I like and admire, my mate Nashy and plenty of other cricketers whose views I respect amongst them. Admittedly, Kevin Pietersen could be his own worst enemy and sometimes defending him – as at one stage I would often do vehemently at the slightest invitation, or lack of one, to anyone I heard slagging him off – could be a thankless task. There is a good argument that he was not cut out for leadership – I get that, even if my own information is that in the specific case when that was removed from him by England it was a two-sided story of which only one side has been heard. I am no longer his apologist, and I accept that others who worked more closely in his company may have good grounds for their decisions in his regard. That's not my point here – I'm speaking from a fan's perspective, and the bottom line is we were denied watching something special. Fine, don't have him as captain, but do whatever you can not to remove him from us completely. Yes, the bloke was different, but he made watching England unmissable. He is what I watch sport for. Again, from my relationship such as it was with him, I know that, like Gower, playing for England meant more to him than people would assume (whether or not that was in a quest for personal glory is by the by for me as a fan) and that he had his own element of insecurity. There will be plenty who disagree with me, and many who argue he was given chances aplenty, but I do have a well-respected supporter in the writer Simon Barnes who titled his *The Times* article on Pietersen in 2014 'Master of his art who will always be worth the trouble' and proceeded to give voice perfectly to my emotions, insisting that 'England are all the poorer for turning their back on a genuine world-class player', referring without too much of a derogatory tone to KP as 'the classic arsehole genius', comparing him to the character Deco in *The Commitments* who was hated by the rest of his band as a complete pain in the arse but who could sing like an angel, and they were nothing without him. Barnes concluded with a recollection of the great swimming coach Bill Sweetenham demanding of the Great Britain squad, 'who wants to be ordinary?' and suggested the rest of English cricket had just put their hands up. The bottom line *from a fan's perspective* is that through an inability again to manage a different, difficult certainly, and out-of-the-ordinary personality, I lost a good five years of watching one of the greatest batsmen of my lifetime. These years of Gower and KP are years I'll never get back.

The nineties were not off to an auspicious start – as a welcome to the real world and a marker for the rest of the decade, this deflating beginning was at least not pulling its punches. And I was going to have to face the rest of it without Mr Gower to occasionally lighten the darkness.

SAFETY DANCE

Following the watershed moment of Italia '90, there were to be significant changes coming in life and sport. The following spring, I took my next step into adult reality by saddling myself with a mortgage and buying my first house. The two-up two-down brought me down from the picturesque gentility of Saddleworth Moor and into the less salubrious surroundings of Lees on the outskirts of Oldham. It may not have been the dream house, but needs must, and as a bachelor pad for the first few months, it had its moments. But freedom and fecklessness were now heading off over the moor to be replaced by the safety of a more routine domestic existence – I was now officially part of the rat race, wedded to a working day to pay the bills. Moreover, my pad and I between us had snared a first serious girlfriend by April the following year, and with my new-found maturity and sudden apparent penchant for settling down, this developed into something with increasing potential to be a lifelong partnership. Ultimately, that role was to be filled more successfully by the next significant other to arrive in my life on the 15th of August: the Premier League, aka the FA Carling Premiership.

The tide of optimism and renewed love of all things football instigated by Gazza and the World Cup hadn't faded, and these laid the ground for long-mooted changes to the national game. Rupert Murdoch's belief, or that of his marketing men, that sport was the way to capitalise most effectively on deregulation and dominate the new satellite TV market had not been diminished by the testing of the water with England cricket. But if he really wanted to shift dishes, the big prize was football and its biggest clubs, and it was worth paying for. Much like my personal life, the sport was about to enter some commitments from which there would be no going back.

The full story of the Premier League and Sky's revolution in our other sports requires, and has been served by, many other books. What we sports addicts realised it meant for us was football on the telly as we'd never had it before. Not just the games but the debate shows and all the other filler that would be needed for dedicated sports channels. This was good news. What was less good news in my case, when ideally a new house of my own would have been the vehicle in which to gorge on this whenever I felt like it, was that the price for this was that of a dish, an expensive system and a monthly outlay to be allowed into the magic kingdom. Sadly, a combination of a fledgling wage, a ninety-five per cent mortgage, the ERM, John Major's recession and the joys of negative equity left this outside my budget. Here

I was being offered the chance to get through the depression of a working Monday by looking forward to the new utopia of *Monday Night Football*, and I couldn't get at it. Love's young bloom was to somewhat cushion this blow at the outset, proving again that at this age, when the opposite sex entered my life, sport could still be moved to the periphery. This solution was only going to be effective for so long, however, and with the end of the romantic relationship three years later came my submission to the charms of the new mistress. As the girl moved out, so the dish moved in and the pain of an emotional break-up was somewhat assuaged by Tony Yeboah's volley against Liverpool and the fact that I could watch it as a member of the exclusive club for the first time, Monday night, tinnie and club sandwich at my right hand and spared any interruption. Perhaps a spell of freedom and bachelorhood was in order after all.

From here, my two football teams were to head off in different directions for the rest of the nineties. Whilst Southampton steadfastly adhered to the narrative that this decade should be one of nerves and disappointment, Manchester United managed to be the one shaft of light that bucked that trend. Heading back to the theme of my supernatural powers, I'm going to claim a credit for both of these things. Having already helped Saints to the FA Cup, promotion and another Wembley final in our first five years together, in the first half of the eighties, they averaged a seventh-place finish in the top division, unheard of in their history before my arrival on the scene. At the same time, having last won the title three days after I was born on the outskirts of the city, United were still trying and failing to win another one. I swapped Southampton for the northwest for good at the turn of the nineties, whereupon Saints reincarnated as a pretty desperate team with an average finish of fifteenth and surviving relegation on the last day five times in seven years. Meanwhile, immediately upon my arrival, United won the FA Cup in 1990 and a further eleven trophies in the next nine years, including their first title for twenty-six years and four more before the end of the decade. Now, please don't try to tell me I had nothing to do with this. The facts don't lie.

The yin and yang of my footballing decade were based on two teams providing constant light and shade, almost, it seemed, on a daily basis. As United were winning their first two titles in '93 and '94, Saints were introducing me to the season-long trials and tribulations of a relegation battle. At the time, this was new ground but was something I have had to learn to live with ever since. Once you realise that, even at the start of the season, your team is a strong candidate for the bottom three, the whole year becomes a point-by-point calculation of how you might get out of it, who might be even worse than you, how their results are going and so on. (I've even started to watch the Championship promotion battles, hoping that the smaller teams will come up who have a better chance of going straight back down again, thereby improving our chances the following year.) You can't help but get mired in a quicksand of negativity. You set out the season's fixtures and work out how you can possibly get near forty points. Every game that you'd marked down as a must for points that ends in defeat is an arrow to the heart; on the other hand, should you get anything from one of the 'free hit' games you'd written off, the weekend was made, and *Match of the Day* couldn't come on quickly enough. This is why, for the fan on a regular diet of relegation campaigns, a game at Old Trafford or Anfield is part of a far more relaxing weekend than one containing a home game with Fulham. The whole thing becomes wearing in time and can hardly be termed enjoyable. There was a time when I would rationalise this by trying to convince myself that being involved in games that mattered was at least more interesting than mid-table mediocrity. This is an argument that was first put to me by my Millwall-supporting south London mate. Mind you, he was also the one who, when the inevitable relegation eventually came to pass in 2005, congratulated me and welcomed me back to what he called 'real football', which he suggested was a far better place to be. These are both comforting positions to take if you actually believe in them, but I have finally come to the conclusion that both are nonsense. Give me forty points by January and half a season of completely meaningless games any time. It's not a very brave or exciting stance to take, but there you have it. In fact, when this scene starts to be played out every year, you almost wish they would get relegated – somehow, I felt cheated when, year after year, I expended months of emotional energy on the 'will they, won't they?' of the battle, only for them to survive and make the whole thing pointless, leaving me feeling rather stupid.

Saints were to perform this safety dance for me, more often than not on the last day of the season, for most of the nineties. The only relief came in the form of Matthew Le Tissier, my footballing ray of sunshine equivalent of David Gower. There was this oddity that such a poor side should feature the most talented player of the decade and that he had no desire to leave. Without a shadow of a doubt, he saved Saints at least three times entirely on his own. In 1994, he scored more goals than the rest of the squad put together whilst appearing to be holding his own personal Goal of the Season competition and scoring a hat-trick in the game that saved us in what was otherwise a pretty horrible season. For this, for his genuine love for our club and for the entirely appropriate way he left the stage, his last touch being the last goal ever scored at The Dell, he will remain forever revered by most Saints fans as their favourite ever player. We may have been terrible for ten years, but Matt somehow made the misery bearable. 1994 was his year, and on the 30th of April, with two more goals against Aston Villa, he had saved me from what I thought would have been the ultimate misery. Forty-eight hours later, I wasn't to be so lucky.

JIMMY, JIMMY...

> 'We die a little every day and by degrees we're reborn into different men, older men in the same clothes, with the same scars'
> MARK LAWRENCE, KING OF THORNS

Ah, Jimmy White. This guy captivated me from the first time I saw him as he hardly looked like my idea of a sportsman at all – he had taken the Hurricane's careworn look and dialled it up a couple of notches. Not that he would've cared much, but Jimmy was not going to be top of the list for a Lucozade Sport advert. There was only one tonic he seemed to recognise, and it wasn't isotonic. Night Nurse might have been a better option as he seemed to arrive on-screen for each match looking like he'd walked straight there from the nearest nightclub. It might have been an idea for the organisers to have laid out a bed rather than chair for him to return to each time a ball rattled in the jaws. Here was snooker's Rolling Stone who did a good imitation of Ronnie Wood walking home from the casino after a bad night's work. In fact, during Jimmy's occupation of it, the snooker table often seemed more like a roulette wheel – a white ball spinning all over the place before landing on reds and blacks in a delightfully random manner. The ride of watching him had that game's same sense of excitement and adrenaline but unfortunately also the same nagging realisation in the back of the mind that there was very rarely a happy ending. But as with most gamblers, he and we were drawn back time and again by the tantalising thought he might beat the odds one day. It was long odds that Kenny Rogers was going to make an appearance in this book, but in *The Gambler*, he offers the advice to the likes of Jimmy that 'you've gotta know when to hold 'em, know when to fold 'em, know when to walk away and know when to run'. It was perhaps to his detriment in terms of world titles that Jimmy didn't really know when to fold 'em, which made our devotion exasperating at times. To this day, it appears he doesn't know when to run, which just makes us love him even more.

'You don't lose six times. You lose five times and then you win. You beat the bad guy'. Richard Osman was referring to Jimmy White and the 1994 World Snooker final. It was what we all felt. What many of us still feel. Two of the toughest of the various English sporting disappointments heaped upon us in the nineties were the stories of Jimmy White and Tim Henman. White spent the first half of the decade getting ever closer, but not close enough, to his ultimate ambition. Then, from the mid-nineties, Tim took over the mantle and did pretty much the same at Wimbledon. Jimmy from 1990 to 1994 is the one thing in sport above all others I would want to go back and change if the gods granted me but one wish. Simon Barnes once compared watching sport to an anxiety dream – a recurring nightmare where you can't control the fact that the objective in your sights is continually, fractionally slipping from your grasp. Jimmy's world finals were the ultimate sporting anxiety dream, except that with the dream, you wake up with a sense of relief; in the reality, there is no such release.

In both cases, what made the whole thing that much worse was the lazy and erroneous label applied by a good proportion of the public, attempting to parade their own no doubt constant perfection and their disdain for Britain's acceptance of second best, notwithstanding the fact they themselves hadn't been good enough to achieve any success of their own. I assume they believed that their pronouncements, from the comfort of their armchairs, that our Jim or Tim has 'shat it again' somehow portrayed them as altogether tougher characters. The refrain was 'they're losers' with the implication that they were forever letting us all down. I've never seen it like that. I get irritated a lot, not least when it comes to sport, with the Great British Public. That body of people that queues up to make utter fools of themselves on the skin-crawlingly crass medium of the sports phone-in programme continually prove that their opinions fall some way short of judicious and informed sporting analysis. Sport is all about opinions, I hear. Well, fine, except when those opinions are wrong. Too many of these people fit the Danny Baker-identified profile of 'sometimes right, sometimes wrong, but always certain'. In my eyes, people who peddled the 'White/Henman equals *loser*' myth were just jumping on the safest of bandwagons. It's the sports-following equivalent of the inherent coward strutting around with his bull mastiff on his arm. Sporting small man syndrome. Disproving what I see as people's dumb opinions is one of the main reasons I yearn so much for certain sporting results. It heightens my desperation for a specific victory. Top of this list would always be Jimmy shutting the naysayers up by taking that world title he all but won and then lost on several occasions. Ah, I hear you say – this very example proves the *loser* evaluation to be spot on and undermines your entire argument. I don't deny it would've made the whole thing easier if the bugger had actually won the thing but still, I beg to differ. You don't make six world finals, several of them after heroic comebacks and last frame deciders, or reach four Wimbledon semis in an era of truly great players, if you are a *loser*. And stop and think for a moment what each of these tournaments would have been like in the nineties without Jimmy and Timmy. I for one would've been a lot less interested if it had been Neal Founds, Nigel Bond and Graeme Dott trying to topple Hendry every year. And let's not let a certain Andy Murray (Scottish rather than

English anyway, so they are at pains to tell us) cloud our memories that Tim was the first English player we could get genuinely excited about at our special tournament for sixty years. They both brought something of huge value to their viewing public and should forever be lauded for having done so. These were two world-class English sportspeople who had the misfortune to be playing at a time when each of them had to contend with a sporting automaton that just happened to be better than them.

With that off my chest, you can perhaps see why their attempts to attain their respective summits meant as much to me as it did to them as the years and the near misses slowly ticked by. Both had their carpe diem moments: Jimmy in 1992 and 1994; Tim in 2001. If it was going to happen for them, those were the times, and the fact that we sensed it at the time made the watching and the outcomes that much more agonising.

Jimmy White was the perfect English favourite. Full of flair, full of flaws and above all, so obviously a great bloke that you'd give anything to go and have a night out with him. Still the most heartbreaking moment, and in a way the most admirable, in the story of Jimmy and his world finals was his one-liner immediately after the most traumatic final of all, his fourth against Hendry and his last. 'He's starting to annoy me now...' said Jimmy with real comic timing, but the weak smile which accompanied the words convinced nobody that he wasn't shot to pieces inside. It was just Jimmy, and we loved him even more for it. Richard Osman again: 'it was heartbreaking to hear his speech afterwards. He's such a good loser, such a class act'. Note the qualification of 'good loser' as being in the sense of 'class act'. Yes, I personally would've sacrificed a lot of other sporting triumphs for him to come back and win it, and every year we began the fortnight with that faint hope that the story's final chapter was still to be written, whilst the reality was drip-fed to us year by year (sometimes teasing us just a little more with a couple of successful rounds) that the chance was gone as Jimmy slowly slipped towards the inevitability of non-qualification and the passing of his baton to Rocket Ronnie. After the sixth final defeat, *The Independent* referred to his quest to win the title as 'a trial of patience worthy of a saint he would never claim to be'. The fact that he still turns up to qualify each year, and professes he still believes he can win it, endears him to us set against Hendry's clear admission that if can't win every time, he won't play anymore. (In fact, Hendry eventually had a change of heart and by 2021 was making a comeback as a rather less intensely driven, if still competitive, character. As I write, the draw has just been made for the first qualifying round for the 2021 world championships which paired Hendry with… Jimmy White. Are you kidding me?) But the one thing we wouldn't trade a win for is Jimmy's personality. We wanted him to win it precisely because of who and what he was. Jimmy insists that it hurt the rest of us more than it did him – that he was OK with it, that it didn't bother him at all – and he was more interested in getting out for a drink when it was done. I'm not totally convinced, but if anyone could genuinely feel that way, I think it would be Jimmy. Therefore, I'm sure he'd find all this love for him awkward, unnecessary and, I'm guessing, a little patronising, but sorry Jim, that's the way it is.

It's easy to forget that he had reached a world semi eight years before, and a final six years before, his arrival in his second final, his first against a young kid called Stephen Hendry. In all, therefore, he made six finals in ten years. That semi-final defeat against Higgins in '82 didn't seem so terrible at the time as, at his age, he was surely going to win this thing several times. In fact, losing it the way he did foreshadowed what was to come now. So come 1990, he was still trying to achieve something he'd begun chasing nearly a decade before. The loss against Hendry was disappointing, the 1991 defeat to John Parrott even more so, given it wasn't Hendry. But those of us feeling the pain hadn't seen the half of it yet. By 1992, Jimmy was playing the best snooker of his life, the flair still there but a new maturity to decision-making and match play which, when allied to the pure ability, had him taking all before him. This was surely the one. By the time he had played Hendry off the table in the final to lead 14-8, just four frames from victory, even we confirmed doubting Thomases felt we probably had enough slack to relax and enjoy the last session. Some of us still had our nagging doubts, for which we blamed ourselves, as the nightmare unfolded. Jimmy could lose the next thirteen frames 9-4 and still be world champion. What he in fact managed was to lose the next ten frames 10-0. I saw excerpts of this final again when lockdown in April 2020 meant Crucible reruns on the BBC instead of the real thing. It shocked me just how horrible it was. The completely haunted look Jimmy wore as he sat in his chair hour after hour was almost unwatchable. At the time, I think I consoled myself with the thought it couldn't get any worse…

So, of course, Hendry beat him again in '93, though with the blessing of not having let Jimmy or me get even a sniff of victory this time. The good news was that in doing so, Stephen was kindly shifting the law of averages so far in Jimmy's favour that if they ever got there again, it simply had to be his turn. Sure enough, with Jimmy back to his form of two years before, they arrived in the final together for the third consecutive year. It was excruciating viewing from pretty much the word go and got steadily worse. I think my subconscious may have tried so hard to erase the memory that I can't be sure, but this may well have been the first occasion I declined to watch for large portions of the match, avoiding the very event I had been waiting for and willing to happen. Either way, I'm pretty sure that how it finished and the scars it left me with produced the first seeds of the condition of non-watchability which was to flourish fully ten years later. I also know for sure that I watched the deciding frame because I'll never forget it. Jimmy was given a chance and was going round the table building the lead which would prevent Hendry from being able to do anything about it. This time, it was he who wore the chastened look. How do you like it then, Stephen? Thirty more points, that was all, the balls available to get them without huge difficulty. This was going to be Jimmy's present to himself on his thirty-second birthday and to me just fifty-eight minutes before my own twenty-seventh. Then the black off its spot. Missed. The stunned silence of the crowd gave way to a collective sigh. I simply froze where I sat, about an inch and a half from the telly by that stage, ready to punch the air. This wasn't a final going up in smoke; it was a decade of devotion. Even worse, I'm not sure there has ever been anything more inevitable in sport than Hendry's nerveless clearance to win it. We may have been willing just one unbelievable moment of fallibility – even on this occasion, we would have accepted a fixed result had he had it in his cold-blooded heart to miss on purpose to let Jimmy and everyone else get what they wanted and deserved. But we knew it wasn't happening.

Having not been brave enough at the time, or since, to have watched the Aguero title-winning goal in 2012, I can safely put the feeling of utter dejection of this moment alongside the second Lions Test match of 2009 and Turin 1990 as the worst moment of my sports-watching life. It upsets me to this day. And others too. In the 2020 reruns documentary, Stephen Fry said with genuine compassion and regret that, for him, it was 'heartbreaking. I mean *really* heartbreaking'. Some may be nonplussed by a sporting contest having such words and emotions attached to it, but at the risk of upsetting such people, this is how it was; something akin to a bereavement.

Steve Davis subsequently put it to Hendry in an interview, 'to some extent, you broke millions of snooker fans' hearts on many occasions… was there any part of you that felt sorry for Jimmy?'. Here was the chance to make us all feel a bit better. The answer was an immediate and unequivocal 'no'. Not surprising and commendably honest, but boy did we want to see him beaten every time, by everybody, from this day forward. If Jimmy couldn't retaliate, somebody else was going to have to do it for him, hence the new-found support for the likes of Ken Doherty and company whenever Hendry was in their sights. Given Stephen's record as a serial winning machine, this 'anyone but' approach was going to fail more often than not. The moment of at least an element of closure coming with the sublime 18-17 deciding frame win for Peter Ebdon in the 2002 final – one of the ultimate schadenfreude moments.

Jimmy wasn't giving up. Others may have just walked away, utterly broken, but Jimmy was a que sera sera sort of guy who just wanted to keep on living his life. He seemed far better able to take it than I did. It reminded me of my cricket-watching mate. Perhaps it's a south London thing. This getting up off the canvas was, however, a double-edged sword for us devotees. Sticking around, Jimmy was inevitably foisting upon us yet more moments of hope and disappointment. That he made it to another semi-final the following year was, in the circumstances, a show of quite incredible mental strength, but the 16-12 loss to someone called Stephen Hendry was almost inevitable and, for me, just another drip of torture. But bless him, even if it didn't deliver the ultimate prize, Jimmy gave us a few more moments to cherish. In 1998, drawn against Hendry in the last thirty-two, we knew what to expect. Even when Jimmy went 7-0 up, I for one was resigned to his defeat. It didn't do to go around humiliating Hendry. For a moment, there was a wobble, but the ultimate 10-4 win which sent our nemesis home had a sweet taste, if only partly laying any number of ghosts.

Although all very sad, there was an element of relief when it became obvious that Jimmy wasn't going to get there. At least we could give up the cycle of hope and anticlimax. Unfortunately, as Jimmy was playing out his 1994 final tragedy, Tim Henman was heading for his first Wimbledon championships that June and the baton of unresolved disappointments landed in his grasp.

SCREAM IF YOU WANNA GO FASTER

'Still nursing the unconquerable hope, still clutching the inviolable shade'
MATTHEW ARNOLD, ENGLISH POET,
THE SCHOLAR-GIPSY 1853

'Watching a Tim Henman match on the Centre Court is like being seven years old again and riding a rollercoaster; all the time you're on you scream to get off, but as soon as you're off, you can't wait to rush round to the end of the queue to get back on'. This was *The Telegraph* columnist Robert Phillip's introduction to an article following Henman's last famous edge-of-the-seat win at Wimbledon in 2007. It is the best summation I have found, not just of following Henman but of the essence of my whole sports-watching life. That was scary and horrible – *let's put ourselves through it all over again.*

The significance of Tim Henman in this overall story initially surprised me; after all, I'm afraid I'm one of those 'tennis fans' who is a fan of the English sporting institution that is Wimbledon and the need for it to complete my summers, rather than a year-round, can't miss it, dedication to the sport. That's not to say I don't get hooked by great players and great matches – the 2008 Federer v Nadal final is in my top ten moments of sporting ambrosia – but these tend to start and end within the ivy-clad confines of SW19. But Henman's story fitted the Jimmy White template – highly talented, entertaining player, good bloke, unfair perception as lovable loser and misfortune to be playing in the era of the best players ever to have played their respective games – and therefore the template for those sportspeople I was desperate to see get over the line and give us the fairy-tale moment. Add to this the seventy-seven-year wait between Fred Perry and Andy Murray (eighty-five years and counting if you're waiting for an English champion) and the fact that Tim's attempts to scale this Everest began the month following Jimmy's last unsuccessful final, and this is how it came to mean so much.

In my first summer of watching cricket, the grey-haired, bespectacled David Steele came from nowhere to be voted Sports Personality of the Year by being parachuted into the Ashes to repel the two-man assault squad that was Dennis Lillee and Jeff Thomson. *The Sun's* Clive Taylor gave him the memorable moniker of 'the bank clerk who went to war'. Watching Tim in the cauldron that is the Arthur Ashe Stadium in New York, he seemed more like the accountant who suddenly found himself in the Coliseum. But, as with Steele, this impression masked a true competitor. That there was so much nonsense talked about Henman prodded at my irritation gene as much as had the unintelligent categorising of Jimmy. To me, there was a little too much of the class struggle about the pigeonholing of him as both a toff and a loser. Admittedly, I would be tempted to join that crusade on occasions when faced with what *The Telegraph* called his 'tiresome battalions of cheerleaders and their exhibitions of manufactured hysteria'. This was one of the downsides of Henman at Wimbledon over which the poor guy had no control. The hordes of travellers from The Cotswolds, the Home Counties, The Richmonds and Cobhams using their lunchtime Tupperwares as pom-poms and giving constant renditions of chants of the 'hotdog, sausage roll' primary school playground variety actually undermined his talent and skewed his reputation. *The Telegraph* goes on, in its Henman retirement piece, having noted how Tim himself had appraised his career better than anyone with dignified realism, 'the tiresome parading of chauvinist sentimentality, Henmania always seemed tainted with distressing exhibitionism and insults the true merit of a career its creator can contemplate with undiluted pride'.

Those who see Henman's sporting epitaph as 'the bloke who never won Wimbledon' don't get it and will receive my rebuff at every turn. Tennis journalist Mark Hodgkinson was right when he wrote that to define him by what he didn't accomplish rather than what he did misses the point. Remember what life was like following Wimbledon before he came along and gave us something to get excited about? You had to manufacture some support for a Borg or a Becker as there was no other option. Yes, as Sue Mott, a journalist who followed every up and down of his career, recalled, there was a sense of emotional agony in sitting astride a gigantic, serrated edge watching him at Wimbledon – he had an unerring ability to play his matches in such a way as to leave us watching 'on the edge of doom, causing maximum distress through hours and hours of angst'. But as this whole story is attempting to articulate, that is what English sport is about. This is indeed borne out by the facts. In six tournaments out of seven around the turn of the millennium, he played at least one tortuous five-setter, putting himself and everyone else through the mill but delivering us a level of excitement and allegiance we had never known before. In 1996, he gave notice of what awaited us all with an epic five-set win over Yevgeny Kafelnikov, way above him in the rankings; a year later, as we began to believe, he took us to 14-12 in a fifth set before beating Paul Haarhuis; 1999 was the next progression – to a quarter-final against Jim Courier – sure enough won 9-7 in the fifth before his first semi-final defeat to Sampras; 2000 his departure was via a loss to Philippoussis 6-4 in the fifth. 2001 deserves more detailed contemplation; 2002 he beat Kratochvil in five sets and lost a semi-final to Hewitt. The tennis scoring system is a piece of genius in its ability to create so many possibilities. It is the ultimate challenge for the pessimist such as myself. If Tim is 40-15 up, please god don't let it get to 40-30. Set point and potential relaxation can become 'advantage' the other way in the blink of an eye. And don't even start with me on tiebreakers. Consequently, every one of these titanic struggles swung constantly between potential triumph and disaster in a dizzying fairground ride of stomach-churning emotion. And this was only tennis for crying out loud.

It was what Mark Hodgkinson referred to as the 'Nice But Tim' perception which, as he says, belied the best British player for sixty-odd years that irked me. The idea he was an underachiever doesn't bear much scrutiny and is debunked by the likes of McEnroe and Federer. In fact, writer Martin Amis suggested he might have been the first human being called Tim to have achieved anything at all. (My own apologies here to Tim Berners-Lee who may have something of a claim.) As Rafa Benitez might say, a few facts: a loser? Statistically yes, in terms of Grand Slam semi-finals. An underachiever? Of course not. Six Grand Slam semis, eleven ATP ranking titles, top ten in the world five times in ten years. What's more, in an era of baseline clubbers, his style was a throwback, which gave us something different – a far more satisfying aesthetic – serve-and-volleying with a grace so much more pleasing on the eye. It wasn't his fault he didn't have that extra little bit of power to beat the very best. To consider Andy Murray a significantly better sportsman, rather than a more frequent winner, I think is a mistake. Robert Phillip makes a strong case that Murray might have become the main man, but Tim was the inspiration.

Winning those five-setters through moments of unbearable tension was not the mark of a weak character. To revisit the previous metaphor, Phillip felt such victories showed that 'beneath the accountant's exterior beats the heart of a gladiator'. The fact I could see this but so many others seemingly couldn't was the thing that made it all the more vital he should eventually come through for me. In the end, he wrung every last drop out of his talent to try to give us what we wanted, and we could see what it meant to him. 'Did the country want me to win more than I did? The answer to that has to be "no"', he once said. It is why it is so hard not to share any of his regret, such as it may be.

Just as Jimmy White had his Hendry, Tim was trying to make his final step in the company of Pete Sampras and Roger Federer. This always seemed to be the way for my heroes – there was a boring sod in the way who was a little less entertaining and just a little bit better. Which is why three days in early July 2001 will go down as one of the great missed opportunities. Sampras's last Wimbledon title of seven was achieved in 2000; Federer's first of eight was in 2003. So, there was a two-year window – just a chink of light. And in 2001, the light burned more brightly with Sampras and Agassi sent home early. Tim himself got rid of Federer in his quarter-final and would play wild card Ivanisevic in the semi. Carpe diem. I doubt there has been more hope, tension and anticlimax across three days of the tournament in its history. One of the more inclement Wimbledon fortnights meant the match which started on the Friday was stretched out over an entire weekend, cruelly prolonging the 'what ifs', the hopes and the fears. Tim himself said on his retirement, 'if I could go back, it would be that one I'd ask to have again. I'd ask for it not to rain'.

On Friday night, he was playing the very best tennis of his life; having lost a close first set, he put me through the usual hell of a tiebreaker to draw level. Then we headed into dreamland. The third set was won 6-0 in under fifteen minutes, losing just four points; now 2-1 up in the fourth, we probably needed just another fifteen minutes to have the whole thing done so we could look forward to our weekend and the prospect of Tim's final on the Sunday. Only, come Sunday, this match was still going on. When the rain came on Friday, Goran had as good as given up. Saturday saw a refreshed Croatian banging down his aces again with enough accuracy to put us through the joys of another tiebreak. These tennis equivalents of penalty shoot-outs were followed in much the same way – you just had to be ahead. And then if you were, you just wanted that one more mini victory for the breathing space. So it was with Tim 3-1 up. Touching distance again. But he lost it. OK, if this is going to be painful, at least make the kill swift. Personally, I wasn't sure I could stand any more of it. But at 3-2 to Goran in the fifth, rain decided it was going to bring us back on Sunday. Goran broke at 4-3 and served out. We forgive the rain a lot in this country. Without it, we know our green and pleasant land would be nothing of the sort. This time, however, we would not forgive, and we could not forget.

Cue the strangest final I can remember on the Monday – all I could see out on the court was a phantom Henman playing every point in the pursuit of our moment of history. Pre-Henman, we English champions of the underdog would have loved Goran's victory, his clear love of the tournament, his redemption from both a final defeat nine years previously and a constant losing battle to right that wrong ever since. But now he was holding the trophy and talking about his moment of destiny without, it seemed to me, the appropriate sense of acknowledgement and guilt that he had ruined everything.

Unfortunately, just like Jimmy, Tim would not let us crawl away and accept that it was over. The chance was gone, couldn't we just leave it at that? But he kept coming back and prolonging the agony. His prerogative, of course, and admirable, I suppose, except that it meant the hope went on, with ever decreasing justification. We knew it was done but couldn't help clinging to the faint possibility of the fairy story. Six years later, just as Jimmy had with his beating of Hendry in '98, Tim gave us one last pipe dream and, of course, in his own signature fashion. Rolling back the years, he beat seed Carlos Moya in the first round, 13-11 in the fifth. Just perhaps...

He lost in the second round and that was the end of the story of Tim Henman and Wimbledon.

Jimmy and Timmy were not losers, other than the fact that when it mattered, unfortunately they were. Life without them would have been much the poorer, but if you wanted two definitive illustrations of hope over experience, look no further.

MY ADIDAS

I arrived in 1995 in something of a sporting rut. We'd just been hammered in another Ashes series in Australia; Saints were engaged in their now annual scramble towards forty points; and England were shortly to see another Rugby World Cup pass by in the blur of something called Jonah Lomu. Even United had let me down this time, somehow contriving to lose the title on the final day with Andy Cole doing a fair impression of an overexcited under-10s striker hammering the ball everywhere bar the back of the net. They backed that up by losing the FA Cup final. There was a general downer to the year which was once again reflected by a personal life which also seemed to be struggling to go anywhere. The loss of the beloved family dog in April was followed by a difficult end to my first serious relationship, and after six years in my first job, the excitement of presenting shin guard ranges at quarterly sales meetings was wearing thin. My new boss was seeing my future on the parent side of the business and marketing elasticated bandages to the pharmacy retail sector was not what I had sacrificed Southampton or London for. I felt something had to give.

My approach to getting over my break-up took the form of an attempt to recreate the debauchery of the summer of 1986, many a sunny weekend spent outside local pubs with a full bottle of wine, chatting up all and sundry and various dalliances and weekends away, aiming to mask the upset, but in reality, it was all pretty empty. I knew I was drifting, and even sport, with the exception of Dominic Cork's hat-trick that morning in a Lake District hotel, was holding only passing interest. I was also vaguely aware that there was some cultural stuff going on that may also have been passing me by...

That a change was needed was best summed up by two gigs in the space of a couple of weeks that autumn. I was not averse to presenting myself, even at twenty-eight, as fashion conscious and music savvy with my finger on the pulse of the cultural zeitgeist. This was rather offset by the fact that I also fancied myself as something of a crooner with a love of all things Sinatra, Dean Martin and the rest. On a long car journey, I had been known to delve so far as Neil Diamond for a singalong and that, for some reason, was enough for me to consider going to see him at the Manchester Arena as a suitable second date with a new girlfriend. I grew increasingly uncomfortable with this decision as the alarm spread across her face, surrounded as we were by Wilmslow housewives swinging their handbags and worse things besides. I would estimate we were the youngest there by a good twenty years. That the relationship survived this perhaps indicated she was more interested in it than I was, but I was given a second chance when I was dragged to see Pulp play a hometown gig in Sheffield two weeks later. I had to admit, this first taste of what would soon be Britpop probably edged 'Love On The Rocks', and I felt back in the game. Thank you, Lyn, for putting me back on the right track.

It was another watershed moment. At around the same time, I was approached by adidas and asked to join them down the M60 in Stockport. Being headhunted for the first and only time in my life by the most iconic sports brand in the world just when I needed it most further bolstered the missing self-esteem which had been reignited by Lyn and Jarvis Cocker, and by the following March, a new chapter was underway. If 1995 had been depressing, '96 would prove the total opposite and would be the start of the two longest and most rewarding relationships of my life, played out in a whirl of Britpop, three stripes and sporting drama.

Not everything about the adidas move was immediately easy. Having been hired for my unique expertise in the less-than-critical shin guards sector, I was not necessarily the man best placed to help take our national sales team past their challenging targets and deliver their bonuses. Therefore, I had to fight extra hard for acceptance in a hard school where first impressions tended to last. adidas were nothing if not committed to product innovation, but having to present and sell their new idea of a shin guard you baked in the oven before use, to a room in which the banter was tougher than any dressing room I had ever inhabited, was one of the trickier assignments of my professional career. Something must've gone right, however, as, bit by bit, I seemed to pass my initiation rituals and tests of credibility and became part of the best group of people with whom I have ever worked.

Everything was different in this place in 1996. adidas had been on its uppers as never before in the early nineties, as evidenced by a review of their product catalogues from those years each Christmas. These were the days before Beckham and Naz – instead, the pages featured Tom Selleck lookalikes in budgie smugglers posing as if for C&A, in one case incongruously holding a Yorkshire terrier on a lead. Then, legend has it that sometime around 1995, as I was undergoing my own renaissance, Madonna was snapped walking out of a New York nightclub in a three-striped top, and within twelve months, the brand was the hottest thing on the planet. Now, I don't like to mention again my propensity for turning around fortunes just by turning up, but there it is.

By the summer of '96, we couldn't make stuff quickly enough to sell it; our UK office was headed by an entrepreneur who believed in the work hard, play hard philosophy, and that was the culture – for a while, it felt like I had joined one long party. Over the next few years, that party was to have stop-offs all around the world, from Jersey to Monaco, Florida to Sydney. That's how we rolled. Perhaps taking our cue from the ever-increasing sense of irreverence and excess permeating the country, from Chris Evans' Radio One show and *TFI Friday*, the arrival of Oasis and the Gallagher brothers and the antics, lapped up by the media, of Keith Allen, the YBAs of Damien Hirst and their gang, behaviour was not always becoming. Breaking in – non-violently but half-cut, by teetering along a ledge fifty feet above the Grand Prix starting grid – to the rooftop swimming pool on the top of the Grand Hotel in Monte Carlo for a not-significantly-clothed midnight swim and the 'naked bar' takeover at a well-to-do Cheshire hotel were just a couple of examples. Various accommodation bans were dished out and accepted as badges of honour. These were the times, and I had landed in exactly the right place to make the most of them. The 'second summer of love' may have officially been announced in 1988, but for me it was 1996, ten years on from my first. And having access to a wide range of three stripe Gazelles and LA Trainers hardly lessened the sense that I was at the centre of it.

To get back on track, there was of course a proper sporting context to being with adidas. Whilst Noel and Liam were parading their Gazelles, the likes of a young David Beckham, Denise Lewis and Jonny Wilkinson would regularly wander through the office door. Although sport had never completely left me, going to live sport had become increasingly rare over the previous few years. Now, opportunities to be at the best events and biggest stadiums came thick and fast and without the bother of trying to secure tickets or pay for them. This was another major step in my sporting reawakening, as was a relatively new route to consumption. The advent of Sky, when combined with the bar culture of the Britpop summer, meant that those events that couldn't be attended were often viewed in groups in pubs as part of what became day and night-long parties. This wasn't the summer for sitting in front of your own TV. To this day, for me, it is often hard to call which is the better experience – most would say being there, and perhaps an increasingly ability to be so has made me too blasé about it, but there are times when the addition of drink, food and company of your choosing, with the only travel required being from one watering hole to the next, seems to have greater pull. Even at the games themselves, there have certainly been occasions when it has seemed a pity to leave the bonhomie and picnics of the Cardinal Vaughan car park at Twickenham to go and watch the match, and a visit to the Harris Garden at Lord's usually demonstrates that there are plenty who prefer watching an England collapse on the screen next to a table full of champagne buckets than in the stands themselves. As I've said, sports watching is often about the occasion as much as the contest, wherever that might be experienced. During that endless summer, both methods were to be employed, particularly over the two events that live longest in the memory.

Sunday the 5th of May was a mix of the sporting and the personal which perfectly summed up the times. That it might be special was perhaps foretold when the Sunday of a bank holiday weekend in Manchester dawned to azure blue skies, and by mid-morning, it was clear this was going to be an unusually hot and sultry spring day. That fitted our plans for the day nicely, given the Loughborough old boys crew had arranged this as the first of the annual reunion matches to be played outside the university. Taking the 'sport as party' route, the jamboree was to start at midday with a match played on the AstroTurf in Didsbury, followed by an afternoon taking in the last day of the football season at the Red Lion in Withington. The weather seemed perfect but in the end was better suited to the second activity than the first, a bunch of late twenty-somethings finding ninety minutes in eighty degrees somewhat sapping, with the reverse of injury time being employed to bring things to an early conclusion. It had, however, given everyone a thirst. That summer's obligatory Gazelles and 'ballooning shirts' were donned, and we joined the congregation milling around outside the pub. However, whilst everyone else chilled in the sun, the next two hours weren't to offer me the same relaxation. Having closed a twelve-point gap, United had to win away at Middlesbrough to beat Newcastle to the title. They managed to do this at a canter on one of those rare and joyous occasions when even I couldn't see any potential disaster looming. The sense of fun in the Manchester pub reached new heights. Only, at the other end of the table, things were not so straightforward. Manchester City needed a result to avoid relegation. There was a strange mixture in the beer garden of United fans, whose day would be topped off by seeing City go down, City fans, desperate for their own reason to join the party mood, and me… the only team that could keep City up was Southampton. For the third time in four seasons, Saints reached the last day on the precipice.

Playing this game of brinksmanship was going to end in disaster one day. Please not today on this most perfect of all days. City needed to better Saints' result, and at 2-0 down to Liverpool, they seemed bent on giving me my second stress-free game of the day. However, when they equalised, and Saints were locked at 0-0, the ache in my stomach was no longer just the lactic acid left over from the lunchtime exertions. I was now the only one of my group who was actually inside the pub, surrounded by a sea of City fans. Injury time, purgatory and suddenly City's players were holding the ball in the corner… I didn't know why and cared even less. I'll never be able to find, and therefore never be able to thank, the person who got the erroneous message to Maine Road that Southampton were losing. But, unable to watch, I was stood at the urinal as a City fan came in to give me the news that City were down, assuming, I suppose, that I would be as crushed as he was. My ability to contain my utter elation would now determine whether I was to continue my afternoon in Withington's pubs or its hospital. That I was successful in this endeavour changed my life.

The feel-good factor, and the many pints of Guinness which were embellishing it, ensured the day was not to end as originally intended in the early evening as the sun went down. It had long since departed by the time we set off in search of the nightclub which we deemed the only appropriate place at which to round things off. This proved more problematic than expected, given we were into the depths of a Sunday night, no matter how much it might feel like a Saturday. Venue after venue was either closed or not overly keen to admit the rather shambolic group we now made up. Undaunted, this had now become a matter of principle, and the team decision was to keep walking until we found somewhere. This policy was taking us further from the trendier suburbs of Manchester towards those that sober people wouldn't venture into after dark. I personally, tired and emotional, had given up, and when we finally arrived at the Irish club in Hulme which was prepared to accept us, I did so in a shopping trolley. This didn't suggest my chances of sweet-talking a young lady into submission were high – in fact, for once, I'm not sure that was on my agenda. And yet, fate and Stella combined to have me half asleep on the shoulder of a stoical girl called Mary. Four years later, she became my wife. This was a significant day and a significant year indeed.

THREE LIONS

In my time at adidas, in fact in my lifetime, my country has hosted just two events of a sporting magnitude great enough to become moments in time in the national consciousness: the London Olympics and, first, Euro '96. For the latter, I had arrived in the right place in the nick of time. adidas's global clout, not to mention its sponsorship of UEFA, put us in the centre of the thing, and my new professional responsibility for the tournament's official match ball meant I felt justified in considering myself a part of it and in accepting the various tickets which were to come my way. The English are prone to a degree of cynical naysaying in such situations, and for months, there had been dire predictions and homilies on why we shouldn't have been hosting it in the first place. But we can sure as hell do events when the time comes. For those not born at the time of the '66 World Cup, there was something magical about the air of anticipation, the idea of Holland v France at Anfield and so on. By the time England opened against Switzerland on the 8th of June, it felt like the whole country (almost) had caught the mood. Being part of the world's biggest football brand at the time meant this could be marked down as work as well as play – I was just starting to think I was living my dream.

On reflection, the hope v expectation parallels between following England at Euro '96 and Italia '90 were surreal. England had been building a decent squad under a genuinely world-class coach. We had a half-decent song, which like New Order in 1990 made it to number one but, unlike 'World in Motion', produced crowd renditions which came to define the tournament. As Nessun Dorma is for 1990, so Three Lions has become a nostalgic trigger for those three weeks in '96. The run-up was again beset by various scandals, at least in the eyes of the press, from dentists' chairs to the manager's alleged financial impropriety, the newspapers still more focused on winning the circulation war than encouraging any sense of national togetherness. Then, England began with the anticlimax of a 1-1 draw before suddenly blossoming into a team that could play football and proving so against the Dutch, inspired by a certain Paul Gascoigne. Familiar? Followed by a quarter-final they were lucky to win and the only obstacle to glory being a semi-final against Germany.

It's hard to articulate to anyone who wasn't part of it just how wrapped up the country was in this by the time of that semi-final. It wasn't just the football; it felt like the whole nation was having a summer party, and we couldn't stand the thought it could be shut down before it reached its climax. History may have been repeating itself, but surely this was where we were due to rewrite it? It couldn't happen again. This wasn't Jimmy White. The buzz in the stadium and the pubs up and down the land that summer night seemed to me to reflect my own state of mind, betraying both an excitement in the hope of potential victory and closure on the events of Turin, and a terrible fear of the reverse, my default position as an English sports fan but dialled up to an almost unbearable level.

I still find it hard to believe that the gods could be so cruel as to play out the repeat scenario to the letter. Another fantastic game, obvious mutual respect and little to choose between the teams, an extra-time moment when England were millimetres from releasing us from this torment, for Waddle's shot off the post read Gascoigne's desperate far-post lunge to connect, the ball scraping off his studs and away. So, it was back to that 'brutal relationship' with penalties, and I for one knew the outcome before it started, making the process of having to endure the inevitable over fifteen minutes, which felt like several hours, even harder to bear.

The downside to the football-in-pub experience is that when it goes wrong on such a scale, the comedown is even more clinical. From a bubbling cauldron of noise and support, there is silence split by the odd curse, the bar emptying faster than a stadium and the melancholy debris of empty bottles and St George's flags all over the floor. You have to drag yourself away, trying to rationalise it as one of those things but actually with that depressing knowledge that it's still going to be with you ten years later.

This one somehow seemed like the ultimate insult. We had been kicked out of our own party, the hosts locked out whilst a group of guests stayed behind to finish our champagne. Summer packed up and went home – party over, just the hangover to look forward to. Two years on from Jimmy, I was left wondering how many times I was going to have to suffer such things before one went my way.

PERFECT

'I think it's one of the most incredible things I've seen in sport. I think I could watch it every day'.

Although I concur completely, that's not me speaking but Stephen Hendry, and he should know. Arthur Conan Doyle wrote that 'mediocrity knows nothing higher than itself, but talent instantly recognises genius'. Hendry was referring to my favourite individual sporting performance of all time. Other split-second *moments* have delivered more euphoria as the realisation of a long-held dream – Jonny's drop goal in Sydney, Ole's goal in Barcelona and Geraint Jones's catch at Edgbaston – but for sheer jaw-dropping quality over a longer period, Ronnie O'Sullivan's maximum break at the 1997 World Snooker Championship is out on its own. I say a longer period – it took five minutes eight seconds. Terry Griffiths had been known to take that long over a shot. And Ronnie had to stop to pick up his chalk.

Now I may be partisan most of the time when it comes to sport, and of course it helps when genius comes in the form of one of your favourites, but I do still love what sport can do, regardless of its perpetrator, when watching it simply blows you away. And this was the closest thing to perfection in sport I've ever seen. Like Stephen, I could watch it every day, although I now restrict myself to about once a month.

Genius has become a glib word in sporting commentary and analysis. It can be defined in terms of both an individual in our midst and a more ethereal presence. The OED has it as 'a person of exceptional ability especially of a highly original kind' and 'the guiding spirit who attends a person from birth to death'. You could argue a case for many in the history of sport who meet the first description. Myself, I would have a McEnroe, a Messi, a Best, reluctantly a Maradona (I'm fighting hard the urge to put Matt Le Tiss on this list), a Bradman, occasionally a Warne or Pietersen, a Higgins (Alex) and perhaps a Ballesteros. Some might be shouting for Sampras or Federer or Navratilova, Woods, Hendry or Jordan. But for me, these are extremely talented sportspeople who had an inner drive to practise and develop their skills and with an almost psychotic need to win. They are serial winners but don't for me fit the genius definition as it sits in my head. Some may disagree, and this is a staple pub argument when sports followers get together.[1]

You make your choice. Take a look at the names on my list – with the exception of perhaps Bradman and Warne (who perhaps sit better in the other group), these are sportspeople whose drive came from a different place. They are indeed 'of a highly original kind'. OK, perhaps they didn't win as much as they could have, but they treated sport and their own talent as something which should be measured in more ways than that and, to me at least, they gave more pleasure and brought me to the TV more often. They changed the games they played, came at it in a different way. The other reason I, amongst many, am drawn to them is their fallibility. The fact they were as likely to lose as win, often through something going on upstairs, some inner turmoil, made me all the more desperate for them not to do so. When Ronnie or Mac was knocked out, when KP was dismissed or Best left the stage too early, the life went out of what I was watching.

The twentieth-century satirist Max Beerbohm said, 'I have known no man of genius who had not to pay, in some affliction or defect, either physical or spiritual, for what the gods had given him'. If that applies to those on my list, it explains our greater love and gratitude – they were paying a price for keeping us entertained. At a more basic level, let's be honest, we also wanted the character they brought and the moments of weakness or eccentricity; call them what you will. The pomposity with which some preach and pontificate on such occasions irritates me immensely. There is hardly a more jumped up, self-important charge than that of 'bringing the game into disrepute' when in fact sport needs at least some of its participants to go off the rails occasionally if they are to retain our interest. I'd suggest there are far more administrators and media people who have tarnished our games.

Look at the list again. Messi excepted, it reads like a who's who of sport's troubled souls, so yes, perhaps this is one of the signs, even one of the criteria, of genius. And it encouraged empathy. Who of us didn't have our weaknesses, our skeletons? Ronnie was the latest incarnation of this and,

---

1 *see appendix*

especially given his genius was announced just three years after the still fresh crushing disappointment of Jimmy White, we treasured him even more.

We had a new Jimmy but just, perhaps, a version that might win the ultimate prize for us as well. So, we cut him some slack. The regular pronouncements of how much the game bored him and how he was probably going to pack it in became a bit tedious and fortunately a bit less credible each time. And deciding at the 2006 UK championships that at 4-1 down to Hendry he'd had enough and would simply walk out of the arena and the tournament let us all down. But in his case, it just made us even more ardent when the time came for the penitent comeback. We want the story not just the sport. Back at the same event a year later, he played Mark Selby in the semi-final, and it went to a deciding frame, for snooker fans, the equivalent of the penalty shoot-out, with about the same level of enjoyment. Ronnie's answer was a maximum break to win the match. That's why we watch him.

As the wheel of my sporting fortunes began to turn and take me down a more positive road as we left the nineties, Ronnie played his part, and he did deliver for me. Six world titles starting in 2001, meaning six tournaments I could be fully committed to all the way through, each one chipping away at the pain of the Jimmy White years. Even then (and even now) I find it hard to watch, though, fearing by the Ian-Botham-getting-out-next-ball principle that my tuning in would ensure the next red would rattle in the jaws. I'm aware this was senseless, partly because history was showing me that whether I watched or not, he was going to win quite regularly, but more so because the idea that I couldn't watch because I was too concerned he might go out, thereby denying me the chance to watch him, didn't hold a lot of water if I wasn't watching him in the first place. Sad, I know.

Supporting someone with the potential for genius is one thing. Actually seeing it happen is another. Watching his 147 again now, I simply cannot believe he made it happen in the way he did. Those who would banish it from the sporting Valhalla on the basis that snooker is not a sport I cannot entertain here. If you have ever tried to play this game, you will understand just how ridiculous this was. I could not beat any professional even if I were allowed to put every ball a foot from the pocket and place the white wherever I wanted by hand. These guys do it all with a stick. What's more, if you want to make big breaks, you have to be able to see the game four, five, six shots ahead whilst concentrating on the one in front of you. And to do it over potentially thirty-five frames, over two weeks, actually takes physical as well as mental strength. One of the things about sporting excellence is that the participant makes it look easy. Don't be fooled. The best players ever to play the sport, which is what it is, can barely comprehend what Ronnie did that day. You may like snooker, you may not; you may like sport, you may not, but I urge you to watch it before you depart this earth. For me, it is a piece of art which stands alongside any other. The final word on it I'll leave to former world champion Peter Ebdon: 'it's artistic; it's creative; it's clairvoyant; it's psychic. He's tuning in to a higher energy'.

ONE MORE TRY

> 'Hope is the feeling you have that the feeling you have isn't permanent'
> JEAN KERR, US WRITER, 1973

One month on from Ronnie's bout of perfection, the England cricket team seemed to be finding some higher energy of their own. An aggregate score of 14-2 to Australia over the last four series didn't suggest the summer's Ashes series was going to lift my spirits greatly. So, it was in a state of some bewilderment that I sat in the open-plan office on Thursday the 5th of June and saw Australia win the toss, normally a prelude to watching them bat for two and a half days, and then England reduce them to 54-8. Had this been the other way round, few would have batted an eyelid, and it was almost more difficult to cope with this turn of events than it would have been if we had been able to trot out our pre-prepared castigations. What sort of emotion were we supposed to employ here? Well, in my case, of course, it was still fatalism. As that annoying sod Warne was helping to double the score in a ninth wicket stand, I had visions of a world-record partnership putting the world back on its axis. One of the more frustrating elements of following England's cricketers over the years has been their inability to push home an advantage. I've no idea if statistics bear this out, but it's always felt like England are worse than anyone else at getting rid of tailenders when on top. On those occasions (more than you might think) that England had the might of the West Indies five wickets down for not much, they would fail to deal with a Deryck Murray or Andy Roberts in the way they had Gordon Greenidge and Viv Richards. This was an intensely annoying trait that did nothing to dissuade me from taking the 'it's all about to go tits up' stance, regardless of the strength of any position. The summer of 1984 may have left enough of a scar in this regard that it never really healed. As one example, at the close of the second day of that series, England had fought valiantly from a tough position by taking three wickets for three runs in the last few overs of the day to leave the opposition 421-7 overnight. An early summer Saturday watching Gower, Lamb and Botham was the prospect laid before me for the next day. But that Saturday morning, the combined might of bowlers Eldine Baptiste and Michael Holding managed to put on 150 for the ninth wicket – the ninth bloody wicket – and by the time I got to see the players I'd been waiting for, West Indies had over six hundred. And I didn't get to see them for long either. Two months later, we'd lost 5-0. So, there was some reason for my nervousness as Warne did his thing. But they made only 118. The next natural reaction of 'the worst cricket supporter in the world' was that if that's what Australia could manage, what about England? Making these guys cross had rarely ended well before. A pound to a penny England would be bowling again before the close. Instead, they were 200-3. The next day, Thorpe and Hussain took their stand to 288 and the nemesis that was Warne had one for 110. Everything was upside down. Then, Australia batted like Australia and set England 118 to win – more room for pessimistic forecasts – had an England side ever lost with a first innings lead of 360? But they didn't, and by the time rain had given us a draw at Lord's despite a return to normality in being bowled out for seventy-seven, we had the long-forgotten riches of 1-0 up a third of the way through an Ashes series. Here again we were being offered hope… and we were being lured in. Three crushing Australian victories in a month and the Ashes were gone again – as far away as ever. I was irritated I had been dragged out of my default position and vowed it wouldn't happen again.

Having thought for a brief moment that the nightmare that was the sporting nineties was about to be halted with an Ashes miracle, only for it to have simply added to the ongoing misery, it was clear some more drastic action was needed to turn my sporting world around. It was time for one of my life changes which history told me had achieved such great things in the past. Worth a try.

One of the more appealing consequences of joining adidas was the need, the opportunity, to move out of Oldham and the two-up, two-down. My involvement in the work hard, play hard culture in which I now found myself wasn't easily maintained from that distance, and the increasing number of post-work summer evening invitations to the nineties fleshpots that were The Rectory and Brazzingamans opened my eyes to a different world in leafy Cheshire. A different world at different prices, however, and negative equity and a not much more positive bank balance meant that two years on from my arrival at adidas, I was still stuck in Princess Street. A breach in the impasse was made when my girlfriend suggested that I might look at areas other than Cheshire given a) I couldn't afford it and b) even if I could, I wasn't the sort who would enjoy for long walking down the high street every Saturday and bumping into ninety per cent of the people I worked with all week. What she might really have been saying was that I was too old, too poor, too antisocial and not quite cool enough for the cafe society and that slippers and solitude in the country somewhere might be more the ticket. She already knew me better than I knew myself. So, it transpired that by '98, we were ensconced in our chocolate box two-bed cottage out in the Peak District, well out of harm's way. Or so we thought. There is a common misconception – there certainly was at adidas – that compared to the nightlife of Manchester, village life must be safe and boring. In fact, I was to learn that a mini society which is based around the local pub, or pubs, with not a huge amount else to do, was a recipe for a social scene with more than a hint of the Ollie Reed about it – one that I am still enjoying to this day. It may have been naive not to have sensed what might lie ahead when we bought a cottage which was semi-detached to the local pub. It was literally nine yards from my front door to that of the pub, which in 1998 was the hub of the village life. Having moved in on an utterly unremarkable Tuesday in March and spent the afternoon and evening unloading and making home, we thought a quick visit next door to introduce ourselves quietly to a few of the community would be a good tactical move. We began the long journey home at 1am, the curtains in the pub long since having been drawn closed but the door left ajar. So, this was to be village life. One of the various half-cut proclamations made that night was that one of my new ambitions was to have a good enough time in the Oddfellows Arms that I couldn't make it home. Oh, how we laughed. But before we left that cottage, a particular day's sports themed revelry was to bring me to the brink of realising that objective.

The village and the pub brought a new dimension to sport. Every major sporting event (and many minor ones) was watched from the wooden pews next door. A village full of Manchester overspill contained a fairly even mix of United and City fans which made derby days in particular lager-fuelled banter-fests. The demographic mix had enough variety to justify sessions watching things that in the past would largely have passed me by. One of my closest friends being a committed blue Glaswegian meant that Old Firm games were now must-sees. Understandably, in order to lessen the impact of drink on the fans attending these bear pit affairs, they tended to be scheduled at noon on Saturdays or Sundays. For us, of course, this had the opposite effect of that intended for those going to the game. It meant that weekend alcohol consumption regularly had an excuse to start as the sun was just passing the yardarm. Add to this the fact that Sky had started to schedule Premier League games at these times each weekend – often featuring Manchester United, and that in a sleepy village there wasn't much clamping down on illegal feeds that would also give access to any of United's 3pm games – and it often became a gradually more unsteady village version of Gillette Soccer Saturday, with us playing the Merson, Thompson, Stelling roles in pontificating and analysing the day's action through ever more hazy eyes.

Was the life change producing the sought-after change in sporting fortunes? The initial signs weren't propitious this time. What it actually delivered for the time being was more of the same from the hope-disappointment graph. That first summer brought another World Cup, and Glenn Hoddle's team had actually maintained the promise of Euro '96 enough to have us believing. I could see my new venue being the perfect one for the tournament, offering the fun of the shared experience without the difficulty of getting home. And we had a team of enough quality, experience and decent coaching to be able to anticipate a reasonable showing without accusations of blind English arrogance. That didn't mean we had forgotten how watching England in knockout games, successful or otherwise, could reduce us to burnt out husks of men in 120 minutes. So, when the big night duly arrived – first knockout game, Argentina of all people, and packed pub – that old devil on the shoulder was back whispering to me all the things that might go wrong. Even the devil didn't manage to paint as tragic a scenario as was to unfold before our eyes. A high-quality first half ended 2-2, including one of the greater 'hope' moments in England's football history: the arrival of teenager Michael Owen being announced via the goal of the tournament, which suggested we might have unearthed, and for once actually picked, a gem that could help us win the thing or at least get damn close. Just get over this hurdle tonight. To now be taken back through pretty much the same desperate journey for the third time in five major tournaments beggared belief. Injustice rained down on us for the rest of the night. Some say he was naive; some say he cost England the game, but it was the machinations of the Argentinians, the play-acting of the archetypal footballing schemer, Diego Simeone, to get the other great English hope, David Beckham, sent off which damned us again. There are few more irritating sights than that of a puffed up FIFA referee looking to make a name for himself, acting with all the pomposity and apparent certainty they can muster whilst plainly getting it wrong; it isn't just the fact that they are the only ones who can't see they've been conned silly but their certainty in their own misjudgement which makes you want to climb into the TV and physically shake them into admitting they've fucked up. If that had been Kim Milton Nielsen's only such moment of the evening, we would have found it tough to forgive, but he ruined his chances forever before the night was out. The Waddle post/Gascoigne outstretched toe moment duly arrived nine minutes from the end of normal time. An England corner, a Sol Campbell header, surely the winning goal, and the pub went bonkers. That release of tension moment followed by the punch to the solar plexus. Alec Lindsay time again. Our friend had disallowed it for the most tenuous of fouls elsewhere in the area.

This was the first World Cup to use that instrument of torture: the 'golden goal'. FIFA apparently used this term instead of 'sudden death' as it was felt that might have negative connotations. It could in fact have potentially been a perfect epithet several times over the next thirty minutes in our pub. This idea had in effect simply extended by half an hour the sudden death nature of penalty shoot-outs and hearts hovered close to failure every time the Argentinians got into our half. The upside to the golden goal, of course, comes if you score it. But this was England. Mr Nielsen's final contribution of note was to miss a clear Argentinian handball in their area in extra time which could have spared us the inevitable. The renditions of the national anthem when a penalty shoot-out was confirmed didn't fool me. We all knew what was coming. Twenty horrible minutes later, we were out of our misery; only we weren't – as usual, that lingered for months. Sometimes I *create* a sense of injustice to help me through the worst of the losses, but this time it was one hundred per cent genuine, and the fact that the Argentinians seemed able to perpetrate these larcenies at will and without a hint of a guilty conscience made them even more galling. The need for redemption, both Beckham's and ours, had now become a burning desire. The pub was not to let us down next time.

So, the football hadn't yet turned; the cricket had built us up only to let us down again, but we had been building an exciting rugby team – perhaps here was the route to salvation. Their new coach Clive Woodward gave the impression that he was nothing if not a visionary in his own eyes, but he was backing that up by building an England team which made leaving the Range Rovers and gazebos in the West Car Park to watch the matches easier for the Barbour crowd to cope with. Tries were raining down from everywhere; youth was being given its chance; and they were a pleasure to watch. And yet England, who had kicked off my nightmare 1990s by throwing away a nailed on Grand Slam, were about to close them in the same way, the symmetry of this bookending of the decade rather lost on me in my fog of despair.

I've argued that playing entertaining, try-scoring rugby is nine tenths of the reward for England rugby fans, perhaps because it has not often been our role over the years to be the cavaliers of the sport. But losing Grand Slams, especially when the efforts of the previous few months deem them as deserved, is tough; losing them to Scotland is tougher; losing them to Wales is a torture beyond imagination. The 11th of April, 1999 didn't on the face of it hold too many terrors. England were the best team by a distance in that year's Five Nations; Wales were making a good case for being the worst. An away game in Cardiff would have made the task stiffer for sure, but this one was moved to Wembley whilst the Millennium Stadium went up, effectively becoming a home game. A full Wembley, a sunny spring day and a Grand Slam ahead. If there was less complacency than there had been nine years before, a complacency which you could argue meant England got what they deserved, I don't recall that this time. There was just a sense of confidence a job would be done. Even I had it. But England were somehow going to conjure up their own rugby version of a golden goal disaster. Although the game had fluctuated more than England may have envisaged or wanted, as it entered the last two minutes, England led by six points – a converted try was all that could beat them, and they were in the Welsh half and in possession. Wales gave away a penalty. All England had to do was kick it to win the game for sure. And they decided not to. Kicking for the corner instead, they turned the ball over and then conceded a contentious penalty. Neil Jenkins' boot walloped it into England territory. The fact that England had a pack to deal with any such situation was rather offset by the sense of foreboding that the events of the last few minutes must have happened for a reason. There was a strange feeling that everyone knew something was about to happen. That something was Scott Gibbs bursting through England's defence for the try Wales needed and Neil Jenkins converting it as I tried one of the most desperate Ziggies of all time to somehow rescue the situation. To no avail. I'm still not sure how England lost that game (too familiar a refrain). To lose it in that way to anyone would have hurt, but the utter glee with which the Welsh players and nation revelled in my pain did nothing to diminish my hatred of defeat to the Celts. Which is a shame, given that the following year England were denied a Grand Slam by the Scots and the year after that denied yet another one by foot-and-mouth and the Irish. Every defeat celebrated as one by all three nations rejoicing in the obvious English pain. Come on, England, let's have one more try. A year later, we beat all three and lost to France. Four 'finals' in four years; four defeats – this was Jimmy White does rugby. To borrow Jimmy's words, they were starting to annoy me now.

SUNSHINE AFTER THE RAIN

And yet, and yet… there were signs of recovery. Over the next couple of years, the new millennium seemed to consider itself sufficient reason for a break with the past, and perhaps my move was gradually having its effect after all. Not consistently, but every now and then, a sporting moment would come along with our pub at its centre, offering us further excuses for celebratory excess. There is not much more satisfying to the sports fan than a story of redemption, or revenge if you prefer to make it more aggressive, and for a time, this was to become our sustenance.

Once again, I would hate to underplay my own role in this turnaround, for this was the age of 'The Guru of Chinley'. The title bestowed upon me resulted from a tactic we started using to make the most of my perceived capacity to influence the future as if by supernatural power. If a game was not going in our favour with five minutes to go, I would be dismissed from the pub and sent back the whole nine yards to watch the closing stages on my own TV. This had begun with the odd United match as they chased the reclamation of their Premier League title, but at its peak, it allows me to claim that I personally played my part in securing United's treble and England's qualification for the 2002 World Cup.

Despite the hangover, literal and metaphorical, from the Argentina defeat, that '98 summer saw England win a five-match Test series, admittedly with the help of the good auspices of umpire Akhtar, for the first time in eleven years. Of course, the Ashes thrashings continued unabated but were now interspersed with series wins against West Indies (the first one for twenty-nine years), Sri Lanka and Pakistan, which added to the sense that change of a sort was afoot. That August also heralded the start of the greatest season in club football history.

By 1998, I'd got used to United lightening my mood through almost constant successes, which made the previous season's effort, winning nothing as Arsenal won the double, something of a shock. If they were going to start disappointing too, I really was in trouble. It didn't help that that Arsenal team seemed to have been created specifically to irritate. On the pitch, the likes of the delightful Martin Keown had a propensity, apparently deliberately cultivated, to wind up both the opposition and me personally; off the pitch, the self-confessed ultimate sore loser, incapable of accepting any defeat had been justified, came in the person of Arsene Wenger. To me, the guy had a chip on both shoulders when it came to Alex Ferguson and United – he came across as believing utterly in his superior intellect, both footballing and otherwise, and becoming increasingly frustrated by the fact that whatever he achieved, Fergie went and topped it. This was not, therefore, the team to which you wanted to cede hegemony. The wrong of '97–98 needed to be avenged. If Arsenal had done a double, the only thing that could truly put Mr Wenger back in his box would be a treble. A fanciful idea but it's why, as the prospect continued to develop through the season, I became so desperate to see it happen. Every game therefore became more tense than the last. This was no cruise to glory – the teams were so evenly matched that one slip anywhere might be fatal. One by one, the games were ticked off through a combination of pub viewing and Guru departures to my lounge. When the two were drawn together in the FA Cup semi-final, I was well aware this was going to be one of those occasions which would offer no enjoyment whatsoever. The prospect of defeat was too painful to contemplate, and I would almost have accepted an offer of being beaten by Newcastle in the other semi to avoid having to look at a victorious Wenger at Villa Park. That's how bad it was. 0-0 in the first game confirmed the difficulty in splitting the sides and meant we all had to go through the mill again three days later. For 120 minutes plus, it was indeed horrible; in the twenty-two years since, it has been watched again more times than I could count as one of my favourite footballing experiences of all time. This made me realise that watching these things when you know the result is so much more pleasant, which was to influence my behaviour more significantly in the years to come.

Sport is littered with sliding door moments – the 'what ifs'. It is why it's so hard to shake narrow defeats – those alternative scenarios simply will not leave your head. Alongside Italia '90, Euro '96 and Edgbaston '05, this was probably the ultimate example. At 1-1 in injury time, down to ten men, United conceded a penalty, causing my heart to consider whether this was really worth the bother and it should just pack up for a while. The worst-case scenario, the sight of Wenger in delirium, was about to be played out. But of course, Schmeichel saved it; Giggs scored the best FA Cup goal ever and somehow it was won. Ecstasy and still on course.

This had been achieved without the benefit of the Guru tactic, I think possibly because I had decided that night that I was too nervous to watch any of the game in the presence of others, but come the afternoon of Sunday the 16th of May, I was back in play. Needing to win to secure the title, United were 1-0 down at home to Tottenham, opening the door for Arsenal again. This was classic Guru territory. This time, it was five minutes before half-time that I received my marching orders. Three minutes later, David Beckham equalised; two minutes into the second half, Andy Cole scored what was to be the winner. I was readmitted to the Oddies to slaps on my back, thanking me for my achievement. Treble part one in the bag; the following week, part two was completed in such a comfortable Cup final win that I didn't have to leave the pub for a single minute.

Four days later came the date with destiny; United had been trying and failing to make a Champions League final ever since their renaissance began in the early nineties, but their nerves had always got the better of them. Another miraculous semi-final comeback win, against Juventus this time, had got them there at last. The only issue for me was that the opposition in the final were Germans, and we knew what that meant. Everyone knows, I assume, what transpired that night, but few are aware of the credit I'm due. At 1-0 down in the last minute and the dream dying as Bayern were bound to close things out with clinical efficiency, I was duly dispatched home in a last forlorn throw of the dice rather than in any expectation. By the time the picture flickered up on my TV screen, United were equalising. It took about ninety seconds for me to regain some form of composure and set off back to the pub to take my plaudits, in which time United scored the winner. Cue one of the most delightful lock-ins of my life. Fergie, Ole and the rest became United legends; I am happy that my own contribution remains less feted but no less critical.

Germany, however, simply would not get out of my life and leave me in peace. A year on, England found themselves in the same qualifying group for the 2002 World Cup and around the corner was yet another German-inflicted disappointment, another encounter with Celtic animosity and another unexpected redemption.

Saturday the 7th of October, 2000 was a day of unusual tension, and for once, it wasn't the sport which was the primary source of the problem. I had a much-loved great aunt who had something of a public profile, having been a cabinet minister in the Labour governments of the sixties and seventies. As a youngster, her fame didn't register much as she was just Great Auntie Barbara to me, the family matriarch who hosted all our extended family gatherings and gave us Christmases which will never be forgotten. My only real frisson of excitement was her referencing as 'Castle Barbara' in *The Two Ronnies* series *The Worm That Turned*. That was something of which a thirteen-year-old could be justifiably proud. Like any good left-wing Labour politician, Auntie Barbara had a beautiful, converted farmhouse in the Chilterns, from whence she further endeared herself to the adult population as Transport Secretary by introducing seventy-mile-an-hour speed limits and breathalysers, not just as a woman but as one who didn't even drive. Her home was not just the base for family gatherings – it also hosted various events at which it was not unusual to come across a famous face or two. One such was the occasion on that October Saturday of Barbara's ninetieth birthday party, and I was tasked with playing a role which was responsible for my stress levels that morning: making the public toast to Great Auntie B. This was my second significant appearance at one of these dos, following on from my debut in 1969 as a two-year-old. On that afternoon, a garden party had been arranged at which the chief guest was the then Prime Minister himself,

Harold Wilson. I'm advised that as Harold got up to make an impromptu address of thanks to the assembled throng scattered in a circle on the lawn, my mother suddenly realised her youngster was no longer with her, and with horror, her eyes next spotted me crawling around the back of the circle, picking up and downing each champagne flute which lay idle. The dilemma for Mum was whether to interrupt a prime minister in full flow or let loose a two-year-old, for whom she was responsible, in a full flow of his own. That she opted for the latter might explain my weakness to this day for a glass or two of fizz on the right occasion. I slept well that night by all accounts.

How I could've done with another twelve glasses of Moët now. Although I'd made a few passable attempts, amidst the odd disaster, at speeches and stage presentations in my professional life, this one was rather different. My anxiety during a lunch I couldn't eat was by no means lessened as the guests to whom I would be speaking started to take their seats: Melvyn Bragg and Jeremy Paxman, not well known for suffering fools, on one side, Neil Kinnock and Jack Straw on the other. The England v Germany qualifier would be taking place around an hour after my moment in the spotlight, and as a cure for the usual pre-match nerves before such a game, this would never be bettered. Somehow, I got through it and even drew some kind reviews from the likes of Paxo who I was aware was not prone to dishing out such things for the sake of it. It was therefore with a glow of both relief and a touch of pride that I sidled off to try to catch the second half at the other end of the house. Arriving in the lounge, I discovered the only other individual who had seen fit to sneak off was the aforementioned former leader of Her Majesty's opposition, Mr Kinnock. It was a dog of a game on a rain-sodden day, and England never looked for one moment like entertaining anyone. I set that against the fact that I was in the surreal position of analysing the game with someone worthy of a decent story on returning to the village the following day. What I wasn't prepared for was the stream of Welsh invective coming from my right every time England got the ball. When at the final whistle, with England having lost 1-0 to severely damage their chances of getting to the finals, the man who had once hoped to represent me and my nation as prime minister punched the air and let out a whoop of delight; my sudden urge to vote Tory for the rest of my life now matched my desire never to be beaten by Wales at anything again.

Sport in general, and the Germans in particular, added to the petty parochialism of one Welshman, had combined to take the gloss off a memorable day. Perhaps the fact I hadn't been at home and able to play the Guru had done for the chances of an England equaliser. Germany, it seemed certain, were in the process of ruining everything again.

One thing about sport is you never know with absolute certainty what is going to happen next or when that unlikely redemption might be on its way. As we gathered in the pub once more eleven months later, we imagined the return game in Munich would be one of those things you felt you had to watch, but with what purpose, you weren't quite sure. The idea that England might get the win had very few apostles in our group. And it took the Germans all of six minutes to take the lead, a state of affairs which was met with an easy phlegmatism, as I recall. That was not the reaction eighty-four minutes later when the scoreline read 5-1 to England. Now OK, we hadn't won anything as a result, but as a catharsis for 1970, 1990, 1996 and the previous October for starters, this was spectacular. This is why we hope in the first place; the element of sport which keeps us going. Here was our reward for suffering the '90s. Returning to the bosom of a German-dominated company on the Monday morning simply added to the sweetness of the taste. What's more, this now meant we were going to push the unconquerable foe into second place. All that would be required were home wins against the might of Albania and Greece over the next two months. No problem.

But this was England. Even they could beat Albania, but a sunny October Oddfellows Arms afternoon watching England beat the Greeks to qualify transformed into one of the most excruciatingly frustrating afternoons the pub had yet hosted. As Germany drew their game, England now only needed a draw themselves, which gave us a safety net we weren't expecting to have to unfurl but was a reassurance, nonetheless. Even going behind in the first half didn't cause much concern; there was plenty of time for the goals required; once we had gone past an hour and not got a sniff of one, however, the atmosphere was getting decidedly more anxious, and I was genuinely annoyed with England that they were putting me through this feeling yet again. Relief all round when Sheringham eventually equalised – all good now. Utter disbelief fifty seconds later when we let them score again. This time, there was not the same serenity – this was going properly pear-shaped. So, with five minutes to go and the miracle of Munich about to be undone came my inevitable departure from the pub to my lounge. This time, five minutes brought no reward. Nor did three minutes of injury time. I'd told them – *don't* abuse the power; there's only so many times you can go to the well. Then David Beckham took *that* free kick – definitively the last chance – and in it sailed. Cue Beckhammania and the rather unnerving confirmation that my own powers still endured. This time, the physical manifestation of my relief took me at full speed past the door of the pub and down the hill screaming. The Guru lived on.

On to the summer of 2002 for one final story of redemption and the near fulfilment of the ambition not to be able to make those nine yards home. The World Cup was to be the last hurrah before we left the village. I'd finally been convinced that the lifestyle we were leading wasn't one that could be sustained without lasting consequences and that perhaps it was time to draw back a little from the frontline. It may seem a little unappreciative to present as a problem the idea of too much enjoyment, but it probably wasn't conducive to a serious professional career, especially as my ability to bounce back from overindulgence the following morning was diminishing with the passage of time. Some may consider this a fairly pathetic complaint, but there were occasions when I would return home on a summer Monday evening, glad to have made it through a day of work at three quarters capacity and even happier to see the inside of my cottage, having had the strength to politely decline the offer of refreshment from the mates sat in the sun on the benches in front of the pub. A knock on the door would often follow as I changed upstairs; I would go down and open the door to be greeted not by any human being but by a pint of Guinness sitting proudly on my front step.

One social occasion to which I needed no second invitation, however, was to join a large group of friends on Friday the 7th of June, once more just the nine yards from that very same step. This was to be the perfect storm of sporting revenge and resultant social excess and an appropriate way to bring down the curtain on four years of jollity. There are many ways to consume sport, but when it comes together as it did this day, it is something I'd take with me to my desert island.

The World Cup draw had put England up against Argentina in their second group game. Of course it had. This being Argentina, talk of revenge seemed more appropriate than redemption. If we weren't going to win the World Cup, winning this game was the minimum requirement. An evening game in Japan meant a twelve noon kick-off in Chinley. The early summer Friday had dawned to clear blue skies, and by mid-morning, the mercury was charging up the thermometer. I'd taken the necessary day's holiday and waved my wife off to work confident in the knowledge that there would be nobody around to talk good sense into me until at least the early evening. Pre-match drinks having been taken in the sun, England did their bit, the revenge complete when Beckham scored the winner. This was one professional connection I had with the day's events, Becks being an adidas ambassador; the other was the fact that Argentina were an adidas-sponsored team and I had in my possession for the occasion a shirt with which we now aimed to recreate in a Peak District village the scenes that no doubt would have followed a home team win in Buenos Aires. Attempting to set fire to the shirt whilst dancing around it in the street may not have strictly been an approved use of company property, but it wasn't an afternoon for sticking to the rules. Lord knows what we made them from because it took several varieties of lighter fluid in temperatures of ninety degrees to get the thing going.

The rest of the afternoon and evening disappeared into a sunny, cold lager-infested haze. Not having been an early adopter of the new iPod technology, the only route to the outdoor party tunes which were deemed necessary for the furthering of the day's pleasures was to wind down the windows on my car parked in front of the cottage and stick on every reggae, two-tone and SKA CD in my collection. I was past the point of assessing what this might do to the car's battery, and the afternoon proceeded unhindered.

I'm told that on her return home, my wife found me having made it ten yards before eventually bowing to the inevitable. In other words, I was asleep on the doormat. The following morning, I opened my eyes to a sight which never bodes well; on the floor on my side of the bed was a bottle of Dettol and a pair of Marigolds. Apparently, the evening concluded with me being asked what I was doing in the kitchen and, on answering, was asked, 'since when have we had a downstairs toilet?'. Possibly unable to face the physical challenge of getting up the stairs, I had dispensed of some of the day's fluid in our swing bin. It seemed an appropriate moment to consider the benefits of moving on. It was at least, according to my wife, the first time I'd ever put the lid down.

PART 3
KEEPING THE DREAM ALIVE
2003–2011

> 'Success is counted sweetest, by those who ne'er succeed
> To comprehend a nectar, requires the sorest need'
> EMILY DICKINSON, US POET C.1859

YOU ONLY GET WHAT YOU GIVE

Mary believes in fate; I'm more of a 'make your own luck' man, but I admit that three of my most life-changing happenings may give her the stronger argument. Meeting on a night on which she wasn't intending to go out, at a venue I only arrived at having been refused entry to four others in the previous hour; being gazumped on a house two weeks before we spotted, and ultimately bought, our house of the last twenty years and possibly the next twenty too; and landing the job of my dreams as the convoluted result of a new MD arriving at an opportune sporting moment. My counter is that we still played a role in determining the subsequent outcomes – I had to be good enough to be offered the job; we had to find the house and negotiate its purchase and I had to find the ability to stand up long enough at the end of a long, liquid day to make the necessary impression on my future wife.

This is why I don't go for the 'fate' line in sport. Some would believe in a certain sporting fate. Was it written that Bob Champion and Aldaniti should win the 1981 Grand National after life- and career-threatening issues? 'Their name's on the Cup' is something trotted out most years, but in fact, such predictions are rarely borne out. Luck and injustice certainly play a part in sport, but fate suggests some element of predetermination whereas luck, whilst still something outside one's control, is more about chance than a preordained inevitability. One thing sport has proven to me is that nothing is inevitable, which is the reason it remains compelling and keeps dangling hope before us in the face of the more likely, less palatable, outcomes.

Unfortunately, sport isn't *fair*, which, for those of us who invest so much emotional energy, can be hard to live with, as it is for those actually taking part, I'm sure. In 1986, Nigel Mansell had put himself through the wringer in search of an elusive first Formula One World Championship. I wasn't really a big Grand Prix fan, but in those days, the idea of a British champion was a big deal, and the guy deserved it. It had been one of the greatest seasons, and the final race was to be one of the most dramatic. Mansell needed to finish third or better to win his title, and with nineteen laps to go, that is the position he occupied comfortably, just needing to cruise the final few laps to his career pinnacle. At which point, his left rear tyre exploded at full speed. He may have said the right thing, that he was happy just to be alive, but I couldn't believe the poor guy's luck. Move on twenty-two years and Adelaide '86 lost its crown as the most exciting ever finish to a championship to Interlagos where, a year before, Lewis Hamilton had thrown away his chance of becoming champion. Now Hamilton entered the last race of 2008 needing to finish no lower than fifth to become the youngest champion in history. Running fifth with a lap to go, he was overtaken, and the title was lost. Except that it wasn't quite – on the last lap, almost the very last bend, the car ahead of his suddenly seemed to be going backwards. On the wrong tyres, it had slowed to a crawl, Hamilton nipped past and nicked the championship. Neither Mansell nor Hamilton had any control over their respective outcomes, but one got his title after two seasons and thirty-five races; the other missed out in his ninety-second race and had to wait for six years and his 184th to finally achieve his goal. Both were unforgettable pieces of sporting drama – one was cruel, the other extremely kind. Luck. But not fate.

Those two things which I find particularly difficult to take in defeat – injustice and not getting what you deserve – aren't quite the same thing. Injustice is unfair and involves being wronged; deserving something in sport is about getting a result you may feel you are worthy of and have earned by your efforts, sometimes over a period of time. Maradona's 'hand of God' was an injustice, but Jimmy White's world final defeats were not – you may say he was deserving of a win for everything he'd given us and how close he'd got over the years, but missing a black off its spot was not an injustice. Australians might argue that England's 'sliding doors' win at Edgbaston in 2005 was strictly unjust if you accept the last man Kasprowicz had his hand off the bat when he gloved it, but few would challenge the view that England deserved the result. United didn't deserve to win their Champions League final in 1999 based on their performance on the night, but they certainly deserved it for being clearly the best team in Europe that year.

You can argue all you like about different levels of injustice – a deliberate act of cheating, such as Maradona's, is surely worse than an incorrect decision from a referee. But is not walking in cricket when you know you've hit one the same or different? And if that's also cheating, then is there any difference between standing there when you've cracked one to first slip and not going when you've got the faintest edge to the keeper? In other words, does the level of barefaced cheek make any difference? I'm not sure I have my own answers to these questions – any sports fan will know that your position tends to be flexible depending on whether or not it's gone in your favour. When England were kept alive in the 2019 Cricket World Cup final as a result of the ball ricocheting freakishly off the back of Ben Stokes' bat to the boundary, it wasn't injustice as it was within the rules, but it sure as hell was luck. The injustice was subsequently discovered to be the umpires awarding the incorrect number of runs for the incident, but as England fans, what did we care? We had lost three finals before; we had been the best, most exciting, innovative team in the world for the last three years and we *deserved* the damn thing, even if not on the day and even if via a touch of injustice. What I do know is that both are hard to take – it's just, which is worse?

You might consider the obvious answer is that a clear injustice, especially a piece of cheating, leaves the worse taste in defeat, but that can depend on whether you feel you deserved to win and on your own personal point of view. Peter Shilton will go to his grave unable to forgive or forget Maradona; his teammate John Barnes has less of an issue, suggesting most players would do it and the English would have been less censorious if it had been he who had punched one in. So, you pay your money…

On reflection, I find my anxiety is most intense when England or Jimmy or United 'deserve' a success, regardless of injustice. It's why Jimmy's story hurt so much. To be fair, following England, this has rarely been much of a problem given the number of times they'd ever actually deserved to win anything up to this point. These probably amounted to two Germany semi-finals and possibly the odd Grand Slam. But it's precisely why 2003, 2005 and 2019 were to be moments of both ultimate joy and relief that this time there would be no 'what ifs' to suffer. We and England deserved these moments, but England being England, they weren't going to let us have it easy.

TOP OF THE WORLD

We moved up to our dream home on the hill in the summer of 2002, and as we ascended, so we moved further away from the nineties, and my sports-following fortunes continued to take a turn for the better and even, occasionally, the unprecedented. In my lifetime, England had never been world champions in a major sport, and the last time they won an Ashes series, I hadn't reached my twenties. Patience and forbearance were about to be rewarded, and although the words of Emily Dickinson at the start of this chapter put it better than I could, it's true that the wait, and the despondencies of the past, were to make success all the sweeter.

To recap, that perfect storm of elements which go to make up my most treasured of sporting victories, ideally the ultimate success, the one which can wear out the DVD for years afterwards, comes against one of your biggest rivals and after a period of sustained defeat. It should be one that is deserved and can be justified as such to others based on performance, often over a period of time. If that performance can be of a style which is deemed un-English, this is another tick. Another reminder: England sides have traditionally been scared to be brave, to risk losing in pursuit of a more glorious outcome. Interesting that the three successes which were to light up my life in the twenty-first century came off the back of a new approach: brave, attacking, damn the torpedoes. It's something the England football team might like to try again, having taken a stab at it under Gareth Southgate in 2018 and almost ended up with a World Cup. The next criterion is for it to be either close (see Rugby World Cup '03, Ashes '05 and Cricket World Cup '19) or so close to perfection that it delivers a thrashing, the extent of which goes past the point of any debate or excuses (see Ashes 2010–11). The problem with the 'close' stipulation is that, whilst it might improve the enjoyment of the DVD in due course, at the time, it is virtually unbearable. I'm aware there are some fans who live for these moments; they love a conclusion like the super over at Lord's – it's what they watch sport for. I admire and envy them because that isn't me. I love a conclusion like that as soon as I know for sure it ends well. Still, a knife-edge denouement does add to the perfect success. And whilst you would like that to be achieved under your own steam, the alternative scenario is equally appealing: the implosion of a supposedly more mentally robust opponent who blows it from a point of certain victory. This one can add comedy value and schadenfreude to your joy. Examples of this breed would include the dear old Aussies at Headingley 1981 and 2019. I can't recall a more amusing and gratifying sight than the face of Nathan Lyon as he bungled the run-out that could have ruined the greatest Test innings and run chase of all time. That's my next screensaver sorted.

A loudmouth on the opposing side that can be shut up by the victory, along with a set of smug, overly complacent opposition supporters and a partisan press, is another positive, and overcoming adversity, such as an official that doesn't seem keen on the idea of you prevailing, completes the satisfaction quotient. All these things are features of my ultimate sporting utopias. As you might imagine, such a list doesn't come together very often, but when it does, oh, the rapture.

The 2003 Rugby World Cup was set up nicely to meet a good percentage of these criteria, hence the desperation that England should now go ahead and win it. As we know, their recent record with regard to finishing off exciting performances with ultimate victory had not been unblemished. The four Grand Slam hiccups of the previous four years meant the faithful could be forgiven for seeing a 'what might have been' final or semi-final anticlimax coming that November. However, with me now in place on top of my own world domestically, they began to get themselves sorted out too and deliver the results their domination merited. The much-awaited and frequently mislaid Grand Slam arrived in some style in Dublin in March, and the northern hemisphere press flagged England amongst the favourites, to audible scoffing from media and public alike in New Zealand – where the idea of installing anybody but themselves as potential winners was incomprehensible, regardless of the fact they hadn't won the thing for sixteen years – and Australia, the true home of England-baiting and the hosts of the tournament. How many times had England won down under, they asked… how would they be able to do it in the giants' backyard? That view looked a little shakier after England went to Auckland in June and beat the All Blacks in their own country for the first time in thirty years and only the second time ever. The fact that they did so whilst playing with thirteen men for a chunk of the game only increased our amusement and their discomfort. When we followed this with a comfortable win against the Australians in Melbourne, the sneering lost a little of its lustre and the likes of that adorable wind-up merchant Malcolm Conn in *The Australian* had to default instead to the 'England are boring' backup plan. The Australians in particular, under the direction of cheerleader-in-chief David Campese and his acolytes in the Australian media, were always good at playing these mind games, casting England as miserable pragmatists, a grey team from a grey country whose tactics ruined the game, whether the pigeonholing had any real justification or not. To my frustration, England were equally good at falling for it. Twelve years earlier, this had probably won Australia the World Cup at England's expense. England had reached the final, using the forward power and penalty-kicking game which had won them a Grand Slam that spring. The Australians of Lynagh and Campese had joined them in the final via an undeniably more adventurous, if far from foolproof, style of play. The entire week leading up to the game resounded to the wailing of any Australian you cared to listen to (not many in my case but too many in England's) that England didn't deserve to win a World Cup playing this way. The reason for this was that Australia realised if England didn't change, they themselves would almost certainly lose. But change England did, taking the bait as naively as the mouse that thinks its luck's in when it spies the treat on a piece of wood. England threw the ball about, lost narrowly and their forward pack are still chuntering about it to this day. Now the southern hemisphere recalled the success of the tactic and, increasingly concerned about England's threat, decided to resurrect it, although with less validity this time. England could play any number of ways now – yes, their forwards were better than anyone's, so was their goal kicker, but the likes of Greenwood and Robinson in the backs were as dangerous as any All Black.

So it was that as England duly arrived in the final in Sydney, despite an utterly Englandesque wobble against Wales on the way, to play the hosts and old enemy in their own stadium, we had the same old cliches ringing in our ears. We couldn't lose to this lot now. We'd cruised past them in June; we deserved this trophy for being the best in the world for at least twelve months; and we'd lost two finals before, and this was our time. As I've said, the edge-of-the-seat finish only offers any pleasure after the event, so my desire in any England rugby game is that they get as far ahead as possible as quickly as possible to manage down the percentage chance of having to call an ambulance towards the end of the game. Instead, England set off in the opposite direction, conceding a soft try after five minutes, and the sinking feeling that the Aussies were going to do us again began to take hold. The sense of foreboding was not diminished by the stone-cold silence of my watching experience. This time, there was no pub – for a start, it was breakfast time (which had actually never stopped us before but anyway...) and, as with that United v Arsenal semi-final, this was just too important for me to watch in anyone else's company; the idea of either not being able to see properly or having to endure some would-be expert's pub commentary was a non-starter. So, there I sat, cross-legged, about three inches from my TV screen. Furthermore, my raging tonsillitis was reducing my patience levels with England and everything else and forcing me to internalise my angst rather than releasing it by screaming expletives at every knock-on or poor refereeing call.

England steadied and scored a glorious try. 14-5 up at half-time was breathing space if not safety. And then for the 'injustice' bit. The referee Andre Watson, as if personally committed to the idea of a more exciting finish than looked likely, or simply concerned that England might win, started giving penalties against England at the scrum to everyone's surprise. The fact that England clearly had the stronger and more skilled prop forwards, and that Watson as a South African should have been as well qualified as anyone to understand this, increased the sense of persecution and rising panic. What the hell was he up to? No matter, last minute and England were still 14-11 up despite Mr Watson's best efforts. So, he tried again and pinged England for a penalty in injury time. Over it went despite the Ziggy and, joy of joys, we now had extra time to suffer as well. And suffer we did, but we'd won it again with three minutes left at 17-14 up. Enter Mr Watson – scrum penalty, 17-17. It was beyond belief after 1990, 1996 and 1998 that we were about to have England's destiny handed over to a bloody penalty shoot-out. Somebody was playing a cruel joke. At which point, Martin Johnson and Jonny Wilkinson, bless them for eternity, took matters out of the referee's hands and into their own. The drop goal in the last minute needs no description here. Burning tonsils or not, I let out a monumental scream. So, this was what winning a World Cup felt like.

Many boxes were ticked; Australians having to attempt the role of magnanimous losers was nectar indeed. It would be churlish not to record that the following day's Aussie papers managed this with some dignity – apologies from *The Sydney Morning Herald* and from Malcolm Conn topping off England's coronation. The English Sunday papers were bought first thing and pored over for the rest of the week and beyond. I still have them. For once, no need for carping, no inquest required – the whole country united in pride, and those of us in the rugby community were in an even higher state of bliss. This feeling would never be beaten, of that I was sure…

Except that under two years later it was, in a sporting summer never to be forgotten. But there is no such thing as a sporting free lunch. A price would have to be paid. The Earl of Rochester might well have been foreseeing 2005 when he penned *The Imperfect Enjoyment* (but the perfect title…) including 'all this to love and rapture's due; must we not pay a debt to pleasure too?'.

Increasingly, there were some sporting contests I so acutely wanted England to win that I started to make trade-offs, with whom exactly

I'm not sure, but in some sort of celestial negotiation that I felt might increase the chances of the sporting gods delivering me the most sought-after prize. These attempts at paying my own debts to pleasure began with that 2003 Rugby World Cup. At the start of that year, I made my peace that in return for a victory in that competition, I would accept a thrashing in the Ashes in Australia at the turn of the year (duly achieved) and an early departure from the Cricket World Cup that followed (also completed without difficulty). Once they had got there in May, I was even debating offering up Southampton's FA Cup final as a sacrificial gift, before realising that this wasn't much of a bargaining chip, given our slim chance of beating Arsenal, so in a wise decision akin to turning down the chance of a desperate DRS review, I kept this one out of it and we lost anyway.

The ultimate success of this strategy first time around meant that by the time we got to 2005, I was willing to forego everything else in return for my first Ashes win in eighteen years. As England followers, we'd got used to living through one Ashes humiliation after another by employing a macabre, self-flagellating humour. It became something of a skill in which I think we took some perverse pride. But enough was enough. I was now right behind the words of Edmund Burke, 'there is a limit at which forbearance ceases to be a virtue'. Did we now dare once again to get drawn in by the faint signs of hope? Since beating South Africa in a Marcus Trescothick-inspired against-all-odds performance to draw their home series in 2003, and then narrowly losing in Sri Lanka, England had won fourteen out of eighteen Tests in a most un-England-like display of ruthless consistency, giving them series wins over New Zealand, West Indies, South Africa in South Africa and Bangladesh. Under the new stewardship of Michael Vaughan, they had built a side of real quality and just begun the assimilation of the final piece of the jigsaw: the X factor which was to be Kevin Pietersen. For once, there was a line-up which could run straight off your tongue as you closed your eyes at night. More than that, Vaughan was very clear that playing a generally inhibited, safety-first style of cricket had brought precious little success and therefore, win or lose, England's best chance was to change their spots. The US historian Henry Adams suggested that 'chaos often breeds life, when order breeds habit'. Well, we were in the habit of losing, and I had no issue if we were to be dished up a little chaos. Vaughan understood this and insisted his team be brave enough to stick to their approach regardless of any hiccups and suddenly, we were watching an England team playing an attacking, risk-embracing brand of the game. All of this had us daring to dream again as the '05 Ashes series headed up over the hill – this must be the best chance yet of at least competing with them, surely? Back to the principle of 'just desserts', all of this success of the last two years would seem wasted if we bowed the knee timidly to the Aussies. But surely, we wouldn't dare to keep attacking against possibly the greatest side in history? We all knew that one defeat and we would climb back behind our collective metaphorical sofas. So, when it didn't happen and England more than held their own, it made it even more imperative that it should end in victory, utterly, unbearably so. In short, therefore, this was the next sporting moment to become the one I wanted to win more than any other in my lifetime, and I was prepared to barter my way to it if I had to, with anything else that year becoming, if not meaningless, dispensable in pursuit of the greater good. Unfortunately, whoever it was with whom I made this pact took me at my word, and by May, I was beginning to have second thoughts. If I were asked to sketch out the worst possible six months to start a year of sport, it would have gone something like this one. Firstly, England had a dire Six Nations, losing to Wales, France and then Ireland by two points, one point and six points respectively. Manchester United won nothing, giving up the title to Chelsea and then losing a dire FA Cup final to an Arsenal team that barely deserved it, via a penalty shoot-out of course. After twenty-seven years, Saints were relegated on a desolate last day of the season. It had to happen sometime after the tightrope walk of the last dozen years, but had my pact with the devil been responsible for the fact it had happened now? Then, enjoying seeing a Liverpool side of a vintage you wouldn't expect to win European trophies being pummelled to 3-0 down at half-time in an unexpected Champions League final, I had to stomach one of the most spectacular comebacks in the competition's history as they recovered to 3-3 and won the bloody thing – yes, on penalties. And to top it off nicely, Jimmy White, who somehow had found the bravery to reach another world championship semi-final and have us hoping again that this might be the redemption year, was of course knocked out by Stephen Hendry. I couldn't think of much else I could have offered the gods, so I had done my bit, but the Ashes simply had to come home now, or I would have sold my soul for a year of complete disaster.

It is a matter of record that what followed was not only the greatest Test series in history but the most agonising to watch for any committed England follower. In fact, great though it might have been, on many occasions, I *couldn't* watch. This one also met all the criteria on my 'perfect storm' list: intense rivalry; an opponent that had beaten us out of sight for eighteen years, building up in the process a superiority complex in team, press and public alike, bordering on the smug; the opposition were also one of the two best sides in history, so any win would carry a true badge of honour; it was excruciatingly close in every game bar the first and was still in the balance on the last afternoon of a nine-week series on what Wisden called a 'surreal final day'. I had another adjective for it. England deserved to win it overall but looked as if they were going to throw it away at the last; it included some of the greatest individual performances I had witnessed, the finest of all coming on that final afternoon, and throughout, it was played in an attacking and courageous style that was more than worthy of success. So, to win this now would make it my utopia of all sporting moments; to lose it the total opposite. It truly felt on the afternoon of Monday the 12th of September, 2005 that England held my future happiness in the palms of their increasingly sweaty hands.

Many a whole book has been dedicated to the detail of the series, which is not my purpose here. What is relevant is that these nine weeks cemented in me a new form of sports consumption (or rather non-consumption) which has grown into a significant psychological issue ever since: the idea that not watching is actually a better tactic than watching, which, let's face it, rather undermines the point of following sport in the first place.

Being present at Lord's on the first day of the series simply intensified my almost insane desire that we should prevail at the end. Lord's for the first day of an Ashes series in blazing sunshine must be my ultimate sporting ticket. I don't remember how I had come by one, but it would forever be an 'I was there' moment. There was an electricity in the air I'd never felt at Lord's, and the clamour for seats apparently led to octogenarian fist fights in the pavilion as seats temporarily vacated for the frequent comfort breaks that both their time of life and the nervous atmosphere in the ground necessitated were instantly squatted in by those with the more controllable bladders. England then proceeded to bowl out, and perhaps even scare out, the Australians in a frenzy of partisan support with cheekbones and stumps being splintered at regular intervals. By tea, they were all out. Those who are familiar with the best way to enjoy Lord's will understand that after two sessions in the stands, it is an acceptable call to spend the post-tea to end-of-play period in the Harris Garden at the back of the pavilion, seeing how many tipsy City boys you can find to supply free Veuve Clicquot. Today in particular, this seemed the best way to get through England's first attempt of the summer at confronting Glenn McGrath. We pessimists recalled McGrath's liking for the Lord's slope which had brought him seventeen English wickets in his two previous Tests here. But surely now, with the momentum with them and the successes of the last eighteen months at their backs, England would press home the advantage. Being in a location in the ground from which you can't see but can hear the action is a strange sensation and one which brings its own unique sense of anxiety if things start to go wrong. When England are batting as they were now, what you want is a general calm silence punctuated by the odd smattering of applause so you can almost forget it is going on, at least until England are in safer waters. What causes the heart to leap and fall like a cardiovascular Dick Fosbury are the gasps of the crowd and the distant whoops of a converging fielding side indicating wickets falling. This is made worse by the time lag between these noises and the action appearing on the screen in the Garden. It gives you the hope that when the pictures come up you will somehow have been mistaken and someone dropped the catch. It is a forlorn hope as the confirmation of your worst fears is played out before your eyes. That evening, there was barely time for a pause between gulps of fizz before another of these audible daggers to the heart rang out, and by the time I could bring myself to peek back through the gap at the side of the pavilion to see the lumbering frame of Andrew Flintoff dragging itself up the steps, England were 21-5. By the time I took my leave and staggered down Lisson Grove towards my train, we had closed on 92-7 and another Ashes series was well underway. Ah well, we'd had some fun. I think the champagne temporarily dulled the pain of realisation that the dream was as far-fetched as ever it was. KP made his first statement over the next few days, but the only comfortable victory of the series went to Australia. Had England then thrown in the towel as meekly as expected, it would have been disappointing, but we had learnt how to live with this before and no doubt would be able to do so again. There would at least be no great tension. But when they didn't, thereafter it was a matter of a rapidly decreasing ability to remain in front of the action as four Tests of incredible quality and excitement played out.

In *Emma*, Jane Austen lamented, 'one has not great hopes from Birmingham'. Now I knew how she felt ahead of the second Test at Edgbaston. When, on the excruciating final morning, England looked to be handing the Ashes to Australia in a game they had already won several times, I settled for marching along the landing to and from the bathroom facilities but generally always returning to the scene of the unfolding horror. Sliding doors moment number one: Australia need four to win. Brett Lee hammers a full toss through the covers, and it's all done, except he had directly picked out the one man I'd forgotten was stationed on the boundary out there (it seemed to take the TV camera about half a lifetime to pan out far enough to reveal him). Moments later, we had won and phone calls to all and sundry were made in a gabbling burst of relief.

Third Test Old Trafford, final day, England bowling out Australia and going 2-1 up. Warne and Ponting dug in. Every ball that didn't take a wicket was its own little anticlimax, with me having convinced myself the next ball would be the one. Something guruesque was needed; time to walk the dog. This time, I was brave enough to keep in touch with TMS on the headphones and by the time I returned, mission accomplished – both Warne and Ponting were dismissed. Four overs to take one wicket. I was strong enough to get back in front of the telly, cursing myself with every wasted ball that I wasn't still out on the hill with Rocco, securing victory. Match drawn. That the public's imagination had been more than just caught by this point in the summer was evidenced by never-before-seen last-day queues at Old Trafford with the ten thousand locked out at 9am becoming the lead story on *News at Ten*. If I didn't know at that moment what the result would mean for the rest of the series, I was equally unaware of the influence these final-day scenes would have on my future life.

In the 'need to get what you deserve' stakes, the fourth Test in Manchester was right up there – it was revelatory to watch the confidence and excellence of England's all-round performance – their most accomplished of the series, making Australia follow on for the first time against anybody for fifteen years. Given a team following on had gone on to win only three times in 128 years, victory would surely be ours, and for the first time in a couple of decades, at least we weren't going to *lose* a series to Australia. The Sunday was part of the bank holiday weekend, so the opportunity was taken for one of the summer's last day-long sessions at the pub. This might help get me through the fact that, rather than dismiss Australia for a low enough total to avoid putting me through having to watch England bat again, we had now been set 129 to win that afternoon. When *Wisden* referred to the next couple of hours as 'another stomach-churning climax', they were sadly referring to the cricketing variety. This was certainly no time for any other sort. As Warne and Lee worked their way with increasing confidence through England's batting, that old impression of rabbits in headlights appeared before us again, and that had never ended well before. From a position of huge excitement, we were suddenly going to enter the evening with Australia carrying away the urn again. At which point, I could stand it no longer. To general bewilderment, I announced I was off for a walk. Given I was the biggest cricket nut in the place, there was incomprehension and derision. But these people had no idea how much this meant to me, and I couldn't stand their apparent ability to take it or leave it. This time, there was to be no radio and no stopping to chat to anyone who might give me an update. I marched up past the chippy and newsagent, round the corner and then did it all over again – four times. I was no less in hell than I would have been in front of the TV, but somehow, it seemed the only thing to do. If I'd been culpable in watching and not tried anything to change the tide, I would never have forgiven myself. By the time I returned, Matthew

Hoggard was playing one of the most unexpected and iconic cover drives in history, and a few moments later, England squeaked home. The next pint was one of the finest I'd ever tasted, but the relief and excitement couldn't completely mask an irritation that England had put me through this again. They weren't finished.

The final Test and another competitive effort, but this time the Aussies, knowing they had to win, had got some of their old cussedness back. Still, going into the last day, England just needed to bat it out for a draw for their greatest achievement of my lifetime after a summer of inspiration. England's then head coach, Duncan Fletcher, admitted in a recent television interview with Ian Ward that the morning of this final day was the only time in his entire playing or coaching career he had felt nervous, an emotion he had previously neither experienced nor been able to understand in his charges. Given Fletcher comes across as the sort of real-life-hardened southern African who, if stuck in a cage with three hungry lions, smeared in the blood of a recently slain antelope, would consider this unworthy of fuss and see it as just another interesting challenge; if he was unable to face his breakfast on this particular morning, what hope was there for the rest of us? Of course, I personally had a different way of dealing with what was ultimately to be the most cherished day in my sports-watching existence: to hide from it for as long as possible. This was a working Monday, and our open-plan office had a TV up on the wall which pumped out sport all day, usually another benefit of employment at a major sports company; this counted as research, after all. On this one day, however, it was a distinctly double-edged sword. Again, I was antagonised by the que sera sera attitude of everyone else in the office. For sure, there were cricket fans in there who wanted an England win, but none seemed to be as paralysed by fear as they should have been. Everything started surprisingly smoothly with few alarms at 67-1. But when Flintoff departed at 126-5, and with England undoubtedly about to undo nine weeks of supreme effort, the nightmare scenario loomed before me. Forget the deal, I wanted my FA Cup back. I'd had enough. There were too many people around me making uninformed and unfair cracks about England and cricket and a grating number of 'I told you so's. Fearing I might punch someone and destroy a career I rather enjoyed, I stood up and announced to the office that, working day or not, either the TV was turned off or I was off myself. Deemed far too melodramatic, the ultimatum was rejected out of hand, so into my car I jumped. I set off around Stockport and the M60 ring road and continued to lap it for the next two hours. My hand hovered over the radio button to my left that would, with one tap, have updated me on events, but I continued to reject its siren call. This was certainly a novel take on sports 'following'. The innocent intoxication and enjoyment of my early years had come to this. But it had worked before and must do so now. I pulled back into the car park and with a hitherto unsurpassed trepidation, pressed the radio button – there was certainly no way I was going to face other people before I knew the worst. Jonathan Agnew advised me that Kevin Pietersen had just reached his hundred and England were to all intents and purposes home and hosed. I sat in stunned silence for some moments – the dumbstruck sort of moments that up until now had meant trying to deal with an intense disappointment. Had this one really gone my way? Had the drive done its job? I wandered back into the office, trying to give off an air of insouciance, challenging any idea that I might have been predicting defeat before I left. The state of the match still gave me time to create one last doomsday picture in my head. Once the runs needed versus time left calculation had left Australia needing at least six runs an over, most commentators were suggesting the game was over. Were they mad? Had they ever watched England before? Even as the required rate ticked into double figures, I could still envisage some arena of damnation in which Matthew Hayden would come out and have a go at it. But in the end, the bad light came, Billy Bowden tipped off the bails with as much panache as he could muster and the greatest moment in my sports-watching life was upon me.

It's only when it's all done that such things can be properly enjoyed. The actor Hugh Grant was interviewed for *Test Match Special's* 'View from the Boundary' at the point of greatest hope and foreboding – tea on that last day – and was in rather an understandable mess. I only heard this recently, hibernating as I was in my silent car at the time, but it once more reassured me I wasn't alone in my conflicting feelings. Said Hugh, 'I'm suffering more than anyone in the whole ground – I can barely speak.

It's hell. You spend all this money on tickets [really, Hugh?] and then put yourself through two days of unmitigated misery'. Which pretty much encapsulates the greater part of my sports-watching life. Now though, I headed home, knowing I had an evening of wall-to-wall highlights to watch and rewatch and papers to pick up the following day. The first phone call was a gushing one to Dad, who had been brave enough to resist the call of his own car and watch all afternoon. He had been through this fifty-two years ago and would understand. I headed off to the Lakes to share the first bottle of champagne that evening and to toast a combination of ourselves and Michael Vaughan. The DVD now sits alongside Ronnie's 147 and, more recently, the Ben Stokes summer of 2019, as the most worn-out piece of nostalgia in my collection. Not only can I not quite believe what happened in that series as I watch back the quality and the drama, but I still find myself genuinely nervous about the outcome. That was the Ashes 2005. The culmination of, and reward for, a lifetime of hope.

IS IT A DREAM?

'I felt if I could spend my life in football that would be a relief because I want to understand how the world works, but I don't want to spend my life in it'
ARSENE WENGER

As if that series hadn't given me enough, back to Old Trafford and the third Test… and more of what I call good fortune and my wife would call fate. Moving to adidas had certainly been a good call, but where I was now ten years on, although paying the bills effectively, was not everything I had envisaged it being. Selecting and allocating exclusive shoe models to a bunch of ungrateful national retail buyers in the middle of a price war was neither rewarding, nor what I considered the best use of my time at the world's best sports brand. I cast envious glances at those involved more directly in the real world of sport in our sports marketing team. To keep myself going, I maintained a fanciful notion that we might yet get into cricket and had even floated a couple of proposals for how this might be done under my own direction. These were treated with a weary disdain by those above me. The idea that a football-led brand based in Germany, where the majority of strategic decisions were made, would divert time, effort and resources into a sport of which they were barely aware was laughable. But you've got to have a dream…

Just prior to Christmas 2004, our UK business welcomed a new MD. As a Belgian who had joined from adidas France, it was unlikely he was going to arrive with Andrew Strauss and Ashley Giles as his top priority. Sure enough, his initial vision was not one that seemed likely to create the opportunity I was looking for. However, he was still willing to approach his new position with an open mind and consider what might be most influential in a market about which he still had things to learn. And didn't it just so happen that his first summer in England was that of 2005? On witnessing television scenes from just down the road in Manchester of queues around the stadium, and a sport which was on the front as well as the back pages of the newspapers and often the lead item on the national news, he decided that this was something with which we needed to be associated. I for one wasn't about to explain that this was the most remarkable one-off cricketing summer in history, that the sport was more the preserve of the middle class forty-something and above than our target fourteen- to nineteen-year-olds and that successfully commercialising any involvement in it was nigh-on impossible. The instruction came down – go and sign the England cricket team. The guy who did these deals for the company seemed to be playing his own game of Happy Families – someone called *Robin Money* responsible for negotiating contracts wasn't something you could make up. He couldn't have been more astonished or sceptical but did as he was bid. Now my previous badgering of my own boss didn't look like quite such a waste of time. He could see what was coming. Summoned to see him, I was advised we now had a position to manage the England cricket team alongside the individual players we would need, our British and Irish Lions rugby partnership and our rugby players. He sensed this might be my dream job. He sensed correctly. He called it my two-year holiday, giving the lie to the rather low level of importance he assigned to this role. It mattered not a jot to me. Twelve years later, I was still doing it. I had finally arrived at the place to which my seven-year-old self could barely have dared to aspire. Just like England before me, as was soon indeed to be living the dream.

The 2007 Rugby World Cup coincided with my arrival in my new role and, given a trip to watch England could now justifiably be expensed, it would have seemed remiss not to accept the suggestion from my cousin and his mate that we should travel to Marseille to take in the quarter-finals. Tickets to England's game in the Stade Velodrome that Saturday were duly acquired, and we were all set up to take in that game live and follow it with an evening in the square of the old port watching France play the All Blacks. This seemed a perfect plan but for my perennial pessimism, which saw both games as shoo-ins for the southern hemisphere, much to the ennui of my travelling companions. England were some way from the 2003 model and had muddled their way this far unconvincingly. My confident prediction was that we would have to sit through Australian revenge. The open stadium in ninety-degree heat was an invitation to cook ourselves on one of those beer-ahead-of-sun-cream days, as England actually increased my discomfort by staying closer to the Aussies than anticipated. Andrew Sheridan was waging a one-man assault on their forwards, and into the second half, England had the lead. Now, of course, the relatively manageable level of tension I'd felt when steeling myself for defeat was transferred up to defcon one as the prospect of a victory came closer. When Jonny put England two points ahead with twenty minutes to go and took me to the top of my distress scale, I remembered the success of the 2005 Ashes tactics in such moments of high drama – namely that I should get the hell out of there. Only this time, I couldn't just switch off the TV or get into my car, and I'd travelled the length of France to watch this game. It was therefore with some incredulity that my mates digested my announcement that I was off, as I got up from my seat and marched to the exit steps. I reminded them of my prediction that Stirling Mortlock would ruin everything with a controversial monster penalty in the last minute and that I for one couldn't stand the sight of celebrating Australians when this came to pass. So, for the final quarter of the game, I wandered around under the concourse trying not to process the various muffled crowd reactions coming from above me. If I felt a little guilty about this self-conscious behaviour, I felt more justified when I passed the only other person who appeared to be in the same state – both with our heads in our hands, we exchanged the knowing glances of brothers bonded by a common fear. My fellow sufferer, I realised, was none other than former England prop and professional hard nut Gareth Chilcott. If this was good enough for Coochie, it was good enough for me. My second validation for my actions came when, with minutes remaining, Mortlock did indeed get his penalty to win the game. The fact he missed it was neither here nor there – I knew full well I didn't want to see it. Our trip back to the city took place in a state of hazy euphoria resulting from an effective cocktail of unexpected victory, Kronenbourg 1664 (the infamous 'pint of numbers') and sunstroke, whereupon we entered an evening of reconciliation and comradeship with our Celtic brothers as we milled around the bars together and, above all, the French themselves as they dumped out the All Blacks. A night outside a French bistro watching and celebrating with the locals as they beat the favourites, our own unexpected semi-final place already in the bag, is one of my more cherished sporting memories – what I can remember of it. Perhaps only topped by a Sunday brunch at the same establishment the following morning, sat in the sun with the English papers somebody had managed to purloin, watching Aussies and New Zealanders, newly arrived from eleven thousand miles away for what they considered their inevitable three knockout games, trying to sell tickets and find the next plane home. *Quel dommage.*

I wasn't going to complain about my new job – responsibility for England cricket for a start meant numerous meetings at Lord's, the library for a time almost becoming a second office. Sitting in leather armchairs sipping coffee and looking out over a frosted virgin winter outfield, I wondered quite how I had landed here. Dad would scarcely believe it. As regards sport, however, it did have an additional consequence – as in those early days in Oldham, my normal allegiances were once again supplemented by a professional anxiety. An expensive partnership with one Kevin Pietersen, for example, meant that my fortunes were now wedded to his – which was to prove anything but an armchair ride. Every match, every individual performance, now once more had an extra dimension for me. The cricket and rugby future tours schedules hadn't escaped my notice as I took up my post. 2009 had a particular appeal: England cricket in Barbados in February, British & Irish Lions tour to South Africa in June and England cricket in Cape Town over the New Year. These were now all essential working trips, of course. There will be no recounting here of the detail of such trips on the 'stays on tour' principle. Suffice to say that any rugby tour which involves seven weeks in close proximity to Welsh forward Andy Powell will have its moments. The relevance is simply my bafflement at being a part of such sporting tours without having any of the necessary sporting skills to be so. I would have to check myself on a regular basis – how had the seven-year-old excited just to catch a glimpse of the back of Mick Channon's head in The Dell car park ended up here? I suppose I came away with two major insights amidst the surreal nature of the whole experience. Firstly, at the Harbour Lights club in Barbados, I was taught that although part of the party, I wasn't going to be mistaken by anybody for a person of note within the England cricket entourage. My conversation loosened by a number of free rum punches, I got chatting to a couple of young ladies who it transpired were newly qualified young English doctors. Believing my raconteur act had them rapt, I asked if they were here to see the cricket. 'No', came the reply, 'we've flown nine hours to see if we can sleep with two England cricketers'. (They actually mentioned two names specifically as their bullseye targets, but my discretion fortunately gets the better of me here.) I have no evidence as to the success or otherwise of their project, but the fact that was the end of the conversation and the last I saw of them was a timely reminder that I was no international sportsman and it might be time to get back in my box. Perhaps I should've worked a bit harder on my off spin after all.

My second education on tour was rather more relevant to my narrative. To say that being part of a Lions tour for seven weeks was unexpected and unearned would be rather an understatement. What it gave me was a different type of desire for sporting victory than I had experienced before, a different reason. No longer just a fan, I was part of something, even if a rather insignificant part. I saw what everyone – from the players and coaches to the security guards and the cook – put into a common goal which would bond them forever, a culmination of at least two years effort.

I knew how bad I usually felt in defeat, but to come away without victory from this sort of commitment was something else. It was to give me one of my most chilling moments in sport and my most memorable within a week. Having lost a first Test they might have won had they played their rugby of the last fifteen minutes any earlier, everything was focused on the second two weeks later. Lose that and a chasm of anticlimax awaited. Saturday the 27th of June at Loftus Versfeld may go down as one of the greatest rugby Tests of all time, but it sits very near the top of my list of worst sporting denouements, and in the annals of undeserved defeats, it is also right up there. Losing both first choice props and both centres – the critical Brian O'Driscoll and Jamie Roberts – during a game being played on the edge of violence and illegality, the Lions ('we' as far as I was now concerned) still dominated and led until the last six minutes. It took the video referee to award the dubious try which put South Africa ahead. Still 'we' wouldn't give in – an equalising penalty from Stephen Jones, who I'd come to know as one of the nicest blokes ever to take to a rugby field and therefore entitled to such a moment, was taking the series at least to the final game. The penalty the Lions gave away with the last play of the game made my heart drop, but it wasn't critical, surely. It was inside the Lions own half, after all. But this was at altitude, thin air and all, and Morne Steyn kicked the most monumental, numbing penalty I would ever see. I had dodged a bullet with Mortlock – not this time. As my Lions collapsed, looking more like soldiers at the Somme than a rugby team, I sat in the stand utterly stunned. Vaguely aware of the celebrating swathes of green and gold South Africans, I was back looking at those Anderlecht fans thirty-two years before, with that same empty feeling. This situation was not improved by the fact I was hosting guests in the VIP seats occupied by the majority of South Africa's rugby dignitaries, which meant no swearing, no loud denunciations of cheating bastards, no way at all to release the anger and dejection inside. I have never, before or since, been so instantly dumbstruck by a sporting moment, physically unable to move from my seat for five minutes, which felt like five hours. Commiserations from South Africans all around, including commendable admissions that the Lions were the deserving winners, made things worse, not better. I was emotionally invested in this in a way I only realised at that moment.

The week that followed, for most of the group, moved from drinking to forget, veering from the despondent to the defiant, to an increased determination to leave the universally loved head coach with a win to take away with him. And redemption there was to be with a win the following weekend. That week gave me two last indelible memories to take away. For all the talk of VIP boxes, this had a been working tour, in my case meaning some proper, hands-on sports marketing. This included responsibility for finding a business in each city we visited which could, within forty-eight hours, turn around a full set of embellished match-day kit, with match numbers, personalised embroidery and the rest. Every single thing on a Lions tour has to be done to the very highest of standards, and nobody wants to be the one to drop the ball, so this was a job which put me under some pressure; I wasn't going to be sad to pick up the last set of kit and leave the responsibility behind. That week, we were back in Johannesburg where the tour had begun, so I already knew where the kit was going. That was the good news. Less reassuring was that this meant a return to the site of my first kit drop seven weeks before. I was aware that Joburg is not necessarily the place for an unworldly Englishman to be alone in possession of valuable commodities. Here I was at 8am, standing on a back street in full Lions' regalia, guarding two huge bags of kit and waiting extremely nervously for the iron grille on the factory doors to be drawn back to allow me in. It had not passed me by that there would have been a good reason for such security. It is no embellishment to this story to recount glancing to each end of the street to see several large figures looking me up and down. My departure from the factory that day remains one of my more important 'breathe out' moments. Now I had to return but had by now used my initiative to befriend the adidas salesman in the city, a Zulu named Bob. Bob was fazed by nothing in his hometown and his driving me door to door made this return trip a far more comfortable one, with one rather sobering twist. As we departed the factory for the last time and turned the corner, I had my first first-hand encounter with a Johannesburg homicide, which, as Bob explained to me in an offhand manner, would have been the result of a shopkeeper defending his premises by shooting someone stone dead. This put things like second Test defeats into sharp relief, and if it had happened on my first visit rather than my second, what the Lions would've been wearing for the rest of the tour is anyone's guess. At that moment, I couldn't believe anything on the tour would live with me any longer than this. I was wrong. I had spent the first two Tests entertaining business guests in the best hospitality the stadia had to offer, which is not, I guess, something to complain about. But on this Saturday night, I was to sit alongside various other members of the backroom team with the non-playing squad members close to pitchside. I was wondering quite what the hell I was doing there – a question which was still in need of an answer as the final whistle blew on the Lions victory and every one of us was hauled over the wall and onto the pitch. My guilt at feeling an utter fraud was genuine but not sufficient for me to reject the opportunity of joining a Lions lap of honour and dressing room beers at the end of an incredible journey. Seven weeks had played out in microcosm every element within the kaleidoscope of my sporting journey, from questioning why I bothered, to thanking my lucky stars that I did, and they had allowed me to live out a dream never to be forgotten.

So, by and large, I couldn't fault the twenty-first century to date in its efforts to compensate me for the miserable end to its predecessor. True, Saints were now languishing in the third tier for the first time in my life, but somehow, I'd made my peace with that as it actually made Saturday results time far less traumatic, but England had given me two utopia moments and my own personal relationship with sport was taking me to unimaginable places in my life. Those England triumphs had followed one of my two templates for the perfect sporting success but had been tightrope walks, and I'd come to accept my country's teams were never going to deliver me victory in comfort. There is something about English sporting performance which gives you the sense that these moments are as special as they are because if they come along at all, it will be as oases in a desert of disappointment, as though periods of sustained success might ruin us. These were for Australia and Germany, not for us. Which made England's cricket from 2010 to 2011 all the more unusual. It is one thing to beat the Australians against the odds in some nail-biting uber-performance. To outplay them in their own backyard to the point where they are holding their own wide-ranging inquest of the type previously copyrighted by England was something different. But the winter of 2010–11 gave us exactly that in-between two more familiar 5-0 whitewashes. For once, the trepidation of waking on a cold December morning to check BBC Sport or turn on *TMS* was yielding not the expected news of disaster but barely believable results, which meant the highlights packages couldn't come round fast enough. Despite England's dominance, thanks to their one old-school performance of the tour in Perth, we went into the iconic Boxing Day Melbourne Test still at 1-1. This was going to be the pivotal game, and by now, you will be able to anticipate my prediction. Spending Christmas night at the in-laws', I woke on Boxing Day with portable radio and headphones on my pillow next to me, as befitting the seven-year-old I still felt inside. When these relayed to me that in the last over of the day, England were 157 for no wicket, I was very happy to take that, assuming a Melbourne storm had washed out the first half of the day. When it transpired that England had bowled out Australia for ninety-eight and were now fifty-nine ahead, Christmas might as well have begun all over again. The game was won by an innings, by *an innings in Australia* on their most cherished of all cricketing days. The next game was won by an innings too. Then, England beat India 4-0 and became the number one Test team in the world. Had the pied piper, who had started looking after this sporting partnership professionally, done it again? Now I had arrived on the scene, were we going to be the new Australia? Were we as England fans even comfortable with that? We had grown quite fond of our ability to handle humiliation with masochistic comedy; there is something in the make-up of the England fan which enjoys this almost as much as celebrating victory. Nobody else can do it like us. As it turned out, we needn't have worried. The balance of nature was soon to be restored.

PART 4
GET THE BALANCE RIGHT
2012–2021

FOREVER YOUNG

> 'When I was a little boy, I had but a little wit,
> 'Tis a long time ago, and I have no more yet;
> Nor ever ever shall, until that I die,
> For the longer I live the more fool am I'
> AESOP, 1684

For the last ten years, I've attempted to recalibrate my relationship with sport. I'm now fifty-three years old, and with all that's gone before in my sports-watching existence, I'm seeking some sort of perspective, a better balance to the relationship, my emotional reaction to it and the part it plays in my life. I'd like to be able to take the learnings and a splash of self-awareness to up the sangfroid and decrease the angst and enjoy it as the entertainment it's supposed to be. However, for all the good intentions, I fear I still have a way to go. C.S. Lewis said that when he grew up, he put away childish things. Well, I didn't. There hasn't really been anything in my life to make me do so. For a start, I'm sure not having children has allowed me to retain a high level of immaturity when it comes to sport. I know many good people who believe I'm missing out, but it's not a life choice I've ever regretted as I've always known caring for my dog is about as much responsibility as I can handle. My very genuine assertion that I love my dog more than I could any human offspring was not one which found great favour with my grandchild-obsessed mother but still... a stream of four letter words every time Fred gives the ball away or Owen Farrell grubber kicks to the opposition full back with a two-man overlap outside him, which is a lot of swearing across eighty or ninety minutes, is hardly rule one in Dr Spock's good parenting guide. And anyway, if I couldn't watch Botham bat for fear of his getting out, imagine how I'd feel about watching my own child in action. 'Did you see my four, Dad?'. 'No, I couldn't bear to watch'. It's not an exchange likely to encourage a well-adjusted adolescent. I see what friends have to do with their kids (or *want to do*, to be fair), including taking them to watch their favourite teams and having to teach them about triumph and disaster, fairness and equanimity, when many of them don't believe a word of it themselves, and I just think I couldn't do it, certainly not if I had to demonstrate by example. My own dad tried it for a while, but once I'd grown up, he regressed to being more bitter and twisted than I was. So, the fact I didn't have to deal with this, never mind the issue of having to take kids to *play* sport when there was something important on the television, left me free to carry on behaving like a twelve-year-old myself and prolonged the process of trying to reach the right balance, which became longer and less straightforward than it might have been.

In seeking a better balance or some form of remission, first you have to acknowledge that you have a problem. In 2016, Jonathan Liew wrote a piece in *The Daily Telegraph* about getting things back into perspective and asking whether getting so angry about sport is really justifiable. He talked of a 'subconscious resolution to feel something positive again' with regard to sport and to 'reclaim sport for its original purpose: to redeem and revive, to enlighten and enliven and make us believe in the impossible'. This is what I'm now striving for, Jonathan. Call it an obsession, an illness, an addiction, whatever you like, but in trying to readjust so that sport plays a more sensible role in the autumn of my life, I have to accept that this is where I'm starting. For my whole system of long-term memory and my recollections of specific moments in time not just to be based on, but to be reliant upon, the memory of often pretty insignificant sporting events is something of a concern and can start to irritate those around you, which is why, by and large, I aim to keep this in my own head. When I put a book down to go to sleep, in the absence of a bookmark, I employ a method of remembering the page number I've reached through the medium of iconic (or to others, completely forgettable) individual cricket scores. Page 215 – David Gower, Edgbaston, 1985; page 110 –

Viv Richards, Antigua 1986; even page seventy – Ted Dexter, Lord's 1963. *War and Peace* might even call for an 8-15, Stuart Broad, Trent Bridge 2015. And so on. In the admittedly unlikely event that someone in the street should shout out the name 'Desmond Haynes!', I would automatically say (to myself ideally), '180, West Indies v England, Lord's 1980'. Who wouldn't? Or is this strange behaviour for a man well into the second half of his existence?

The obsession starts to determine your mental state. It becomes so important because you are aware of the direct impact it will have on your future happiness. In the short-term, that means what happens with your weekend. Do you or don't you watch *Match of the Day?* Will you be able to buy the Sunday papers to enjoy the afterglow of victory, or are you going to have to ignore them? Can you turn the radio on over the next few days, or will it have to be the iPod? What sort of grief are you going to get on Monday at work or, these days, instantly via a tumble of smart-arsed WhatsApp messages? In the end, this isn't just about the match itself, if at all, it's the aftermath and potential long-term effects, and this is why the truly afflicted can't really get over things. The greater the joy or pain, the longer term the impact will be. It is the chasm that you know the long-term nature of certain disappointments will drop you into which is the greatest fear. That 2005 Ashes DVD has sustained me through numerous disappointments, and I continue to reach for it at the worst moments sixteen years on. What would my crutch have been if Shane Warne had caught KP? It doesn't bear thinking about. To this day, I've managed to switch off the TV or radio, just in time, every time I sense a replay of Aguero's goal in 2012 on the way. Turin 1990, Jimmy White 1994, England v Wales rugby, Wembley 1999. These things still cast a cloud and have to be avoided to this day unless I feel the need for a little self-harm. Of course, I'd like to think this inappropriate level of supposed emotional impact is starting to weaken a little as I begin my second century – that is certainly my intention – but just for now, I wouldn't bet so much as my Saints programme collection on it. I may be fifty-three but, as I say, I'm still seven years old on the inside.

JOY & PAIN

'A sip is the most that mortals are permitted from any goblet of delight'
BRANDON ALCOTT, US TRANSCENDENTALIST, 1877

My attempts to find this balance in the last decade have been rather hampered by the inconsistency of those I follow and my continued inability to suffer it with a smile. The England cricket team must by now be the most infuriating sporting institution in history, even if it remains my most beloved. Not the best; not the worst; the most infuriating. I know they don't do this on purpose, but can it be coincidence that Mr Alcott made his statement above in the same year as the very first Ashes Test? Did he know something? Ashes win 2013, thrashed 2014/15, win 2015, thrashed 2016/17, draw 2019 in a series which was the perfect summation of their vicissitudes. I've just finished following them through a series in India (in truth, following is inaccurate – I'd long since turned off the television by the fourth Test). How do you score 578 runs in your first innings and another 1009 in the next seven put together? Is this the nature of sport or the nature of England? But English cricket wasn't alone in bouncing me through highs and lows for ten years solid. Joy and pain came from every direction. Three weeks in 2012 are a perfect illustration, culminating in another of the moments which would make my top five all-time sporting miseries.

Manchester United had been my rock through the bad times, and there was a real concern that if they were to be usurped at any point, a vital support mechanism would disappear. By 2012, that process was well underway with the reincarnation of rivals City from comical music hall turn to a serious global force underwritten by Arabian oil. For United to hand over their dominance at all would be bad enough, to do so to City, unimaginable. This had to be resisted at all costs, and for now, I retained at least a little faith in Sir Alex to repel the challengers as he'd done for me so many times before. This is why a close title race with City in 2011–12 was so draining and important. In the meantime, Southampton's descent to the lower reaches of the football league and near financial oblivion had been turning around, and that same spring of 2012 saw them on the brink of promotion back to the Premier League. Another three weeks of emotional sporting turmoil began.

With six games left, United held an eight-point lead and, based on recent history, were as good as champions. Despite some hiccups, come the 22nd of April, we knew a win at home to Everton would keep them five points clear with three to play, albeit one of them away at City. It was one of the strangest, most deflating games I'd ever witness. The stadium may have been racked with tension, as was our pub, but at 4-2 ahead with seven minutes left, United started playing as if they had not a care in the world. When Patrice Evra hit a post when it would've been far easier to make it five and put us all out of our misery, he didn't seem unduly bothered and neither did my mates. Of course, I saw it differently – could they not see the obvious danger in this moment? Sure enough, a dominant United conceded one, and then an equaliser, to a stunned silence inside Old Trafford and the Oddfellows Arms alike. Hmmm.

Six days on, I was on my own in front of the TV as Saints needed to beat Coventry that morning to be sure of promotion. This was one I certainly couldn't share. Even my wife and dog were out, leaving me the solitude I required. It was altogether a different day – that rare beast of a vital game that becomes a cakewalk to happiness. Despite a nervy start, after twenty minutes, Saints were two up. The BBC report later suggested victory was all but assured with seventy minutes still to play – yeah right. I was trying to calculate just how far ahead Saints would need to be before I could start to believe. As it happened, by sixty-three minutes in, it was 4-0 and even I was struggling to conjure up the scenario in which disaster could strike. Just don't let them score one…

So rare is it that I have ever been able to watch twenty-seven minutes of an event so important to me in such a state of calm that the next half hour was one of the finest I can remember, basking in success and relaxation whilst toasting my team with a full bottle of Veuve. I just needed United to complete a perfect spring.

Forty-eight hours later, United lost at City who went top on goal difference with two to play. United had shot it. Both duly won their penultimate games, so come the 13th of May, United had to better City's result to save me and the title from a fate worse than death: my own version of the 'Arab Spring'. In fact, by this point, the tension had gone – City were at home to season-long strugglers QPR and had dropped only two points at home all season. No hope worth getting uptight about then. And yet, over the next two hours, hope would rise and then disappear in one of the most famous days in football's history and one of the bitterest in mine. United's game was heading for a 1-0 win; City, somehow, were 2-1 down. Suddenly, the hope was unbearable once more, and with fifteen minutes to go, I defaulted to my, by now familiar, tactic in such situations, this time opting for the 'take the dog for a walk' approach. I wasn't alone in struggling with the moment. At the Etihad, *The Times'* Matt Dickinson recalled:

'There was a woman who looked to be about eight months pregnant right in front of the press box, and she was clutching her stomach, going, "I can't bear this anymore." She wasn't talking about the pregnancy. As a journalist you're sort of loving the story, but at the same time you can't help but think, these poor people.'

Indeed. But the sympathy was to prove misplaced. Once I felt I had given it enough time to be all over and I could turn back on to confirm United's title, I hadn't reckoned on the first image being United players sat on the pitch heads in hands and the first sound being that of Martin Tyler talking about the most unbelievable finish ever seen. I froze for a moment before letting it sink in that United had lost out, not quite sure how or why. Now, I would have been disappointed but able to live with this if City had won 3-0, but learning that in injury time they still needed two goals and then got them was impossible to take in. Sky and Tyler may have been rejoicing in a moment that they knew would live forever; personally, I at least had the consolation that I'd been wise enough not to witness it in real time. It hasn't been easy, but to this day, I've still not seen that final goal in its entirety. Every time (and it's a lot) I sense it is about to appear in a promo or be replayed on the radio, there is a desperate dive for the off button. Occasionally, I've been a fraction too late but always got rid before Tyler can reach his crescendo. Perhaps watching this now should be my first step in the resetting of my relationship with sport – watch the bloody thing and accept the drama. I'll think about it. Nine years on, I fear it's still too raw. As a postscript to that day, the football writer Henry Winter told his own story of being at the City game, which resonated with me:

> 'I saw a father leave with his son at 2-1 because the son simply couldn't handle it. There was a look on the father's face, like, all the things you pass on to your kids, good principles, maybe a few quid and the furniture, but also you pass along your allegiance to a team. And there was a look on this kid's face like, my friends at school are supporting United, and Dad's given me City. This is the worst moment of my life. Dad looked shell-shocked. What have I done? Social services is going to be called for the torture I've put him through.'

There, in one paragraph, is the best encapsulation I can find of the various things that made up my own youthful experience with Dad: the allegiance, the father and son shared experience, the desolation of crushing disappointment and the inequitable nature of it all. And the fact that, sometimes, you just can't watch.

LOOK AWAY

'A man who fears suffering is already suffering from what he fears'
MICHEL DE MONTAIGNE, 1580

This not watching is the issue which most frustrates my friends, and I'd most like to address if I can amend my approach. I'm perfectly clear that it makes a mockery of having an interest in sport because, if it's not entertainment, what is it – what's the point? But the fact remains; if the process of watching something that matters to you more than it should is not actually enjoyable, why put yourself through it? There is a piece of research published by psychology professors at the University of San Diego which suggests that people generally enjoy a story more when they know the outcome in advance. Applying this to sport makes sense to me, or at least it did at around this time. It challenges the regular trotting out of the line that the attraction of watching sport is its unpredictability. Says who? Enjoyment is not really in watching the victory as it unfolds, which is rarely any fun at all, it is in the aftermath. The aftermath of a win offers relief, a ridiculous sense of personal achievement, the reverse being true when it goes wrong and I switch off the TV, ignore radio, papers, everything. But there is a definite linear graph I could plot, using time on one axis and enjoyment on the other, for any contest which is remotely close. There is a level of allegiance at which sport's unpredictability becomes a significant problem rather than a virtue, and to my mind, sport's climactic moments have been manufactured by man to be as unbearable as possible: penalty shoot-outs, golden goals, super overs, tennis's tiebreaks, and the list goes on. Why should I give them the satisfaction? Not watching until the result is known is ultimately a selfish approach – it could be argued it isn't supporting at all. But I still understand, even espouse, the argument for the joy of highlights, which are what my sporting viewing is now based around. A Saints victory will mean watching *Match of the Day*; a defeat means I ignore it. It's also why an Ashes series in Australia is more manageable than one at home. You go to bed and are excused the live passage of the game. You get up and check the score. A good day means you tune in as soon as possible to Sky's highlights. The more common occurrence of a disastrous one and you simply ignore it and pretend it never happened.

I might sit down to watch England bat, but if they lose a couple of quick wickets, I turn off and occasionally check the score on the app. Once the next partnership is past a hundred, I may deign to go back. This, I guess, is an attempt to turn my sports watching into something which only shows me the good things and not the bad. Firstly, that's weakness on my part and secondly, it's impractical. Given that the statistical history of following those that I do proves there will be more bad than good, this is going to severely restrict my viewing. I've thought about asking Sky and

BT for rebates when renegotiating my subscriptions for the percentage of action I pay for but can't actually watch, but I accept this may be a long shot.

In my youth, it was not often my frugal family invested in a new car. If and when we did, however, it was a sure thing that my dear make-do-and-mend mother would immediately cover the smart new seats with some form of home-made cover, quite often old curtain material or similar. The fact that this made the new car look horrendous didn't bother her – the comfort and justification lay in the fact that when we came to sell the car, the seats would look immaculate. In other words, don't enjoy it for what it is, rather do anything you can to protect against disappointment. I used to rail against such behaviour, but I guess this is not a bad metaphor for not watching my favourites until I am safe in the bosom of the highlights.

As previously recounted, this probably began in earnest with the 2005 Ashes. Being sent to watch the last five minutes at home to change the outcome was one thing, and even at the gates of hell that were the last few minutes of the Rugby World Cup final, I had managed to stay with it. But once, in 2005, the genie was out of the bottle, to be followed by the departure from the terraces in Marseille, the thing began to snowball. The 2008 Champions League final had United against Chelsea and was too close to call. As normal time dragged on, it became clear this was an extra-time job and, a pound to a penny, another fifteen minutes of penalty shoot-out agony. Well, I wasn't having it. The moment it went to extra time, I promised myself I would be off for a bath, calculating thirty minutes' play, plus a bit of injury time, ten minutes faffing about before penalties and those fifteen minutes of turmoil, so give myself an hour and I should be safe. Even then, I couldn't bring myself to unpause the TV to be greeted by potentially scarring scenes with no time to compose myself. Instead, I went to Ceefax (yes, Ceefax), clicked on page 301 and saw the headline: 'United win cup in shoot-out drama'. Elation and relief coursed through me with the knowledge that I could now unfreeze and enjoy every second of the conclusion myself without the slightest tension. Now, what's wrong with that? What's more, when I saw the sequence of penalties on the teletext and the see-saw nature of the shoot-out, I was more convinced than ever this had been the right course. I would've hated every second. But in convincing myself that this approach had saved me from a quite horrible experience and instead allowed me the pleasure of certainty, not to mention the possibility that this had been a good luck charm, I laid the foundations for it to become a staple of the future. It has now developed to a point where, although Southampton are my team, and back in the day I would walk over hot coals to see them on the TV, today I will rarely watch them in any live game unless there is effectively nothing on it.

TIME, CLOCK OF THE HEART

Three other factors have been known to encourage this increasing tendency to look away: that in reality, the anticipation and aftermath of an event are usually much more pleasurable than the thing itself; that the level of enjoyment of any viewing is in inverse proportion to the time left in a game; and that from the early years of being a lucky charm for my favourites, through my phase as the Guru of Chinley, I now sense that no outcome will be positive if I am watching it happen.

Firstly, anticipation. I have reached a point where I can enjoy the anticipation of a big event – although why I am anticipating something which I am pretty sure I won't be able to watch, I'm not sure – and can maximise that enjoyment by watching back, following the reaction and so on, if I heard it was a positive result. There is something called 'the dopamine hypothesis'. It suggests that dopamine – a chemical neurotransmitter which affects how we feel pleasure – is not released with pleasure itself but with the anticipation of it. If a new album is being released by your favourite artist, you look forward to its arrival. It might actually be a disappointment when you get to hear it – we're looking forward to a pleasure which ultimately might instead be a disappointment. In other words, it's better to travel than to arrive. I sat down recently to watch Manchester United play Sheffield United. Stuck in lockdown, I'd been looking forward to having something as an alternative to my wife's Wednesday selection of *Love It or List It*. The previous night, I'd decided not to watch Saints play Arsenal as I feared it might be too painful (good call, lost 3-1). But United were on a roll and at home to the club cut adrift at the bottom of the league. Safe enough and better than Phil and Kirstie, surely? It wasn't entertaining; it wasn't enjoyable; it was full of frustration and irritation, and it sent me to bed tense and annoyed, so it can't be said to have filled any positive purpose at all. But would I be watching them again come Saturday? I really feared so. This is the issue. I watch things which I anticipate being enjoyable – at least I look forward to them – but more often than not, the experience itself leaves me in this state.

Oddly enough, given my inability to watch Southampton, United I watch every time, probably because I anticipate the odds of them winning are greater. This changes, however, if there are fifteen minutes to go and they're hanging on. This introduces the issue of the time-enjoyment continuum, which is the next reason watching can become unbearable. Enjoyment is in inverse proportion to the time left in the game for things to change. Anticipation pre-game sits high on the enjoyment axis; the first half is manageable as there is still time to address any reverse; the second half gradually becomes a nightmare, regardless of whether you're ahead, level or behind. The ebbing of time plays on the pessimist's sense of impending disappointment. The level of angst is increased should your team be showing what appears to be a disregard to the reality that they are running out of time. The percentage of my time watching the game as opposed to the clock in the corner now decreases, at which point the decision has to be made as to whether you have the courage to stay with it or take that bath/drive/dog walk. Unless England or Saints or United are so ridiculously far ahead that even I can't envisage a problem, I think I can say I have never truly enjoyed the second half of anything... a pint of Guinness excepted.

Finally, the third justification for turning off the TV: the perceived possibility of jinxing the whole thing. Back to Neville Cardus and his agony watching Reggie Spooner. I have every sympathy as I always felt that if I watched, Botham would get out next ball or Ronnie would miss. The statistical reality is that Botham had a batting average of under forty and O'Sullivan can't clear the table every time, so the chances are my jinx theory is going to be endorsed by events more often than not. Is that a reason not to watch the greatest sportsmen in action? Over the years, that initial Midas touch which produced a stream of unlikely successes and memorable moments just by my presence, had started to wane. I went from this to a point of what seemed to me to be total 'Jonahism'. Gradually, it got to a point where great things occasionally happened if I wasn't in contact with them but never if I decided to be part of the spectacle. It may have been some sort of divine payback for taking things too seriously, who knows? A couple of seasons ago, Saints were in serious need of points and had one of those 'free hit' games away at Manchester City where a point would have been as good as six. I turned on Jeff Stelling, expecting the news of the thrashing, to find the score at 1-1. Then I realised I'd got my calculations wrong, and the match was still happening. It was, however, six minutes into injury time. Without me, Saints had done the job. Sure enough, Jeff suddenly cut back to the match reporter with his best 'not going to tell you' lead-in, announcing a dramatic late goal. City had scored with the last kick, and I had got involved just thirty seconds earlier. My fault.

Ronnie O'Sullivan had been cruising through the rounds of the 2020 World Snooker and included one of his more spectacular frames on the way. I, of course, had seen little of it, fearing the impact I might have. But at 5-2 up in his semi-final against Mark Selby, I told myself it was a farce not to watch my favourite player as he was beating all before him, so *sod the theory*, I thought, *let's enjoy a bit of it*. So, I watched him lose five frames in a row, mainly from winning positions. I turned off again – at the end of the session, he'd won seven frames in the match, and I'd seen precisely none of them. I vowed not to return, and of course, he won the next day. It even happens when the result is less immediately traumatic, just irritating; this very morning as I was writing this, I turned on England's Test match in Sri Lanka. This was a Covid-period match of little import as Test matches go, but nonetheless… switching on after a long dog walk, I saw England were 300 plus for 3 – miles ahead – and in the middle of a 160-run stand, during which there had been barely a hint of trouble. I thought I'd settle in for an hour. Second ball – wicket. I switched off and got back to writing, reassured that my paranoia had been proven valid once again.

This pattern of joy and pain – the continual oscillation between success and failure – has endured throughout the last ten years and therefore done nothing to discourage my belief in the safety of highlights. It's been the encapsulation of a life of sport in a few years. Manchester United pre-Fergie's departure and the 2012 nightmare versus the recovery of the title a year later, followed by the more frequent frustrations of the post-Ferguson years to come; Ashes wins followed by Ashes thrashings, England's nadir performance against Iceland in Euro 2016 followed by the nation-inspiring 2018 World Cup – a run to a first semi-final for twenty-eight years followed by surely the biggest missed opportunity in their history; England rugby's horrendous home World Cup in 2015, made worse for me by the fact I had access to the best tickets in the house to host guests throughout the tournament, set against possibly their greatest single performance I'd ever seen in beating the All Blacks in the 2019 semi-final, only to not turn up and be battered to defeat in the final. Even Liverpool's pain, and consequently my relief, in 2018 in losing the title and Champions League final, followed by their elation, and my mortification, in winning them both over the next two years. How I was supposed to have maintained any equilibrium watching all this live, I've no idea. If sport is going to continue to be so utterly unreliable, and I'm sure it is, the temptation, or rather the need, to look away and take refuge in the joy of highlights still feels like the best option.

DON'T STOP BELIEVING

'Faith may be defined briefly as an illogical belief in the occurrence of the improbable'
H.L. MENCKEN, US WRITER

I accept that, until this point, I have been a glass half-empty follower, 'the worst cricket supporter in the world', but even I will admit there are things that happen in sport which forever keep us coming back, which reignite the hope versus the expectation and will guide me into a sea of positivity in my new start. If we stop believing in sport's power to deliver the occasional miracle, we are rejecting its ability to intoxicate and inspire us. The last few years have given me a combination of sufficient miracles and performances of such enthralling perfection that my devotion remains. Fortunately, I am still able to appreciate the genius that gave me the Wimbledon final of 2008 between Nadal and Federer, just edging out Borg and McEnroe 1980 for me as the ultimate demonstration of how the sport of tennis can be played. Such quality borders on the unbelievable and can justifiably be deemed to be a form of art. Unbelievable plays an important part – the sporting miracle is still a powerful draw. 2012 gave me the Miracle of Medinah, and another highlights programme unlikely ever to leave my Sky Plus box, when Europe won the Ryder Cup in the US in the greatest comeback in that competition's long history. Golf rarely gets me fixated, but this was compelling theatre. Then there was the Leicester City Premier League win in 2016, which may now live forever as the most trotted out example of a sporting 'miracle'.

Just occasionally, so occasionally that you have to treasure it forever, the unbelievable genius performance dovetails with the unbelievable outcome, in a contest that truly matters to you. As an end point to this story, the summer of 2019 feels appropriate. To paraphrase Sir Alex, 'sport… bloody hell'.

England's cricketing summer of 2019 brings everything together nicely. It included a long-sought World Cup victory – hard earned over several years but ultimately achieved in a fashion only England seem to want to inflict on their supporters; there was an individual performance of such breathtaking brilliance it shall live forever in the annals of sport, and it all became so unbearable to watch that it produced two further moments when I simply had to depart the scene. Above all, it veered from hope, through pessimism to resignation and unimagined elation in a way that reaffirmed what sport can do and encapsulated my journey from innocence, through purgatory to redemption. From the humiliation of the 2015 Cricket World Cup, and a sense that after three losing finals, England might never again have the chance to win the thing, Andrew Strauss, Trevor Bayliss and Eoin Morgan set out to change matters for us. Going back to the notion that sports fans want to see attack and entertainment just as much as trophies, and also the evidence that this approach is the only one which has ever delivered England significant success whilst I've been alive, at long last, England joined everyone else in the twenty-first century version of white ball cricket. Rather than disrespecting the format, with a continued air of condescension, putting us through fifty over innings of Alastair Cook and Jonathan Trott nurdling totals in the middle two hundreds, the penny dropped that everyone else was playing a different game. From a fan's perspective, we weren't only not very good, but we were the focus of every other nation's ridicule. This was one new dawn that was actually going to endure. Within a year, we were watching England break batting records all over the place and beat everyone in sight. Before and including that 2015 World Cup, England's one-day team had achieved a score of 350-plus twice in their history and never got anywhere near four hundred; in the four years afterwards, they made 350 or more fourteen times and over four hundred four times. This included the two highest scores in history and the unfettered joy of 481-6 against none other than those nice Australians. I say unfettered, but the fact I finished that innings feeling slightly disappointed that the five hundred that had looked on at one stage hadn't been reached (and of course, my concern Australia might get them…) indicated how far we'd come.

So, by the time the 2019 World Cup began in England, we were not only clear favourites but commonly acknowledged as the best ODI side in the world over the previous few years. This, of course, doesn't sit well with either me or England. I was perfectly aware that for all their ability and un-England-like aggression and confidence, England were still capable of delivering us moments of catastrophe when it really mattered. Defending nineteen off the last over to win the 2016 T20 World Cup as they deserved to, Ben Stokes' first four balls went for twenty-four and left our superhero a broken man. I didn't feel a whole lot better myself if it's any consolation to him. So it was with a trepidation that falling at the last was an almost inbuilt England propensity that I took in the start of the tournament. On the downside for my stress levels, this whole thing was going to be drawn out over seven weeks. I would've been perfectly happy had it been crammed into one. Let's get the damn thing over with. On the plus side, the format meant you could have the odd disaster and still recover (a safety net which of course England were to test to the full), so the jeopardy levels didn't kick in for a while. However, good old England, having barely lost a game for the last few years, managed to lose three in three weeks to take us to that jeopardy point well before was anticipated. From now on, we had to win four on the trot against the very best if we were to be world champions and had four opportunities to blow it all without that net. History told me at least one of these had to go wrong. From hope, I had already reached the point of resignation to prepare myself for the worst. Then they beat India as they had to, seemingly nervelessly (them, not me), and beat New Zealand to reach the semi-finals. Here was the next problem: the opponents were Australia. I would categorically have preferred to have gone out two games previously than to lose to this lot now. The positive supporters recalled the 481 from the year before; I was more inclined of course to reference the comfortable defeat from sixteen days before, in which the Aussies hadn't broken sweat and our batsmen had barely been able to lay a bat on a bloke we'd never heard of called Behrendorff, or the more obvious threat of Mitchell Starc. And yet, something odd happened – from the moment Australia were 14-3, England broke the habit of all our lifetimes and cleared a nasty-looking hurdle with the utmost serenity. I was still looking for the potential bumps in the road, but at 124-0 chasing 224, even I felt I might enjoy a small part of the day.

Which all left a final at Lord's and the craziest day in cricket history. Sparing the full detail, it is still mind-boggling enough to require a recap, if only to reassure myself it ever really happened. England put everyone through it in their inimitable way. They'd as good as lost the game, recovered it, lost it again and then somehow won it by tying it – twice. As sporting finishes go, I'd seen tight ones, but this was the most ridiculous, preposterous and agonising ever. England 86-4 and losing; Stokes and Buttler add 110 – England on top; more wickets – England seven down, need twenty-four off twelve, almost lost; Ben Stokes the only hope; Stokes caught on the boundary… but Boult's foot steps just over the rope and it's six; England run two, but as the throw comes in, the ball ricochets off Stokes' bat to the boundary – as the BBC had it, 'one of the most insane things in cricket history'. England right back in it. Two needed off the last ball – anybody's guess. Full toss – surely, it'll go out of the ground, but it's patted for one. Super over. After seven weeks, twelve balls would decide it. This was made no easier for me by the fact my most recent signing to adidas was a certain Jofra Archer who was now going to bowl that over. I both knew Jofra and really liked the guy. Brave enough to take this on in his first ever tournament for England, surely, he wasn't going to be broken by a disaster? He didn't deserve that, and neither did I. Personally, I was concerned for both of us. Professionally, six balls could make this the best piece of business in my recent history. All on the line. Sixteen to win, first ball called wide. Great comeback, then the most gobsmacking, stomach-churning six sailed into the stands. All over, lost again. How Jof ever recovered from that, I don't know. I'm still in recovery today. And then two needed off the last, the run-out, a tie, a count back and England win on boundaries hit. 'By the barest of margins', screamed the astonishingly magnanimous New Zealander Ian Smith on commentary. Of course. This was England.

Obviously, all this was far, far too much for me. Away on holiday in the South of France, perhaps things would have been better all-round if we had still been in the seventies and I had to wait to try and find a paper forty-eight hours later. However, there was the BBC and Sky on my iPad, so I couldn't claim a lack of technology as my excuse for looking away. I certainly couldn't watch – I had long since decided this was to be a day on the sun lounger with highlights to follow if needed. I can assure you that wasn't because I didn't care – the precise opposite. But as things got out of hand at the end, I couldn't help myself looking more often than was good for my health at the live score update and running text on the BBC app. This somehow seems easier than the real thing, though I've no idea why. Much like that 2008 Champions League final shoot-out, I felt my approach was fully justified by what transpired – not least that I hadn't jinxed it but also that I would never have survived it. Now there was just the elation and two days of holiday dedicated to highlights, radio, podcasts and everything else I could lay my hands on. Now, I have good mates who not only watched it but were actually present at Lord's. They honestly said they really enjoyed it. *Enjoyed* it. Whilst I believe them, I cannot understand them – they are made very differently to me. The view that this was what they watched sport for, and they loved every minute.

But absolutely no chance, I'm afraid. A footnote is that my strategy has been slightly undermined by the remarkable fact, I assume due to rights arguments and such, that there is no DVD available of the tournament to play and replay. Thank heavens for Sky Plus and the review programme now tucked away for as long as my Sky box is alive. At least this was over now – in all my sporting years, this was one of the very pinnacles, but I wasn't sure I could go through anything like it again. A shame really, as six weeks later, it got worse.

Ben Stokes had contributed significantly to one miracle that day at Lord's; now he created another literally off his own bat, playing an innings which might be best remembered through Samuel Johnson's words 'all argument is against it, but all belief is for it'. Experience and expectation versus hope again. In my world of sporting trade-offs, I admit I had been willing to offer up the Ashes series just this once for that World Cup. However, now that was in the bag and the sight of Australian Test cricketers was back in front of me, that bargain was null and void.

After the euphoria of Lord's, the Ashes series was proving a more sobering experience. Unable to deal with their previous nemesis Steve Smith, England had been thrashed in the first Test in Birmingham. If England couldn't win at their banker venue of Edgbaston, it didn't bode well for contests anywhere else. When they did finally manage to get through a Test without a Smith century, restricting him to a mere ninety-two at Lord's, the rain got in the way and, arriving at Leeds, defeat would mean the Ashes were gone inside three Tests, evoking the 1990s in a depressing way. In attempting to prevent this outcome, being bowled out for sixty-seven in their first innings was probably not the best approach. Cue the public outrage, wailing and gnashing of teeth. For me, it simply meant switching off and attempting to ignore as much of the rest of the game as possible, trying unsuccessfully to convince myself that I was past caring. Having been set twenty-nine more runs than they had ever scored to win a Test in their history, and with a draw out of the equation, at least there was time to accept this was not to be our series and to think of what other sport I might feign interest in to soften the reality. Of course, they then dangled the carrot of hope before us again at 163-4. This was a better fist than expected, although not remotely enough to suggest a miracle. And at 286-9, seventy-three away from their target, I was comfortably able to switch off not just the TV but the app and return to the more controllable pleasure of a glass or two of rosé in the garden on a hot summer's afternoon, reassuring myself once again that there were more things to life than sport. And yet. An hour or so later, I flicked the app back on primarily to check the Premier League scores, whilst also confirming the defeat. I was stopped in my tracks halfway to the fridge and the next bottle of Cotes de Provence by a headline telling me Stokes' heroics had taken England to the most epic Ashes win in history. The TV couldn't go on fast enough. That was the end of the garden and the sun, if not the rosé. And, like the World Cup final before it, when I was taken through the sequence of events, my avoidance of the real-time action could be argued to have saved a couple of years of my life. The sixes which just cleared the boundary fielder by an inch; the tough but nonetheless dropped catch which would've ended the match; the truly incredible botched run-out which simply added to the pleasure of the whole thing; and the blowing of a review which cost Australia the game when Stokes was plumb lbw and the beautiful Joel Wilson decided on 'not out'. Luck yes, fate no. I saw the delirious crowds in the stand, and every time I watched the last hour back, I picked up on different faces and emotions as it all unfolded. I realised that thousands of people had been through it all ball by ball and apparently enjoyed the experience – was I envious? Possibly. Was I incredulous? Absolutely.

In six weeks, I'd been granted the most remarkable finish to a cricket match, possibly any sporting event in history, and the greatest Test innings of all time, resulting in a record-breaking and miraculous victory, and all of these things had quite unfathomably gone the right way. OK, I hadn't been able to bring myself to watch either of them, but that doesn't diminish their place in my heart. Perhaps this was someone testing me again, a tempting call to rejoin the throng. *Come on, we won't let you down – just look at what you're missing. Stop being so damn pathetic about this thing called sport and give it the credit it deserves.* It would be a fair argument. Perhaps I could make this my watershed after all. Certainly, had I known then that it would be my last sport as I knew it for a very long time, it might have given me pause for serious thought.

HOLE IN MY LIFE

Perhaps it was some sort of karma that I was left with a summer like that of 2019 to sustain me through the desert we were all about to enter. A desert which would give me that chance to recalibrate the true value of sport in my life. At the advent of spring 2020, life was progressing in a manner we all took for granted. For me, that meant having just been to Twickenham to see England beat Wales with that sense of relief rather than complete enjoyment which is my lot. At full-time, my phone told me Southampton had been beaten at home by the might of Newcastle and so came the frustration that the day, the whole weekend, had been undermined. My self-pity might have been somewhat reduced if it had been apparent that this was the last time I was going to go through such emotions for the foreseeable future and that I was about to discover how much I would miss them. The following week, something called Covid-19 upped its game and we were stunned by a smack in the face which was the real-life equivalent of the cartoon frying pan. When we woke up, our world was a different place; our reality had changed; and sport had disappeared.

The various lockdowns and life changes that followed put sport into perspective in more ways than one. The situation reminded us that sport was not truly a matter of life and death and that there were times when it needed to be relegated in our list of priorities. But as the absence went on, it also revealed the flip side: that maybe sport was more important than it was sometimes given credit for. Yes, getting too high or low about Saints' result at Swansea was still hard to justify to a non-believer by rational argument, but the part sport plays for so many in the fabric of their lives was laid bare. As people talked of increased incidences of loneliness and mental health struggles, sport for once was dismissed by few as irrelevant, its absence being a cause and its reappearance for many an important part of the solution. It certainly made me reassess.

I shared the view of *TalkSport's* Andy Jacobs, who would probably not take umbrage with a suggestion he might on occasion fit into my glass half-empty club and that he certainly shares a tendency to take the vagaries of his sporting favourites to heart. He suggested in the early stages of lockdown that he was missing football but not missing the stress that ruined his weekends and made him miserable, although he then qualified this with the equally recognisable sense that actually, he was missing that too as it was what made the highs what they are. Joseph Heller said, 'the idea of always being blissfully at peace, always being blissfully happy, is scary'. But I had the same initial feeling that the absence of the critical part of the season, when every game mattered that much more, was a welcome release. This was aided by another consequence of this hole – nostalgia was back and, as you may by now be aware, I need no great encouragement to wallow in it. Given my enjoyment of watching when I already know the result, the endless stream of replayed classics and the emergence of a genre of high-quality sporting documentaries, on which the sports channels now had to fall back in an attempt to make something of the rights they had so expensively purchased, was manna from heaven for a while. All the entertainment, none of the stress. In the early years, rain at the cricket would mean the BBC simply shifting to racing, John Craven's *Newsround* or a still image of a girl holding a teddy bear. Since Rupert Murdoch usurped Lord Reith, this affront no longer happens. If you are going to have a year-round, twenty-four-hour-a-day cricket-only channel, you're going to see the Ashes in the 1980s replayed rather a lot. But the issue of no live sport was more of a challenge to the sports news channels, and there was a certain sadistic amusement in watching the anchors trying to fill twenty-four hours of airtime. This was a tough enough assignment when sport was happening but bordering on impossible now it wasn't. The dead eyes behind which panic was barely concealed and the fixed smiles of presenters still trying manfully to sustain the concept of 'news' were more akin to a 1970's communist bloc state news channel. I wouldn't have been surprised had the camera panned out to reveal that someone had them at gunpoint. The always rather bumptious yellow banner employed with great gravitas for 'Breaking News' and once reserved for a Cristiano Ronaldo transfer or one of Tiger Woods' wilder indiscretions was now reduced to announcing that National League 2 might be considering postponing the season and the reaction of Barrow's chairman to this bombshell.

The feeling of course did not last and the emptiness of sport without the 'now' became apparent. It's another thing the pandemic helped to reassess – it may be safer and more comfortable to watch in full knowledge of the outcome, but one of the fundamentals of live sport is that we *never* know exactly what is going to happen and that's a *virtue*, not a threat. For all the grief live sport could cause, I knew now how much I missed it. The efforts to get some sport back on as soon as possible was a clear indicator that even the government understood its real social value and that lockdowns without it would be even tougher to endure. Football addicts and cricket lovers alike are unlikely to be sated for long by repeats of *The Repair Shop*. We were therefore thankful for the mercies that were the return of football (although it has maybe taught us once and for all that a game to follow every single night is not the dream scenario it may once have seemed), the World Snooker Championship and a summer Test series. Thankful but still ultimately unsatisfied. The lessons kept coming that sport without fans is akin to tonic without Tanqueray Ten, a pale offering lacking the all-important flavour and failing to deliver the sense of intoxication desired. What was the point in beating Liverpool if you couldn't see the faces of their fans behind the goal as the winner went in? So, our passion, rather than being something to be derided, was revealed as an essential component of the whole thing in the first place. I start to feel a little less guilty about the level of my obsession. And sport out of context upsets my 'rhythm of life'. Great to have Ronnie winning the World Snooker, but in August? Worst of all was a summer season without a summer season. No Lord's, Wimbledon, Henley, Ascot; no Veuve, Pimms and Guinness; no nipping for a pint in The Hanover when the Test at The Oval was going the wrong way. We might as well have been on the moon. Of all the things to have to do without – holidays, the pub on Sundays, loo roll thanks to the stricken British public's morbid fear of the worst of all possible consequences of a global pandemic – for me, the loss of the sporting summer was the worst. The cricket was on the T.V but not a true part of our summer, confirming that it isn't just the game that matters; it's everything which goes around it.

So, might 2020 be a watershed for us English sport obsessives? As and when it returns, hopefully as it was before, will I love it more for itself, for its just being there? Will the immaturity of the nerves, the pain of defeats, be something I can place in a better context? Will there be less angst, hatred and schadenfreude involved and more appreciation? I hope so. But I fear that will last about as long as it takes for Steve Smith to score his next hundred. Before 2020, I did feel a creeping sense of guilt over how much I let sport be the barometer of my life's enjoyment. But Covid did allow me some leeway. My emotional state is genuinely directly linked to the fortunes of my sporting favourites and least favourites. It remains a sad admission in many ways, but there it is. This strange time did show the importance of sport to a vast number of people and that it should not be dismissed as inconsequential. When it was taken away, some of us may have been surprised, some of us less so, by the hole it left. For many, melodramatic as it may sound, we had it reconfirmed that it is still the soundtrack to our lives.

LUCKY MAN

'I measure my own life by the experiences I have, the friendships I make and the memories I cherish'
DAVID NASH, CRICKETER, BUSINESSMAN AND FRIEND, 2021

So, at the end, where does this leave me? What have I learnt? I think it is this: that following sport can be painful and as such seems like a strange choice around which to build your life. The journalist and Crystal Palace fan Jon Pienaar considers following his team 'a steady ache interspersed with huge explosions of euphoria'. Although Millwall Den would probably tell him it serves him right for following Palace, does that not sound a bit like life to you? Sport *does* reflect life, perhaps making those parallels I keep returning to between sporting fortunes and my own stages of life less bizarre than they at first seemed. In life, pleasure and pain go together, and if I'm not willing to make an emotional investment in anything for worry it may bring disappointment, I'm not really living. I think I need to adopt the stance of a certain American brothel keeper called Polly Adler (she didn't say it to me in person, you understand) that 'I am one of those people who just can't help getting a kick out of life –

even when it's a kick in the teeth'. And far better I get my sadness from Saints losing at home to Brighton than from things that truly matter and that bring real grief. I think, ultimately, the way to stay sane is to have this self-awareness; I may never be able to completely shed, or even tone down as much as I might like, my overemotional commitment which seeps into other areas of my life, but as long as I can *recognise* it's out of proportion, I ought to be OK and shouldn't worry too much about its influence. Personally, I'm happier to be stuck with an overcommitment to something that ultimately can't cause anyone else much harm than the sort of overzealous religious conviction that just might. Certainly, others may be affected briefly by my related mood swings, but I don't force my views or prejudices on them. There will always be a search for the right level of perspective, notwithstanding that the perspective tends to change with results and will continue to do so. The journalist and broadcaster Louis Theroux, as part of his documentary on the golden age of snooker and its wealth of characters, suggested the sport's popularity back then was because 'we interpret the world through stories. Success, failure, comeuppances, reversals, comebacks'. Which is why devoting emotional energy to the following of sport is perhaps not so strange after all.

Another love of my life is the great outdoors, the wonder of nature and the Lake District in particular. This is partly because it was my parents, who both rest there atop a favourite hill, who inculcated this passion, and I know how much pleasure they got from my inheritance of their understanding of the value of such a place and partly simply because I see it as my own little piece of heaven. Sat at the side of Stonethwaite Beck in the twilight on an early summer's evening with a Mount Gay rum in my camping mug, I don't care one bit about the Champions League final result that night or anything else sport-related for that matter. If I could sit there forever, I would therefore be cured. That is my perspective. To use the words of English playwright Joseph Addison, 'the important question is not, what will yield to a man a few scattered pleasures, but what will render his life happy on the whole amount'. I don't even have to be there to find its solace. After a significant (supposedly) sporting disappointment, I can reach for one of Alfred Wainwright's *Pictorial Guides*, sit in an armchair and take myself back there to memories of the place and take a more sanguine view of the sporting disaster which has just befallen me. I see the guides as a work of true genius and their author's perspective on life something of an inspiration and an aspiration. He once wrote that the top of his favourite fell, one which I have frequented many times, is a wonderful cure for a man trying to get a persistent worry out of his mind. For 'persistent worry' in my case read troubling defeat. In 1991, I missed my first live FA Cup final since that first one seventeen years previously where I started this journey. The only reason good enough for this was to accept a friend's suggestion that we instead head for the top of a Borrowdale mountain. At the end of a perfect day, the realisation that passing on the football was not only not a problem but had left me with a sense of satisfaction and a very happy day was liberating and reassuring in equal measure.

The narrative originally envisaged for this book was heavily weighted towards the 'pain and suffering' the sports addict, and particularly the English sports follower, has to endure and to ask why on earth we bother with it. But now, in writing it, I've moved my metaphorical goalposts. I now see the bigger picture and take heart from the words of the Scottish poet (so he should know) Thomas Campbell: 'one moment may with bliss repay unnumbered hours of pain'.

For every 5-0 Ashes whitewash defeat there's been a Stokes 2019, an Edgbaston 2005, a Botham 1981; for every World T20 or Champions Trophy final disaster there's a 2019 World Cup; for every Tim Henman semi-final defeat there's eventually an Andy Murray (not full compensation, admittedly); for every Kiawah Island there's a Miracle of Medinah; for every Jimmy White defeat from the jaws of victory there'll be a Ronnie O'Sullivan 147; for every Man Utd 6-1 home defeat by City there's a Barcelona '99; for every England semi-final penalty shoot-out defeat there's eventually… not sure, but whatever it is will surely arrive one day. This is the nature of sport, and it has now dawned on me why I am hooked on it after all. Ultimately, the trade-off between the good times and bad is worth it. It just doesn't feel like that most of the time whilst you are living it. This is why we have video recorders, Sky Plus, catch-up TV, YouTube and podcasts coming out of our ears, so we can rewatch the good times and artificially tip the balance in their favour to remind ourselves why we go through it all. The good is just so good that we want more and more of it – it's part of the human condition. What is the light worth without the shade? In his *Desert Island Discs* interview, Arsene Wenger, having acknowledged he wasn't the world's greatest loser, was asked how he coped when a dream didn't come true. I found his answer instructive:

> 'You are guided by dreams your whole life – some come true; some don't come true. You have to accept that you never win everything you want to win, and you have to live with what you didn't achieve. Most important is to be faithful to what matters to you and to find a meaning in your life and walk on the road of your life with the values that are important to you. After that, you win; you lose; it's part of life'.

Wise old owl. I've never before wanted to take much heed of Mr Wenger, but I'm going to try it now.

In his book *The Meaning of Sport*, something of a bible to me and, I would hazard a guess, a better take on the subject than this one, Simon Barnes concludes that sport is so many things – most of them showing different sides of the same coin reflecting every element of life – 'it's everything and nothing, shows superhuman strength and endless fallibility, is beautiful and ugly, a waste of time and something which can enrich all who come into contact with it'. I could go on but shouldn't as the words are not my own, and as a summary of my own relationship with sport, it cannot be bettered – I urge you to read it. But to borrow just a little more, I'd pick out: 'sport is an escape from real life; sport makes real life uncompromisingly vivid'. And that, in a nutshell, is that.

I have no doubt I will continue to be addicted to the hope amidst the reality of disappointment because, to employ the wisdom of Simon Barnes one final time, whilst some of us are addicted to the past (and if this book tells you nothing else it tells you I am one of that number), all of us are addicted to the future. We have to be. It gives us that hope, 'that's always the most prudent way to enjoy the future – before it gets here'. This is why the anticipation of United's next Champions League semi-final will always be better than the thing itself.

So yes, if we want to be a part of this at all, we have to suffer the sorrow, but we should try to embrace it. That will be my ambition from now on. The future's bright; life is good. Losing might be bad, but on balance, I will keep reminding myself it's better than nothing at all. I'm aware that I'm probably only one last ball Ashes defeat away from a relapse. If a perennial winner such as Martina Navratilova can voice the opinion as she did in 1989 that 'the moment of victory is too short to live for that and nothing else', perhaps I can now start living by that. At first glance, Southampton getting beaten 9-0 for the second consecutive season, this time at Manchester United, might have seemed a cause for several months' worth of brooding and humiliation. Far better, I realised, to enjoy the ridiculous nature of it all and announce it as our own particular party piece, for which we have become rightly famous, offering up to others the chance to take their turn in line next season. I know such an attitude will at best wax and wane and that I will constantly have to check myself to see if I am following my new dictum. Aristophanes said old age is a second childhood – well, let's hope so because I'd certainly relive mine just as it was; let's see how it goes. In the end, sport has been an absolutely life-enhancing entity and writing this story has made me realise that. To see only its capacity to disappoint occasionally in the relative minutiae of its results rather than the benefits it brings in its wider context would be a waste of any years that remain. It is our own call whether we let it add to, or subtract from, the joy we take from being on this planet, so what are you going to do? I'm going to keep repeating to myself the words of Anne Bronte: 'but he who dares not grasp the thorns, should never crave the rose'. I think what she meant was 'get over yourself'. What matters above all is that sport is there regardless. And if at worst it allows us an excuse not to join in the Wednesday night viewing of Phil and Kirstie, it is making a contribution.

I've been incredibly lucky, no doubt about that. Setting off in the world had I known what sport was going to bring me, I would scarcely have believed it. One more visit to my new favourite guru and philosopher Mr Wenger. Asked for his definition of success, he paused before saying:

> 'Success is finding the meaning of your life and to be capable to live it. After that it's never enough. But if happiness is to have a

life you want to have, I can say I have been very happy until now because I had the life I wanted to have.'

Moi aussi, Arsène.

A glorious irrelevance? It can be glorious, Danny, for sure, but an irrelevance? The results at 5pm on any given Saturday perhaps, but not the bigger picture. There were seven words we used to try to live by at adidas: *sport has the power to change lives*. It certainly changed mine. And what might I urge others to take from all this, if anything at all? Enjoy sport and everything it brings. If you can avoid being the me that gets bitter and twisted, please do – learn by my poor example and I'll be delighted. But if you get the chance to be me by spending your life in and around sport, grab it with both hands, live every moment and be thankful for it. And remember, when all is said and done, it's not life and death, it's only chasing rainbows…

POSTSCRIPT

July 2021

'The future bears a resemblance
to the past, only more so'
FAITH POPCORN, THE POPCORN REPORT, 1991

NEVER-ENDING STORY

The challenge in writing a book interwoven with sporting events is finding the place for the full stop... because sport doesn't stop (if you accept the brief halt in 2020 as a one-off). This is one of the reasons we keep coming back; whatever has just happened, something else is about to, and who knows, perhaps it will be the elusive fairy tale somewhere over the rainbow. It's the never-ending hope. I may have thought the story was done, but sport had a different idea of how things might conclude in a way most in concert with all that had gone before. 2021 was to encapsulate in its first six and a half months the essence of the previous forty-seven years. At the end of 2020, I had also left adidas and started a whole new chapter – another reset and the last example of sport and my life seemingly running in improbable tandem. This would be another hole in my life but also another opportunity to change perspective, to approach the future differently... so, welcome, 2021. Even if the lockdown Christmas just gone had had to be a little more subdued than those which had gone before, Monday the 4th of January dawned with that familiar sense of anticlimax. And the once mighty FA Cup couldn't save me these days. As Mary left for work and I contemplated my first day without effective employment for thirty-two years, the future was uncertain but, I hoped, full of possibilities. I could've been back in 1974. I was also aware that my melancholy was unlikely to be lifted by the prospect of Southampton playing Liverpool that evening. If you have made it this far, you will know my take on this – give me any game to win in any season and this is it. Recent history also determined that the odds on such an outcome were not remotely in my favour, and I had again already rationalised away the impending defeat in that attempt to lessen the pain that the last forty-seven years had taught me doesn't work. Then, that evening, at the same time as Boris took to BBC One to announce a further two months of lockdown for the whole country, and the end seemed as far away as ever, Saints were beating Liverpool 1-0 on the Sky channel I paid good money to access. What was that if not a pick-me-up? A 2021 version of the 1974 FA Cup third round and a sign that good things were again just around the corner, that there were still rainbows to be chased. And of course, I couldn't bring my new, better adjusted self and my new sense of perspective to watch a single damn minute of it. Happy New Year again.

Then, to Southampton's subsequent loss of their next twelve games and agonising reacquaintance with a relegation battle were added England's worst performance in a Six Nations in living memory, losing to all three Celtic nations for the first time in forty-five years and the England cricket team losing a home series for the first time in seven years and a home series to New Zealand for the first time in twenty-two. In-between, Manchester United managed to lose a European final on penalties after the prolonged agony (which I followed through intermittent glances at my phone whilst tidying an already spotless bedroom) of twenty-one consecutive potential cardiac arrest moments. Add in the continual England batting collapses and the Lions losing their Test series by three points in a deciding Test which they should have won, together with Southampton's sale of the one man who had kept us afloat for two years, Danny Ings, who claimed he wanted to go up a level and then went to… Aston Villa, and the normal order of my sports fandom seemed to be restored. And then, to confirm my Pied Piper facility had not just come to an end but turned 180 degrees, there was Harlequins Rugby. The club had been the best part of hopeless for the previous seven years whilst I was managing a professional partnership with them. On the day I left adidas, they sat seventh in the league and had just parted company with their coach. Within six months, they had won their first title in nine years via two of the greatest comeback wins in Premiership history. I was getting the message.

These happenings in themselves would not have been enough for me to reach for the laptop again and feel the need to add a final chapter. That accolade was reserved for what came next.

Fifty-five years to the month after I am convinced I was conceived, England finally made it to a second final of a major international football tournament. That in itself seemed neat enough, but would victory be the perfect conclusion to my tale? Well, we'll never know, but somehow, the experience of those thirty days of summer could not have been more apposite; one month which captured everything I have come to know, and tried to articulate, about following sport. Here was the joy of the shared experience, made more vivid in the wake of the hibernation of society for the previous eighteen months. Everywhere, a sporting event was reconnecting people – both with each other and with their nation, their team and their performers within it – here was an antidote to the rise of 'wokism', a green light to wave a flag or two together and a happy endorsement of the right to be proud to be English. Here was a summer tournament which we needed like no other before...

It gave us the usual schadenfreude – England fans seeing Germany coming to terms with defeat by our own hand and Scotland fans no doubt rejoicing in the tournament's final act. As England's young team progressed, it increasingly tilted that balance within us of hope versus experience... the hope that was ultimately to kill us again. It reaffirmed for many that there is excitement in the anticipation of the moment, and a rush of joy in the aftermath of a successful outcome, but little actual pleasure in enduring the spectacle itself, as articulated before and after every increasingly important England match by radio presenter Max Rushden, the personification of this emotional state for those of us whose month was played out to the constant background noise of *TalkSport*. He talked of his almost continuous state of nerves across the entire tournament and the difficulty in the unique experience of wondering how to react to being in a final and how to get through a final day of purgatory which, in reality, did not begin until 8pm. This time, the anticipation wasn't much more enjoyable than the thing itself. Of course, personally speaking, it took me back to that place where I could no longer bring myself to watch. Having announced to the pub at lunchtime that not only was it a cast-iron certainty the match would go to penalties but it was just as certain that I would not be watching them, I stuck to my plan, avoided the drama and once again completely failed to influence the outcome.

And of course, it gave us our England hard-luck story via Pete Davies' 'stupid, heartless bingo of penalties'. I heard there were actually people who thought this time we were going to win it rather than accept their English fate and place it on the pile already containing Turin '90, Wembley '96, St Etienne '98, Lisbon '04, Gelsenkirchen '06 and Kiev '12. It's a hell of a list when you look at it. Lusail Stadium, Qatar '22, anybody?

So, if all this was some divine test of my new perspective on sport and life, how am I doing?

You know what? None of these things seem to have caused me the lasting damage they would have done in years gone by. A couple of things struck me; firstly, I simply wasn't as devastated as I had been in the past, and whether this was influenced by leaving my professional role or the lessons genuinely learnt in the writing of this story, I may just have come through it and out the other side. Secondly, despite the pain of the outcome at the Euros, if we were given the chance now to go back a month and cancel the whole affair, would we do so to avoid the ultimate disappointment? Of course not. A reminder that no matter what lemons sport serves you up, you should really just use them to make gin and tonics and reflect that it gives more than it takes. And then, to reaffirm the difficulty in finding a place for me to stop, Emma Raducanu did her US Open thing as I was heading to the printers, hence this ultimate example of what sport can do receives a sentence rather than the book, or library of books, it deserves. Perhaps it was the final little nudge that sport really is bonkers, bewildering and inspirational and that anything could happen, and probably will, just around the corner. I think I've finally found my perspective and my redemption. It's all a part of living my never-ending story. I wish you all the very best of luck in living yours.

APPENDIX
A LIFE IN LISTS

Not necessarily what I consider to be the 'best' sporting moments and achievements but favourites, and least favourites, that are personal to me from half a century of sport.

FAVOURITE SPORTING 'SUCCESSES'
1. Ashes, 2005
2. Southampton v Manchester United 1-0, FA Cup final, 1976
3. Cricket World Cup, 2019
4. Manchester United treble, 1999
5. Rugby World Cup, 2003

MOMENTS OF GREATEST ELATION & RELIEF
1. Kasprowicz, c Jones b Harmison, Edgbaston, 2005
2. Jonny Wilkinson drop goal, Rugby World Cup final, 2003
3. Steve Moran goal, Southampton v Portsmouth 1-0, FA Cup fourth round, 1984
4. Ole Gunnar Solskjaer goal, Champions League final, 1999
5. Ryan Giggs goal, Manchester United v Arsenal 2-1, FA Cup semi-final, 1999

MOMENTS OF DESOLATION WHICH HAVE ENDURED LONGER THAN ANY OTHER

1. Jimmy White v Stephen Hendry, deciding frame, World Snooker final, 1994
2. Germany v England 4-3, penalty shoot-out World Cup semi-final, Turin, 1990
3. Morne Steyn drop goal, South Africa v British & Irish Lions, Loftus Versfeld, 2009
4. Sergio Aguero goal to win Premier League title, Manchester City v QPR 3-0, 2012
5. Germany v England 6-5, penalty shoot-out Euros semi-final, 1996
6. Everton v Southampton 1-0, FA Cup semi-final, 1984
7. Sergey Kovalev beats Anthony Yarde, World Light Heavyweight title fight, Russia, 2019
8. Goran Ivanisevic beats Tim Henman in five sets, Wimbledon semi-final, 2001
9. Scotland v England 13-7, Five Nations, 1990
10. David Gower omitted from England cricket squad for tour to India, 1992

MOST SPECIAL HALF-DOZEN 'BEING THERE' MOMENTS

1. British & Irish Lions dressing room, Lions v South Africa 28-9, Ellis Park, Johannesburg, 2009
2. Southampton v Crystal Palace 2-0, FA Cup semi-final, Stamford Bridge, 1976
3. Ashes series first day, Lord's, 2005
4. Mo Farah 10,000m gold/Jamaica sprint relay, Olympic Stadium, London, 2012
5. Southampton v Sunderland 4-0, second division, 1975
6. Stuart Broad 5-37, fifth Ashes Test, The Oval, 2009

HALF-DOZEN MOMENTS OF SPORTING GENIUS

1. Ronnie O'Sullivan maximum break, World Snooker Championship, 1997

2. Ben Stokes 135 not out, third Ashes Test, Headingley, 2019
3. John McEnroe beats Jimmy Connors 6-1, 6-1, 6-2, Wimbledon final, 1984
4. Shane Warne 'ball of the century', first Ashes Test, Old Trafford, 1993
5. Nadal v Federer Wimbledon final, 2008
6. Viv Richards 189 not out, first One Day International West Indies v England, Old Trafford, 1984

FAVOURITE HALF-DOZEN INDIVIDUAL PERFORMANCES
1. Daley Thompson decathlon gold, Los Angeles Olympics, 1984
2. Stuart Broad 8-15 and three hundred Test wickets, third Ashes Test, Trent Bridge, 2015
3. Kevin Pietersen 158, fifth Ashes Test, The Oval, 2005 or 186 second Test v India, Mumbai, 2012 (take your pick)
4. Ian Botham, third, fourth and fifth Ashes Tests, 1981
5. David Gower 157, third Test v India, The Oval, 1990
6. Lionel Messi, Barcelona v Bayern Munich 3-0, Champions League semi-final first leg, Barcelona, 2015

MOMENTS OF SPORTING THEATRE
1. Michael Holding over to Geoff Boycott, third Test West Indies v England, 1981
2. Borg v McEnroe tiebreak, Wimbledon final, 1980
3. Dennis Taylor v Steve Davis black ball final, World Snooker Championship, 1985
4. Tom Watson/Jack Nicklaus final round, The Open Championship, Turnberry, 1977
5. Muhammad Ali v George Foreman, World Heavyweight title fight, Zaire, 1974

MOMENTS OF GREATEST SCHADENFREUDE
1. England v Germany 5-1, World Cup qualifier, Munich, 2001
2. Peter Ebdon v Stephen Hendry 18-17, World Snooker final, 2002
3. Germany v Argentina 1-0, World Cup final, 1990

4. India beat Australia after following on, second Test, Kolkata, 2001
5. Portsmouth docked nine points and relegated from Premier League, March, 2010

A BAKER'S DOZEN WHO HAVE GIVEN ME GREAT SPORTING PLEASURE ON OR OFF THE PITCH

1. David Gower
2. Matt Le Tissier
3. Jimmy White
4. Daley Thompson
5. Ian Botham
6. Stuart Broad
7. George North
8. Lionel Messi
9. John McEnroe
10. Malcolm Marshall
11. Kevin Pietersen
12. Viv Richards
13. Ronnie O'Sullivan

This book is printed on paper from sustainable sources managed under the Forest Stewardship Council (FSC) scheme.

It has been printed in the UK to reduce transportation miles and their impact upon the environment.

For every new title that Matador publishes, we plant a tree to offset CO_2, partnering with the More Trees scheme.

MORE TREES
LET'S PLANT A BILLION TREES

For more about how Matador offsets its environmental impact, see www.troubador.co.uk/about/